The Biopolitics of Disability

Corporealities: Discourses of Disability

The Biopolitics of Disability

NEOLIBERALISM, ABLENATIONALISM, AND PERIPHERAL EMBODIMENT

David T. Mitchell
with Sharon L. Snyder

University of Michigan Press
Ann Arbor

Published in the United States of America by
the University of Michigan Press
Manufactured in the United States of America
⊗ Printed on acid-free paper

2018   2017   2016   2015   4   3   2   1

A CIP catalog record for this book is available from the British Library.

ISBN 978–0-472–07271–2 (hardcover)
ISBN 978-0-472-05271-4 (paper)
ISBN 978–0-472–12118–2 (e-book)

About the Cover

The cover design by celebrated graphic artist Selene DePackh (participant and expert commentator on autistic art and culture), *Vitruvian Man with CP*, is based on an idea developed by the authors. The vision is our attempt to depict a "posthumanist" disabled subject existing (and, at times, productively exceeding) the constraints of neoliberalism (that which we define in this book as a tightly limited form of inclusion for "diverse" citizens). The targeted grid that encompasses the figure is ringed with medical terminology denoting forms of muscular atrophy and spasticity—ways in which diagnoses identify muscle groups that refuse to comply with normative expectations of functionality. Inside the grid we find a mirrored figure: akimbo, multilimbed (suggestive of the many limbed Lakshmi or elephant-like Ganesh of Indian myth), and decidedly neuroatypical in posture. *Vitruvian Man with CP* offers an antithesis to the bounded perfection of Leonardo da Vinci's *Vitruvian Man* with his emphasis on symmetry and normative human form. In her narration of cross-species attachments, Donna Haraway describes mongrelized human and nonhuman bodies as participatory in a "multipartner mud dance issuing from and in entangled species" (32). The design captures the multiform alternative corporeality of crip/queer bodies emerging throughout the pages of *The Biopolitics of Disability*. Here we theorize material and immaterial connectedness, as parallel to Haraway's cross-species and ever-mutating revelations: the potentially adaptive (mis)firings characteristic of every sentient body. Like the messy unfoldings of *Vitruvian Man with CP* we chart disabled people's creative productions of living within narrowly devised aesthetics, attitudes, and architectures of contemporary "diversity." The nonnormative engagements witnessed within these pages are world-transforming in ways that crip/queer bodies enrich scenarios in which they have been traditionally narrated as divisive, pathological, and in need of a heavily enforced grid of surveillance to limit their alternative flourishings. Their mere inclusion within neoliberalism is not enough, so runs our argument, without an active encounter with the alternative materialities such bodies and minds bring into being.

Acknowledgments

This book is based on a decade and a half of research devoted to thinking about embodiment and disability's social placement as exceptional deviation. Essentially our guiding question has centered on why, when all species are characterized and sustained by mutation, convergence and divergence, embodied vulnerability and adaptive reroutings, would disability situate some individuals outside of social registers of desirability, creativity, acceptability, private and public forms of participation? Given this state of affairs a more important follow-up question pressed itself upon us: What do disabled people do with themselves once their social inclusion is announced as a finished project of the modern nation state? Much of this research was done in collaboration with other disabled and disability-identified scholars, artists, activists, professional colleagues, relations, and friends.

Our early work on disability culture catalyzed an interest in these research questions as we searched for like-minded individuals with whom to share our comfort in being disabled. Our first professional interaction with disability studies came in 1993 when we presented an essay on disability and Lacanian subjectivity for the "Otras Habilidades" conference held in Mayaguez, Puerto Rico. There we had the tremendous good fortune to meet many of the colleagues who would go on to spur and support our work over the long and winding road of our professional careers: Simi Linton, Rosemarie Garland Thomson, Cindy LaCom, Harlan Hahn, Marcy Epstein, Susan Crutchfield, Martha Stoddard Holmes, Russell Vickery, Pierre Etienne Cudmore, and Nandita Batra. On the island of Puerto Rico we first realized that our experiences of nonnormative embodiment could be shared and turned into some useful grist for academic analysis.

A second moment of revelation about the camaraderie available in disability culture occurred during our participation in a 1994 conference at the University of Michigan, "This/Ability: A Conference on Disability and the Arts." Here we collected the interviews and performance footage that would become the documentary film *Vital Signs: Crip Culture Talks Back* (1995). The film was financed by Northern Michigan University and captured by a group of Sharon's film students who founded the Gonzo Media Student Group: Grant Guston, Nicole Bracy, Matt Bainbridge, and Rick Hart. During the conference we first heard Cheryl Marie Wade read her jazzy version of "Disability Rap" and perform *Sassy Girl: Memoirs of a Poster Child Gone Awry*. The Irish performance artist Mary Duffy staged her memorable one-woman act as a nude Venus de Milo in front of a black plastic garbage bag background in a basement somewhere in the bowels of the Rackham building. Bob DeFelice and Julia Trahan's comedic routines turned disability dead ends into entertaining cultural commentary at a local café on State Street. Carrie Sandahl acted out her medical history in a white lab coat and sweat pants artistically covered with red magic marker to replicate the surgical incisions and social woundings that traversed her disability life. Ann Finger read her imaginative rendition of a meeting between two disability icons in her short story "Helen and Frida" atop the Graduate School with the wind blowing her beige tunic-like top wildly. Eli Clare breathed life into the tremors and stammers of CP in her poem, "Learning to Speak." We love all of these people and remain heartened by the essential contributions to disability studies and arts that they have gone on to make from this brief moment when our lives and bodies all intersected.

Similarly we teamed up with the inimical Rosemarie Garland Thomson in order to vent our frustrations at having disability studies sessions rejected, year after year, by the Modern Languages Association Convention Program Selection Committee. Our late-night phone calls turned into a petitioning of the MLA office in New York, then headed by Phyllis Franklin, to give us a discussion panel from which we might gauge organizational interest in the field. Dozens of people came to that first session in 1994 and signed forms of interest on behalf of the establishment of a formal Discussion Group that would hold a panel devoted to disability studies in the humanities. The original committee, auspiciously titled The Standing Committee on the Status of Disability in the Profession, included some of the most central thinkers in the burgeoning field: Georgina Kleege, Ellen Steckert, Lois Bragg, Rosemarie Garland Thomson, Nancy Mairs, Simi Linton, Brenda Brueggemann, Lennard Davis, and ourselves. In exchange for writing accessibility copy for the program we hosted one special session that ultimately grew into today's Division on Disability Studies (the Discussion Group also remains). The committee's early years celebrated an extraordinary group of books that would pilot the field, including Davis's *Enforcing Normalcy: Disability, Deafness, and the Body* (1995), Thomson's *Extraordinary Bodies: Figuring Physical Disability in American Literature and Culture* (1996), Nancy Mair's *Waist-High in the World* (1997), our own collection *The Body and Physical Difference: Discourses of Disability* (1997), Simi Linton's *Reclaiming Disability: Knowledge and Identity* (1998), Georgina Kleege's *Sight Unseen* (1999), Brenda Brueggemann's *Lend Me Your Ear* (1999), Lois Bragg's *Deaf World: A Historical Reader and Primary Sourcebook* (2001). It was the exceptionality of the insights, esteemed nature of the group, and the momentum created by such an array of foundational works in the field that boosted our own energies and led this small institutional insurrection into a fully legitimated fixture of the organization.

As mentioned above, 1997 witnessed the publication of our first collection of essays, *The Body and Physical Difference: Discourses of Disability*. James Porter brought our work into his influential series "The Body, In Theory" for the University of Michigan Press with great fanfare. Without James's support and recognition for our work we would not have the national and international recognition we gained in the years that followed. His summative phrasing of disability "as somehow too much or too little of a body" continues to reverberate in the field's parlance as the hard kernel of a definition we all share. Our career-long executive editor at the UMP, LeAnn Fields, saw something further in our work and helped us successfully propose the Corporealities: Discourses of Disability series that continues today as one of the research hallmarks of disability studies in the humanities. We celebrate her support of a field that few others would have recognized as having potential in the mid-1990s at a major university press. Today Corporealities has published more than twenty-three new books on disability studies in the humanities and remains the longest-running academic book series in the field.

Following the publication of our second book, *Narrative Prosthesis: Disability and the Dependencies of Discourse* (2000), we were offered the opportunity by Vera Moser to lecture in Germany at the Goethe-Universtät in Frankfurt, Germany, and by Anja Tervooren to lecture at the Free University of Berlin. During that visit we were exposed to a comment from a longtime disability activist about the Nazi extermination of disabled people in psychiatric institutions under the auspices of the T4 program that gave us the materials for the documentary film *A World Without Bodies* (2002), and created the research basis for our third book, *Cultural Locations of Disability* (2006), about U.S. and European participation in cross-Atlantic eugenics.

Keeping with this spirit, in 2002 we were awarded a grant from the German-American Exchange Foundation (DAAD) backed by the generous support of Jewish culture and body theorist scholar Sander Gilman. The grant financed a summer-long research travel group of U.S., Canadian, and Australian scholars to further study the ravages of the T4 program during World War II. That group gave us a reflective community of disability scholars once more as we collectively navigated German memorials and archives that often proved less than accessible and seriously disheartening. Those remarkable individuals included Adrienne Asch, Brenda Brueggemann, Ingrid Hoffman, Rosemarie Garland Thomson, Mark Sherry, Nancy Hanson, Sandy O'Neill, Gerry O'Brien, Walton Schalick, Debjani Mukherjee, Pamela Wheelock, Sara Vogt, Nicole Markotic, Sally Chivers, Sumi Colligan, Kanta Kochhar-Lindgren, and Emma Mitchell. The vitality and professional caretaking these relationships established for us continue into the present.

A special recognition goes out to our colleague in the collaborative critiques we have exchanged of special education since the late 1990s: Linda Ware. Her guidance and depth of commitment to the reform of disability education in the United States gave us confidence that the undertaking of joint research would yield great results. The fruits of our professional collaboration with Linda are summarized here in chapter 2, "Curricular Crip-istemologies." In addition to her professional understanding of the SPED world, Linda's innovative parental investments in making a life for her cognitively disabled son, Justin, gave us much of the wherewithal to pilot our own disabled daughter, Emma Mitchell's, difficult journey through a life of medicalization, stigma, and lifesaving surgical interventions. What greater gift of professional, policy, and personal insight could anyone give?

The *Journal of Literary and Cultural Disability Studies* gave us a forum for developing early drafts of several of the chapters included in this book. David Bolt's leadership on this journal and at the Centre for Culture and Disability Studies at Hope Liverpool University has reinvigorated the field of disability studies in the humanities right at a key moment when many of its founding energies were flagging. From life in a council flat (the U.K.'s version of public, low-income housing) to one of the most visible disability studies senior lectureships, David has given us all a model of how commitment to the promotion of the work of others feeds back into one's own. His students and colleagues in DS at Hope Liverpool University provide an incredible portrait of what shared devotions between invested scholars can look like (one we will say is largely unmatched by anything in the United States we have experienced to date).

Of course, we could not complete the work that follows without key funding support provided along the way. In addition to the DAAD scholarship and key documentary film funding from the True North group, *The Biopolitics of Disability* was generously augmented by a grant for "Projects of National Significance" by the Office of Post-Secondary Education, U.S. Department of Education, as well as numerous stipends for international travel to disability film festivals, where the bulk of materials for chapters 4 and 5 were developed. These visits to present our work and judge other independent disability film productions were financed by the London Disability Film Festival, the Breaking Barriers Film Festival in Moscow, the Government of Milan Italy Public Affairs Division, the School of Disability Studies at Ryerson University in Toronto, Picture This! Film Festival in Calgary, the Emotion Pictures Disability Documentary Film Festival in Athens, Greece, Western Australia University in Perth, and the Munich Film Museum. Finally came the provision of a Norman G. Freehling Visiting Professorship in the Institute for the Humanities at the University of Michigan during the 2012–13 academic year. Our time there was greatly enhanced by the work of our colleague and women's autobiography scholar Sidonie Smith, as well as the impressive group of fellows she helped assemble at the institute. A special thanks go out to Daniel Herwitz and Gregory Dowd for helping to organize the original appointment. Also much appreciation to the institute staff, including Terry Jansen, Jan Burgess, and our longtime friend Jane Johnson in the Department of English for making our time in Ann Arbor so without worries.

At the University of Michigan no other colleague has propelled our work than that of our friend, fellow theorist, and disability studies traveler Tobin Siebers. It was Tobin who played an instrumental role in the Freehling Visiting Professorship appointment, and nothing has proven more sustaining than our pleasurable weekly conversations held in the recesses of Café Zolá. From Shakespeare's Falstaff to our shared critiques of dismodernism, Tobin's wit, insight, and stoic endurance buttressed us when our own lives felt in disarray. He and his partner, Jill, always made time for our own needs, and we love them greatly for their friendship and heartfelt devotion to our best interests and those of the field to which we are all committed.

While little value can be claimed in the course of an acknowledgments page for the unnecessary obstacles encountered during our time as faculty at the University of Illinois at Chicago and as director of the Institute on Disabilities at Temple University—largely due to the neoliberal pirating of disabled people's lives by those involved in the DD network—we continue to be buoyed by the success of our best graduate students. These persons include a diversity of disability activists, academics, and policymakers, such as Sarah Triano (Executive Officer of the California Committee on Employment of People with Disabilities under Governor Jerry Brown); Meenu Bhambhani (Vice President and Head of Global Corporate Social Responsibility at MphasiS in Mumbai, India); Michelle Jarman (Associate Professor of Disability Studies at the Wyoming Institute for Disabilities); Eunjung Kim (Assistant Professor of Gender and Women's Studies at the University of Wisconsin); Vladimir Cuk (Acting Executive Director at International Disability Alliance); Jessica Cooley (from an MA at Temple University to a PhD program in Art History at the University of Wisconsin at Madison); Kelly George (from a PhD in Media and Communications at Temple University to the mother of a new baby and soon on to her own research post); Sara Acevedo (a.k.a. "Fridita Kay" following the excitement of your recent PhD work in Anthropology and Social Change at the California Institute of Integral Studies and an appointment as Visiting Scholar at Berkeley City College); among many others. Collectively and individually you give us hope in the promise of a new generation of disability studies scholarship to come.

We are writing this acknowledgment at the conclusion of our first year in the Department of English at George Washington University. The amazing group of people here committed to the life of ideas, literature, and social justice help us to realize that we would have gladly traded much sooner our previous experiences in Chicago and Philadelphia for those that awaited us in DC. For Robert McRuer we feel the indebtedness of those who have had their own scholarship enriched by the excellence of his ideas, depth of his camaraderie, and the generosity of his friendship. Jonathan Hsy, Jeffrey Cohen, Ayanna Thompson, Faye Moskowitz, Alexa Huang, Tony Lopez, James Miller, Abby Wilkerson, Holly Dugan, Gayle Wald, Ann Romines, and others have already contributed much to our desired experience of comfort in a new academic home. The depth of your welcome and open embrace of our contributions already makes us feel the care of a shared venture on behalf of future generations of students. We value too the gift of M. Bychowski, whose assistance in a fall 2013 GWU Introduction to Disability Studies class and commitment to the development of Trans theory in medieval and modern literature has renewed our confidence in the value of co-teaching and pedagogical mentoring experiences.

None of these academically sustaining relationships, however, would be worth it without our alliances in the international disability arts community. It was there that our films were first recognized as substantive contributions to the art of disability living that is so central to the arguments and examples of this book. First, a heartfelt recognition of our nearly two-decade-old relationship with the amazing figural artist Riva Lehrer. Riva's vision of disabled bodies as worthy of an arts career devoted to their representation—the loving and yet technically adept sweep of her brush across their idiosyncratic contours—connected with our desire for undertaking an aesthetic transformation of how the world views such bodies. Likewise our invaluable time in Chicago exposed to the artistic creativity of writers and dramatists such as Mike Ervin (Smart Ass Crip), Susan Nussbaum (*Good Kings / Bad Kings*), and Tekki Lomnecki (Telling Tales Theater) kept us bolstered in the belief first expressed by our friend and performance artist extraordinaire, Cheryl Marie Wade: "My work is always for my community. But I also want to do such good work that I get places they don't usually let a gimp in (if you know what I'm saying here)." In tandem with our best friend, James Charlton, whose knowledge of Marxism and Chicago politics continues to astound us, we want to give final cheers to this group who helped to mold so much of our work in the years during and since our time in Chi-town.

As Jack Kerouac says of his prurient interest in the lives of those who do not fit into the normative shape carved out for them by ablenationalism: "the only people that interest me are the mad ones, the ones who are mad to live, mad to talk, desirous of everything at the same time, the ones that never yawn or say a commonplace thing . . . but burn, burn, burn like roman candles across the night" (*On the Road* 1753–56). It is these "mad ones" for whom this book is written.

— *Princeville, Kauai*

Portions of the following chapters have previously appeared in other publications. We thank the publishers for giving us initial forums in which to present these ideas.

An earlier version of the introduction, "Ablenationalism and the Geopolitics of Disability," first appeared in our special guest-edited issue of the *Journal of Literary and Cultural Disability Studies* 4.2 (2010): 113–25.

Sections of chapter 1 initially appeared under the title "Minority Model: From Liberal to Neoliberal Futures of Disability," in Nicholas Watson, Alan Roulstone, and Carol Thomas (eds.): *Routledge Handbook of Disability Studies*. Oxon: Routledge, 2012: 42–50.

Chapter 2, "Educational Cripistemologies; or, Every Child Left Behind," was initially written for Robert McRuer and Lisa Johnson's guest-edited issue of the *Journal of Literary and Cultural Disability Studies* 8.3 (2014): 295-314. This essay was written with our colleague Linda Ware.

A version of chapter 4 under the title "'How Do We Get all of These Disabilities in Here?': International Disability Film Festivals and the Politics of Atypicality," first appeared in Nicole Markotic and Sally Chivers' special guest-edited volume of the *Canadian Journal of Film Studies* (Spring 2008): 11–29.

An excerpt from what became chapter 5, "Permutations of the Species: Independent Disability Cinema and the Critique of National Normativity," was published in D. Iodanova and Leslie Torchin's edited volume, *Film Festival Yearbook 4: Film Festivals and Activism*. St. Andrews: St. Andrews Film Studies, 2012: 81–93.

Finally, an earlier version of the afterword, "Disability as Multitude: Reworking Nonproductive Labor Power," was published in our special guest-edited issue "The Geo-politics of Disability" in the *Journal of Literary and Cultural Disability Studies* 4.2 (summer 2010): 179–93.

Contents

Illustrations following page 114

Introduction

The Biopolitics of Disability: Neoliberalism, Ablenationalism, and Peripheral Embodiment explores how experiences of disability under neoliberalism offer more than exposés of encounters with discriminatory social barriers *or* the contingencies of experiences of incapacity brought about by paying closer attention to impairment. Barrier removal and bodily limitations on public participation have been the two poles between which disability studies research has primarily shuttled since its founding moments in the 1970s.[1] The former (barrier removal) has claimed the lion's share of the field's attention, while the latter (impairment effects) has continued to evolve as a key component of scholarship on disability embodiment. The scholarship on "impairment effects," largely spurred by feminist disability studies scholars such as Susan Wendell, Carol Thomas, and Jenny Morris, serves as a primary course correction for the field through its advocacy of a more visceral engagement with bodies. Both of these analytical interventions have played a crucial role in disability studies as the twin pillars supporting the field's politics and research. However, their significance should not continue to remain exclusive of alternative ways of thinking disability as a more agentive, "leaky" (Shildrick, *Leaky Bodies* 10), or "lively" materiality, in the words of recent "immanent materialists."[2]

While a majority of disability studies research remains focused on pragmatic social changes brought about by barrier removal (i.e., accessible public transportation, universal design in architecture, the right to be educated in the least restrictive environment, exercise of the voting franchise as citizens, deinstitutionalization), the 1990s witnessed an emergence of new work on "impairment" (Morris 10) and "impairment effects" (Thomas 25). The more open engagement with "impairment effects," as Carol Thomas explains, "sought to counter-balance an over emphasis in the social and minority models of disability on environmental restrictions experienced by disabled people wherein the ability to fully participate as citizens in a democracy (for example) is impinged upon by real bodily limits" (125). An emphasis on impairment effects allowed a greater range of opportunities for productively thinking disabled embodiment as not solely limited to socially created encounters with exclusion. At the same time, while these two domains are critical to the developing contributions of disability studies and international disability rights movements, they are largely bounded by the terms of social recognition (i.e., inclusionist practices and civil rights-based policy work) that characterize neoliberal diversity initiatives. They have almost nothing to say, for instance, about *the active transformation of life that the alternative corporealities of disability creatively entail.*

This book shares much in common with the approach to disability as radical materialism that characterize Margrit Shildrick's influential body of work: *Leaky Bodies and Boundaries: Feminism, Postmodernism, and (Bio) Ethics, Embodying the Monster: Encounters with the Vulnerable Self,* and *Dangerous Discourses of Disability, Subjectivity and Sexuality.* In concert with Shildrick's work, the central approach of this book regards neoliberal inclusionism as primarily made available to newly visible public identities such as those labeled handicapped, cognitively impaired, intersexed, deaf/blind, or queer based on a formerly stigmatized group's ability to approximate historically specific expectations of normalcy. Yet, in bestowing these forms of grudging recognition, neoliberal inclusionism tends to reify the value of normative modes of being developed with respect to ablebodiedness, rationality, and heteronormativity. *The Biopolitics of Disability* attempts to push all the way through the sleeve of impairment to explore how disability subjectivities are not just characterized by socially imposed restrictions, but, in fact, productively create new forms of embodied knowledge and collective consciousness. As Alexander G. Weheliye explains, "the flesh thus operates . . . simultaneously [as] a tool of dehumanization and a relational vestibule to alternative ways of being that do not possess the luxury of eliding phenomenology with biology" (44).

The chapters to come address these paired issues of phenomenology and biology as seriously as they do social exclusion. These attentions result in what social theorist Margaret Archer characterizes as a mode of alternative representation that "makes our real embodied selves living in the real world really load-bearing" (22). Integration practices within neoliberalism largely short-circuit opportunities for more meaningful apprehensions of disability subjectivities that involve ways of experiencing and being disabled in the world. What is often lost in relations of neoliberal normalcy are ways in which disabled people's openly interdependent lives and crip/queer forms of embodiment provide alternative maps for living together in the deterritorialized, yet highly regulated spaces of biopolitics. The preservation of disabled bodies in these spaces depends on managing to invent forms of culture that operate as alternatives to the principles of neoliberalism.

Consequently, this book focuses on the emergence of new crip/queer subjectivities at work in a variety of domains including: disability arts, disability studies pedagogy, independent and mainstream disability cinema, Internet-based single-impairment user groups, antinormative novels of embodiment, and, finally, the labor of living in "nonproductive" bodies within late capitalism. The designation "crip/queer" recognizes that all bodies identified as excessively deviant are "queer" in the sense that they represent discordant functionalities and outlaw sexualities. Thus, crip/queer forms of embodiment contest their consignment to illegitimacy because sexual prohibition has proven one of the most historically salient forms of exclusion within biopolitics since the late nineteenth century.

Yet, in the words of Queer and Race sociologist Randall Halle, "queer" designates "not the acts in which they engage but rather the coercive norms that place their desires into a position of conflict with the current order" (117). In tandem with queer, "crip" identifies the ways in which such bodies represent alternative forms of being-in-the-world when navigating environments that privilege able-bodied participants as fully capacitated agential participants within democratic institutions. Such alternative modes of interaction made available by crip/queer lives create capabilities that exceed, and/or go unrecognized within, the normative scripts of biopolitics. It is in these spaces of cultural production that disabled people offer alternatives to what Robert McRuer calls "compulsory able-bodiedness": "the [assumption that] able-bodied identities, able-bodied perspectives, are preferable and what we all, collectively, are aiming for" (*Crip Theory* 372).

INCLUSIONISM AND NONNORMATIVE
POSITIVIST CRITIQUE

Most importantly, this book attempts to register some aftershocks among contemporary disability communities resulting from developments within neoliberalism that have, paradoxically, resulted in greater social visibility and participation for some disabled people. Shildrick explains the historical development of neoliberal disability in this manner: "I concentrate on the continuing discursive exclusion of disability within western and western-inflected societies, and argue that at the very same time such states are making tremendous strides towards the formal *integration* of disabled people into the rights, obligations, and expectations of normative citizenship" (*Dangerous Discourses* 1). This increased presence results from practices of neoliberal disability tolerance to which we refer throughout this book as *inclusionism*. By inclusionism we mean to identify a term specifically associated with disabled bodies operative in the policy world of neoliberalism. Most significantly, inclusionism has found its most robust rhetorical home within the myriad diversity missions advanced by public education. Inclusionism has come to mean an embrace of diversity-based practices by which we include those who look, act, function, and feel different; yet our contention here is that inclusionism obscures at least as much as it reveals.

In queer theorist Sarah Ahmed's words:

> Perhaps the promise of diversity is that it can be both attached to those bodies that "look different" and detached from those bodies as a sign of inclusion (if they are included by diversity, then we are all included). The promise of diversity could then be described as a problem: the sign of inclusion makes the signs of exclusion disappear. (830–32)

Inclusion in this scenario allows for the embrace of some forms of difference through making them unapparent. The magical resolution of diversity-based integration practices is achieved by "making bodies that look different" invisible, more normative. While Ahmed discusses the inclusionist problem specifically in terms of questions of racial diversity in institutions of higher learning, here we intend to use inclusionism in relation to crip/queer bodies as well. Because disability impacts all socioeconomic brackets of existence, diverse embodiments coexist in racialized, sexed, gendered, classed, and disabled bodies simultaneously. This coexistence represents the fraught intersection that inclusionism occupies within neoliberal systems.

Neoliberalism is diagnosed as the arrival, during the latter half of the twentieth century, of what Henry Giroux calls "hyper-market-driven societies [that] organize identities largely as consumers." As such, neoliberalism offers few spaces from which to "recognize (our)selves outside of the values, needs, and desires preferred by the market" (*Disposable Youth* xiv). Within this limiting framework of consumptive recognition, however, neoliberal governance systems have opened up some opportunities for the potential inclusion of formerly excluded groups such as people with disabilities. *The contention of this book is that meaningful inclusion is only worthy of the designation "inclusion" if disability becomes more fully recognized as providing alternative values for living that do not simply reify reigning concepts of normalcy.* While an egalitarian concept of disability has sought to free disabled people from the restraints of able-bodied oppression (i.e., ableism), a nondialectical materialist account of disability—that which we refer to throughout this book as nonnormative positivism—pursues disability as something other than the oppressed product of social constraints (Snyder and Mitchell, *Cultural Locations* 10).

Nonnormative positivisms extend a methodology developed by philosophers of new materialisms such as Diana Coole and Samantha Frost as a "multimodal materialist analysis of relationships of power"; such approaches open up the matter and materiality of embodiment as exceeding its social scripts of limitation, and, via this opening, one may better recognize

> diverse temporalities by examining their more enduring structures and operations as well as their vulnerability to ruptures and transformations—all the while acknowledging that they have no predestined, necessary, or predictable trajectory. (36)

Within this account new materialisms involve a more fleshy grappling with the nature of materiality itself; how bodies go about inhabiting their messy dynamics in ways that exceed the stigmatizing ramifications of seemingly deterministic social beliefs. While none of the contributors included in Coole and Frost's collection apply new materialist approaches to disability, we demonstrate that disability could serve as a critical fulcrum of such work in future philosophies of materiality.

To return to our thesis, then: Disability studies scholars are caught in their lives and their theories between two zones of negativity without something akin to "nonnormative positivisms." Without alternative materialist approaches there exist few ways to identify the creative interdependencies at the foundations of disability alternatives for living addressed in our existing traditions of thought. Disability studies, in the years to come, must be able to address what crip/queer bodies bring to the table of imagining the value of alternative lives, particularly lives that exist at the fraught intersections of marginalized identities such as disability, race, gender, sexuality, and class. As Nirmala Erevelles argues in *Disability and Difference in Global Contexts*, under examination such intersections reveal themselves as "mutually constitutive of each other" (45).3 There is a great need for an ethical methodology from which disabled people can articulate how their lives bring something new into the world that may otherwise go unrecognized. Nonnormative positivisms provide alternative spaces from which to discuss options for living within alternative embodiments (those designated here by lives lived in peripheral embodiments) as a critical third rail of disability experience.

The work of nonnormative positivisms serves as a site for an alternative ethics to be articulated about why disabled lives matter and how we might revise, reinvent, and transform narrow normative practices, beliefs, and qualifications of who counts. Right now, disability studies and global disability rights movements find themselves having to argue that disabled people must be allowed to pursue their lives much as able-bodied people do in order to prove worthy of acceptance and as recipients of equality of treatment. This may be so but, for our purposes in this book, we want to argue that such a goal is too small and often further solidifies the unchallenged desirability of normative lives. Crip/queer lives explicated through nonnormative positivisms are those that believe another world is possible and such worlds will not come into existence unless we vigilantly attend to the nuances of disabled lives as viable alternatives.

The Biopolitics of Disability situates its inquiries along this Möbius strip of relations between disabled bodies, internalized scripts of embodied normativity (their biopolitical imprinting), and the creative ways in which lives experienced within differential bodies transform the environments of which they are a part. The non-normative positivism we employ operates in tandem with that which disability studies scholar Tobin Siebers theorizes as "complex embodiment." For Siebers, "Disability creates theories of embodiment more complex than the ideology of ability allows, and these many embodiments are each crucial to the understanding of humanity and its variations, whether physical, mental, social, or historical" ("Disability and the Theory of Complex Embodiment" 271). Both approaches involve a more rigorous engagement with the ways in which disabled people experience their material lives as alternatively embodied.

For Siebers and ourselves these parallel methodologies shift our approach to non-normative materialities as actively existing in relation to environments and beliefs rather than as passified objects of social forces exclusively sculpted from the outside in (Snyder and Mitchell, *Cultural Locations* 5–11). Disability, within non-normative positivist approaches, hosts debilitating social beliefs born of anxieties about the radical vulnerability of embodiment (i.e., stigma, suffering, and impairment), but also functions as a disruptive force of resistance in sedimented systems of privilege accorded to normative bodies within nationalist imaginaries of ableism. Consequently, new materialist approaches offer an enrichment of the way alternative cognitions/corporealities allow us to inhabit the world as vulnerable, constrained, yet innovative embodied beings rather than merely as devalued social constructs or victims of oppression. Within nonnormative positivisms, the materiality of disability is foregrounded as a site of creative dynamism and bodies become more than inert corporealities (inactive matter) imprinted by cultural beliefs. Instead, disabled bodies become active switchpoints as their alternative navigations offer an opportunity to perceive that, in Elizabeth Grosz's words, "the capacity to act and effectivity of action is to a large extent structured by the ability to harness and utilize matter for one's own purposes and interests" ("Feminism, Materialism, and Freedom" 148).

THE BIOPOLITICS OF DISABILITY

In referring to the biopolitics of disability we identify a marked historical shift in practices evolving initially during the primary eugenics period wherein lives with disabilities found their existences increasingly immobilized within the nation. Institutionalization (chronic human warehousing), marriage prohibitions, involuntary sterilization, confinement within one's home, inaccessibility of shared public space, segregated education, and intensified immigration restrictions are all tactics employed by liberal governance practices not just to physically control, but to statistically graph and determine in minute detail the cultural parameters of life within which disabled people find themselves enfolded. We want to demonstrate throughout this book that control of the coordinates of what Georgio Agamben refers to as "bare biological life" among citizens in market capitalism has been fashioned on the basis of systems of oversight specific to disability and others occupying peripheral embodiments (*Homo Sacer* 1). This approach allows us to situate disability as a primary case of social justice rather than an exception to the rules of human governance. As Martha Nussbaum points out, "issues that seem extremely important for social justice—issues about the allocation of care, the labor involved in caring, and the social costs of promoting the fuller inclusion of disabled citizens—fail to come into focus or are explicitly deferred for later consideration" (431–32). Nussbaum exposes how neoliberalism, by treating disability as an exceptional case to be put off until later, involves national strategies of deferral as part of its efforts to "seize hold of life in order to suppress it" (Foucault, *History of Sexuality* 136).

In our previous book, *Cultural Locations of Disability*, we undertake a historical materialist analysis of disability to show how nation-states (U.S., Canadian, Australian, and European) regularly traded demographic information about the prevalence rates of feebleminded, epileptic, blind, and deaf populations at the beginning of the twentieth century (103). This international exchange of statistics about disabled populations in the space of "the Eugenic Atlantic" led to shared international diagnostic practices regarding plateaus of "trainability" and threats posed to the well-being of local communities and able-bodied ideals of the nation at large (*Cultural Locations* 101). The overall goal was to more actively police disabled people in order to decrease possibilities of polluting the nation's reproductive pool with the generational transmission of inferior hereditary characteristics. During the liberal Fordist period of production such tactics were implemented by the state and other public institutions as active measures of restriction against disabled people; conversely, during neoliberalism's post-Fordist period such state-imposed implementations went underground and seeped out into the capillary life of everyday citizenship.

Neoliberalism, as characterized by the majority of its theorists, involves strategies of the seizure of the very materiality of life at the level of the individual. Such practices divest themselves of their restrictive character within liberalism and now present themselves in a less negative fashion as the regulatory, productive domain of biopolitics. As social geographer Tim Cresswell points out, the state "wishes to control flows—to make them run through conduits. It wants to create fixed and well-directed paths for movement to flow through" (49). Disabled people know all too well the processes by which their lives are fixed on well-directed paths by the state. Key to effectively channeling disabled people's social mobility are techniques of oversight regarding the statistical quantification of "patterns of life." Those data-gathering activities chart resources available to the state in terms of the rhythms, practices, and activities characteristic of a citizenry's embodied patterns of living: mortality and morbidity rates, reproductive rates, disease and disability rates, zones of toxicity and safety, prognostic predictability factors and health risk calculation statistics, age-of-population pyramids, health disparities and quality-of-life coordinates, and so on (that which Patricia Clough refers to as "the biopolitics of an affect economy" ["Future Matters" 15–16]). Such state-authored statistical practices Foucault describes as "an entire series of techniques and *regulatory controls: a bio-politics of the population*" (*History of Sexuality* 139, his italics).

Consequently, biopolitics identifies the beginnings of a shift away from the punitive processes of confinement and legal prohibitions for disabled people. This is in spite of the fact that most of these practices continue today on a somewhat reduced scale, often in secreted for-profit institutions, and as morally questionable practices within neoliberalism. One might read, for instance, our review of Susan Nussbaum's novel *Good Kings Bad Kings* for a discussion of the contemporary operation of neoliberal for-profit institutionalization practices *enacted* on multi-handicapped, racialized disabled youth in the U.S. (Truthout.com). Ultimately, however, biopolitics involves a move toward a productive massaging of ways to live one's life appropriately within the community without disrupting the naturalized, normative activities of citizenship.[4]

The degree of detail operationalized by modern states for channeling national citizens into modes of acceptability governed by norms of appearance, behavior, and functionality, establishes a form of biopolitics within which nationalism and ableism come together. Biopolitics involves the adoption of a mobile series of productive practices taken on by the state in order to "seize life at its roots" (Hardt and Negri, *Empire* 27); or, in Foucault's words:

> If the question of man was raised [within the medical and human sciences]—insofar as he was a specific living being, and specifically related to other living beings—the reason for this is to be sought in the new mode of relation between history and life: in this dual position of life that places it at the same time outside of history, in its biological environment, and inside human historicity, penetrated by the latter's techniques of knowledge and power. (*History of Sexuality* 143)

By situating the "biological environment . . . outside of history" Foucault traces a relation of bodies within biopower that culminates in their transformation into individuated objects of national knowledge bereft of their more dynamic, mutating, idiosyncratic histories. The biopolitical body represents a targeted corporeality that is simultaneously pierced by "techniques of power and knowledge"—for instance, those encased within classifications of pathology that represent the "inside [of] human historicity"—while being shorn of their own particular (and, in a larger sense, evolutionary) material dynamism. Biopolitics, in effect, norms corporealities within categories of abnormalcy. It does so in order to organize crip/queer biologies into hyper-market-driven identities. As such, biologies are transformed into measured capacities assessed by the yardsticks of an increasingly medicalized culture.

Biopolitical identifications of dysfunctional bodies productively assist nations in an improved knowledge of all bodies with respect to the further embedding of universal norms of functionality, appearance, and capacity. As the German disability studies scholar Rebecca Maskos explains in our documentary film *A World Without Bodies* (2002), disabled bodies under-going autopsies after gassings in Nazi psychiatric institutions "were human because they could make references to humans, but they were not human at the same time." This externally fashioned understanding of people living in peripheral embodiments as useful *and* expendable can be imperceptibly ingested into the cultural knowledge base of all bodies as an in-built base-line against which normative developmental curves are assessed. In Judith Butler's terms, disability is constitutive of ability yet culturally and scientifi-cally disavowed as central to the realization of normative living (*Bodies That Matter* 140–41). Disability hauntingly informs formulations of normatively maturing embodiments passing into orderly adulthoods.[5]

Biopolitics designates processes of managing population resources through demographic record keeping at the level of the state; neoliberalism operates as a system of governance particular to the last half of the twentieth century. As such, neoliberalism has been characterized by strategies wherein governance by and for the people is abdicated in favor of strategies that pave the way for new corporate marketplaces.[6] David Harvey identifies the prin-cipal strategy in these state-led openings on behalf of for-profit industries as "accumulation by dispossession": governmental participation in the cen-tralization of wealth and power for the few by dispossessing publics of their collectively held spaces and markers of collective belonging (*New Imperial-ism* 64). In doing so, neoliberalism effectively defaults on its obligations to govern on behalf of the people. Neoliberalism, in other words, increasingly rationalizes the use of public resources for the global expansion of capital by ransacking the commonwealth as a resource awaiting a new generation of corporate exploitation.

These developments disproportionately impact the lives of people with disabilities and other occupants of peripheral embodiments (queer, inter-sexed, transgendered, racialized, impoverished, obese, to name a few key sites of cross-disability compounded identities that prove resistant to pass-ing as normative). Within neoliberalism rests a marked movement to ad-dress disabled people and other marginalized segments of the population in paradoxical terms as new commodification opportunities, evidence of the triumph of American exceptionalism, and/or as threats to the productive mandates of market capitalism. In part, these changes emerge most starkly from an increasing tendency to conflate two critical nodal identity points in the modern subject formations of a people: nationalism and ableism. The convergence of these two divergent ways of being and belonging (or, alter-natively, being but not belonging—the terms of a constitutive haunting of normalcy by disability) emerge most vehemently in countries undergoing processes of industrialization and postindustrialization.

In *History of Madness* (2006) and *History of Sexuality: An Introduction* (1978), Foucault charts the historical contingencies of arrival at this conver-gence of nationalism and biopolitics (what will we call the ground zero of ableism) as the goal of techniques of power to target nonnormative bod-ies through inclusionist practices on behalf of their status as objects of knowledge—inclusive techniques that have less to do with a more expansive tolerance toward formerly deviant citizens than the appropriation of disabil-ity as an opportunity for expansion at the consumption end of late capitalist marketplaces. In this book we refer to the historical period within which these changes primarily occur as neoliberalism and the tactics undertaken as belonging to what Kevin Floyd theorizes in the *Reification of Desire* as par-ticular to the production mode known as "post-Fordist neoliberalism" (158).

ABLENATIONALISM: WHERE ABLEISM AND NATIONALISM MEET

Any openings neoliberalism creates for acceptance of formerly excluded populations comes at a cost. First, with respect to the commodification of necessary material supports (assistive devices, pharmaceutical thera-pies, durable medical goods) within for-profit medicine as a new hawker of consumptive technologies formerly financed by the state. Consumptive technologies of the body arrive on the market with the attendant economic inaccessibility that often accompanies such product development gone private. These developments represent "innovations" at the consumption end of late capitalism (post-Fordist economies) because they, particularly in the case of people with disabilities, focus on the supplementation of bodies diagnosed "debilitated" as opportunities for new product development and market expansion. Within neoliberalism nearly all bodies are referenced as debilitated and in need of market commodities to shore up their beleaguered cognitive, physical, affective, and aesthetic shortcomings. Neoliberal bodies, in this sense, provide opportunities for treating the individual topos of biology as, in-and-of-itself, a site of perpetual improvement for market-based exploitations and informational/affective resource extraction.

Consequently, "incapacity" has become an increasingly fluid, shorthand term for individual citizens' responsibilities within biopolitics for their own body management. Jasbir Puar refers to this tactical expansion of impairment as a central feature of "debility" in her essay "Prognosis Time" (163). Neoliberalism comes replete with an expansive sense that we are all living in relation to the arrival of a prognosis of the pathology-to-come. Second, despite this neoliberal expansion of debility as an emergent characteristic of all bodies, its overdetermined application to an insufficient every-body surrenders the lived alternatives developed by disabled people navigating a world organized around narrowly devised norms of capacity, functionality, and bodily aesthetic. In the chapters to come we will refer to those disabled people who by paradoxical means gain entrance into late capitalist cultures as "the able-disabled"—those who exceed their disability limitations through forms of administrative "creaming" or hyper-prostheticization but leave the vast majority of disabled people behind. Likewise, we also discuss the utility of this new formation of tolerance (i.e., inclusionism) being advertised globally as an exceptional constituent property of extra-national diversity narrated as prematurely accomplished in neoliberal postindustrial nations as "ablenationalism." Both "the able-disabled" and "ablenationalism" develop as late twentieth-century neoliberal strategies for the tightly regulated entrance of people with disabilities into neoliberal economies through what Michel Foucault refers to as "biopolitics" (*History of Sexuality* 141).

While *nationalism*, in Hardt and Negri's terms, is synonymous with "modernizing effects" that unify people by breaking down "the barriers" of other cultural differences (*Empire* 107), *ableism*, as theorized by disability studies scholars such as Fiona Campbell, legislates privileges of citizenship based on norms of ability. Ableism frames disability as a "predominantly negative feature, tragedy, or flaw" that necessarily excludes some on the basis of inaccessibility, stigma, and normative aesthetic expectations of belonging (Campbell, *Contours of Ableism* 52). Thus, ablenationalism conjoins the features of nationalism as a "deep horizontal comradeship" with norms of ability that appear naturally synonymous with the privileges of citizenship (Anderson 7). Functionality, ability, and appearance all serve as determinative of participation in the surface identifications cultivated by nationalism. As such a baseline of expectations about embodiment comes replete with normative notions of nationality. One of the main points of *The Biopolitics of Disability*, then, is to understand how beliefs in disability as a materially devalued existence create one substantive foundation upon which nationalism flourishes. This development is one of the substantive paradoxes within neoliberal disability.

Our formulation of *ablenationalism* begins with an acknowledgment of Jasbir Puar's influential formulation of *homonationalism* in her book, *Terrorist Assemblages: Homonationalism in Queer Times* (39). Both homonationalism and ablenationalism theorize the degree to which treating crip/queer people as an exception valorizes norms of inclusion. A key feature of neoliberalism entails the celebration of a more flexible social sphere; one that is characterized as exceptional based on the evidence of an expanding tolerance—or, perhaps, even a limited "acceptance"—of formerly marginalized differences. Yet, as Puar points out, this new acceptance works in a limited domain wherein "upstanding homosexuals participating in normative kinship models" serve to further reify the inherent value of existing heteronormative social relations (*Terrorist Assemblages* 73). In the wake of this open toleration of some gay lifestyles, a further stigmatization of queer bodies that fail to fit newly normed standards of bourgeois gay sexuality means they find themselves further ostracized, devalued, and dehumanized—abjected at the margins of recently assimilated communities of the formerly stigmatized.

Yet, while going largely unaddressed in *Terrorist Assemblages*, Puar's key usage of "upstanding" in her formulation of homonormativity helps begin the process of assessing the bodily-based nature of privilege in late capitalist societies. Likewise, disability studies critiques undertake analyses of the repetition of human predicaments born of an ever expanding catalog of ways that, in the words of Stanley Elkins, "bodies fall away from true" (223). This characterization in Elkin's novel is made by the queer male nurse, Colin Bible, in his innovative peroration about the unrecognized value of alternative embodiments for a band of disabled youth in his charge. Colin's analysis regarding the ways in which human materiality inevitably fails to meet norms of embodiment would be worthy of Georges Canguilhem's critique of pathological states in *The Normal and the Pathological* (see chapter 7 for a more in-depth analysis of Colin Bible's commentary as a key feature of the antinormative novel of disability).

As people with disabilities encounter the inflexibilities of key social institutions such as health care, religious gatherings, communities, workplaces, schools, families, and so on, such encounters increasingly depend upon the ability of some to "fit in" by passing as nondisabled, or, at least, not too disabled. *Inclusionism requires that disability be tolerated as long as it does not demand an excessive degree of change from relatively inflexible institutions, environments, and norms of belonging.* In particular, the degree to which disability does not significantly challenge the aesthetic ideals of a national imaginary dependent upon fantasies of bodily wholeness and, if not perfection, at least a narrow range of normalcy.

These sites of interaction between fantasies of normative bodies and the disabled bodies that give life to the fictionality of normativity exclude some inhabitants to a greater degree than those enjoying status among the newly tolerable (i.e., able-disabled) within neoliberal diversity initiatives. Throughout this study we will refer to the residents of this surplus humanity as those occupying *peripheral embodiments*; such exclusions result from equality denied to a majority of crip/queer bodies based on determinations of their excessive deviance from culturally inculcated norms. Within neoliberalism's inclusion schemes, those occupying peripheral embodiments cannot be adequately accommodated even under the most liberal, fluid, and flexible diversity doctrine given the in-built limits of community infrastructure, reasonable tolerance, limited economic resources, and traditional historical expectations about who will share the rapidly dwindling commonwealth represented by public and private spaces.

As a historical practice, ablenationalism develops primarily as an outcropping of what disability historian Henri-Jacques Stiker identifies as "the birth of rehabilitation." For Stiker, rehabilitation, as the benign cultural relation of ability to disability, involves the mid-twentieth-century entrance into an age of normalization—one that fully coincides with the development of neoliberalism—wherein all citizens are increasingly subject to the dictates of how to be more alike than different from each other (121). By normalization Stiker references the strategies by which individuals find themselves bound into practices of conformity that exceed a prior era's exclusions based on determinative differences such as race, gender, sexuality, ethnicity, and, in the foremost cases addressed in this study, crip/queer existences (i.e., disability).

Part of what marks transitions to neoliberal forms of inclusion, the rhetorics and practices that allow some members of previously outsider groups to be included under the goals of normalization, regards a changing representational approach to disabled people. Disability within neoliberal orders of inclusion has come to represent a certain kind of embodied value for contemporary nations in at least four specific ways that we chart throughout *The Biopolitics of Disability*: (1) through the bulking up of sheer population numbers by counting disabled people in population demographics—"a nation's wealth is its quantity of people" (here the question of quality of life is deferred to something that can be best addressed by debility-attentive marketplaces); (2) as evidence of a nation's moral commitment to the "less fortunate" (while other, less advanced countries discard their disabled people and leave them to languish in abject poverty, "this" country provides humane supports and care to even its most vulnerable and unproductive members); (3) the provision of health care (in exchange for medical treatment, disabled people's lives allow a nation to collect "data" that assists in improving the health of nondisabled citizens while often degrading their own well-being in the process), and (4) the recognition that access to normative social institutions (privileges of citizenship, education, community living, legal protections against discrimination, marriage, representational inclusion, sexual experiences, etc.) is a right of all citizens.

Each of these claims under neoliberal biopolitics depends upon a widely held public recognition of an almost exclusively negative valence ascribed to people with disabilities predating the era of normalization.[7] Disabled people's national service within neoliberalism occurs to the degree that the nation is enabled by its claims to have relinquished a more restrictive, carceral mode of social treatment (i.e., eugenics) toward its non-productive members. A prior cultural moment's widespread practices of institutionalization, prohibitions, and stigmatizing containment strategies (its formalized, systemic segregation practices) are magically resolved by allowing them to lapse into the distance of a bygone and, presumably, more barbaric era.

We want to make absolutely clear at this point that the goal of this book is not to disparage efforts at the meaningful inclusion of people with disabilities. Rather the emphasis is upon a critique of strategies of inclusion that discount, universalize, and normalize disabled people on behalf of claims to social integration. As Asma Abbas pointedly argues, "[f]or one, it is so centered on the person who is performing the inclusion that the included can be little more than 'beneficiaries'" (39). Such approaches are based on a devaluing of differences disability embodiments bring to the project of living with others. This is an alternative ethics of living that, as we argue in chapter 2 in our application of Jack Halberstam's theory of the "queer art of failure" to disability education, could best be made available by articulating disabled people's productive failure to adhere to the unrealizable projects of neoliberal body normalization schemes.

Thus, while disability has been recognized as a social, material, and manufactured terrain within disability studies and other discourses associated with an array of social deconstructionist approaches, its basis in bodies as well as ideologies also provides opportunities for unique combinations of social becoming (i.e., nonnormative disability materialisms). Attention to the lived intricacies of embodiment offer alternatives to normalization efforts aimed at homogenizing a previous era's social degenerates. Thus, the interactions of more material-based disability arts and cultures, as will be demonstrated throughout this book, are consistently generated around creative alternatives to the politics of inclusion as much as exclusion. This array of alternatives of living interdependently as disabled people is precipitated by the need to navigate the world in devalued differential embodiments.

In order to locate people with disabilities as impacted constituencies within global capitalism one must often look beyond the parameters of even informal economies, or the radical margins of Marxist conceptions of surplus labor, to those classified as the rightful recipients of national charity (welfare and social service recipients, for example), a form of ubiquitous marginalization Jim Charlton refers to as "peripheral everywhere" (195). In emphasizing severity of incapacity as primary to a devalued identity, discourses of policy, economics, health, rehabilitation, and citizenship support practices of volunteerism and charity as instances of what disability historian Paul Longmore calls "conspicuous contributions" to sustain them (144). As a result, this willy-nilly approach to the provision of supports and services by the private sector further demonstrates neoliberalism's abdication of the responsibility of governance.[8] As we discuss in the afterword, whether supplied by nation-state or market, the calculated provision (and purposeful nonprovision) of services based on principles of detecting qualifying bodies as "too impaired" for meaningful labor underscores the degree to which even a catchall category of "surplus labor" operates as a highly guarded space of state-sanctioned ostracization. The people who rely upon public provision of supports are impacted by this situation particularly in the wake of recent austerity measures implemented in the United States, Europe, and Australia, where health care and unemployment coffers are pillaged to make up budget shortfalls.

For instance, in the United States individuals living on Social Security Disability Income (SSDI) are not counted among the ranks of the unemployed. The best result, from the perspective of the quantitatively oriented neoliberal state, may be to have hordes of individuals not fully recognized as existing among the ranks of the unemployed while simultaneously existing at the edges of economic and social sustainability. Further support for such claims of "organized forgetting" *can be demonstrated* by the way census counts are taken (Giroux, *Organized Forgetting* 19). The fact that the U.S. census does not include institutionalized people in most states while each prisoner is counted meticulously in the prison-industrial complex points to another form of invisibility. Such developments entail the creation of forms of disenfranchisement not included in numbers regarding those embodiments failing to be successfully supported by the state.

Further, these new alternative forms of displacement occur in tandem with what political economists and race/sexuality theorists identify as discourses of American exceptionalism (that which we theorize in chapter 1 as "ablenationalism"). Discourses of American exceptionalism reference national claims of moral caring on behalf of the displaced, marginalized, and differentially embodied. Such claims on the part of the neoliberal state are deployed in the interests of supporting U.S. interests in shoring up a perception of its diminishing status as a world leader in a global marketplace (Puar, *Terrorist Assemblages* 4). The cultural forces bringing about this historical move out of the eugenics era are those that act upon peripheral embodiments (we include cognitive and sensory disability in this rubric) through practices of regularization, automation, classification, and standardization. Along with normalizations of racialized, sexualized, and gendered modes of being, neoliberal marketplaces produce modern formations of disability as an increasingly malleable form of deviance tamed for the good of the nation as a potential participant in the inflows and outflows of globalization.

Within the terms of ablenationalism, then, disabled people are increasingly fashioned as a population that can be put into service on behalf of the nation-state rather than exclusively positioned as parasitic upon its resources and, therefore, somehow outside of its best interests. Perhaps the irony of this transition is that it could be argued to fulfill a common precept of disability rights advocacy communities: disabled people want to be treated like everyone else and in such a way that their disabilities are not defining of their value as human beings. The contention appears incredibly reasonable and garners alliance with the "contemporary spectacle of able-bodied heteronormativity" (McRuer, *Crip Theory* 3). For McRuer, and certainly ourselves, the questioning of the assumed naturalness upon which heteronomativity rests is one of the only cultural spaces from which "new (queer/ crip) identities might be imagined" as nonnormative alternatives to the flattened horizons of ablenationalism (149).

NEOLIBERAL DISABILITY

Consequently, this book is about how changes in cultural approaches to disability have come about under neoliberalism: where they might be evident, how disabled people have responded to them, and how the understanding of disability has shifted beneath the order of biopolitics. *The Biopolitics of Disability* seeks to chart avenues into alternative methodological opportunities for recognizing the instrumental nature of such changes upon the lives of disabled people; first, in terms of the advent of depreciating forms of productive normalization, and second, through the creative ways in which disabled people have navigated neoliberalism as a result of finding themselves in seemingly benign, but often intolerable, cultural situations. Such maneuvers require a tricky navigation of public definitions that transition disabled people away from more traditionally patronizing roles as "exceptional Americans" (including special students, super crips, exceptional people, heart-warming inspirations, overcomers, wheelchair explorers, etc.), but avoid falling into the equally worrisome position of proofs underwriting national claims to a completed process of inclusionism paraded as a prime example of American exceptionalism. It is in the interstice of these two untenable positions that we situate our critique of neoliberal disability.

In contrast to our analysis of disability as a product of the segregating era of eugenics in *Cultural Locations of Disability*, the advent of what we will call *neoliberal disability* plays a critical role in efforts to represent the nation as synonymous with an expanding, yet tightly parametered, array of acceptable body types and the uses to which those divergent bodies may be put. Within the logic of neoliberalism this exceptional status is based upon embodiments that are the responsibility of the individual and no fault of the social order.

One might be led to think that within this rubric of undervaluation, disabled populations might find themselves marginalized at the outskirts of cultural utility. Yet recent practices of ablenationalism—those open rhetorical claims to a new era of inclusion for people with disabilities issued by the state and its sponsoring international corporations and charitable networks—have situated some mutant bodies as effectively and normatively disabled. Disabled people now increasingly perform their representational work at the level of globalization as a symbol of expansive inclusionist efforts extended by the beneficence of neoliberal tolerance for unfortunate (read: racialized, heteronormative, non-Western) disabled people around the globe.

Additionally, in the wake of the emergence of practices of neoliberal inclusionism this study seeks to map some of the coordinates of global disability populations—or, more particularly, the interactive spaces, both literal and virtual, disabled people have crafted to share information about their lives. In the words of immanent materialist William E. Connolly, regarding alternative materialist perspectives of being, disability represents an "energized asymmetry that periodically sets the stage, when conditions are in place, for old formations to disintegrate and new ones to surge into being" (181). One result of this "energized asymmetry" among disabled people is the ability to draw some necessary parallels between their material and social conditions around the globe, as we do in our discussion of international independent disability cinema in chapters 4 and 5. The goal is not to perpetuate universalizing conclusions about duplicative states of social rejection (the forms of social rejection experienced by people with disabilities are often quite unique), but rather to gain an understanding of the nuances of ablenationalism's tactics on something approaching a disability studies analysis conducted on a national, even global, scale.

It is also an expressed tactic of this book to analyze whether or not disabled people have been effectively navigating the shifting historical terms of their social treatment under neoliberal governance in a manner that empowers rather than further disempowers them socially, economically, and professionally. Finally, and perhaps most importantly, our goal is to assess the compromises reached at the edges of disability "precaritization" at a time when severe disability serves to identify populations most in danger of rampant social neglect and the necropolitics of expendability (Butler and Athanasiou 5).

MAPPING THE TERRAIN OF
THE BIOPOLITICS OF DISABILITY

The chapters in this book participate in theoretical crossings between disability studies and critical race studies, queer studies, political economy, sociology, cultural studies, literary theory, visual anthropology, and social history, among others—all theoretical movements bringing scholarship into increasingly wider global awareness campaigns around questions of social justice and the strange agencies of materiality (biologies). Such approaches to disability encourage emergent generations of researchers and practitioners to keep alert to the limits of ever-mutating epistemologies that mark disabled people as subjects of neoliberalism, ablenationalism, and globalization. These limits are set by transecting experiences of "otherness" as raced, gendered, and sexed social inequities and the largely immobile status of constituents that disability studies would seek to represent and more qualitatively mobilize.

The identification of these multiple permutations of existence runs counter to Fredric Jameson's formulation of the term "geopolitical aesthetic" in its emphasis on biopolitics (3). Rather than recognize a constructed globe as a single unit of territorial repetitions of experiences of marginalization (what Jameson refers to as "the world system" [10]), the chapters that follow seek to multiply the ways in which disability, as variations on the theme of human variation, navigates local and global political spaces. Disability, in this approach, represents a bounded social identity hemmed in by, and creatively inventive within, the narrow local contexts within which those with peripheral embodiments primarily live. Or, as Carrie Sandahl explains in the documentary film *Self Preservation: The Art of Riva Lehrer*, "as disabled people we're hemmed in by confining normative spaces, but we also find ways to maneuver alternatively within them."

Chapter 1, "From Liberal to Neoliberal Futures of Disability," charts theoretical implications for scholars participating in a "turn to the body" school of criticism as a reaction to the orthodoxies of minority and social model thinking within disability studies. This chapter sets the historical stage for the analyses of disability under the conditions of neoliberalism to follow. Specifically, we query key formulations of the social and minority models of disability that have been integral to efforts by disability rights movements in postindustrial nations to gain access to dominant social institutions. These move in tandem with the contemporary gay rights movement that seeks normalization through policy changes that allow gay and lesbian people access to marriage, adoption, and other middle-class heteronormative institutional practices and lifestyles. Disability rights movements have made similar claims, seeking access to independent living in communities of their choice, the right to free public education in least restrictive environments, the end to discriminatory insurance practices that exclude disabled individuals from coverage for preexisting conditions, accessible housing, barrier-free architecture, economic accessibility to consumptive lifestyles, appropriate inclusive public transportation, and the pursuit of sexual experiences of their choice. In taking up these normalizing practices, many minority groups have articulated arguments that attempt to divest excessive differences from stigmatized populations as deterministic projections of ableist society. Disability rights movements have argued, for instance, on behalf of disabled people's similitude to the universal human aspirations of able-bodied people as the basis for their demands of integration alongside others.

This emphasis on integration alongside others marks the historical emergence of disabled subjectivities into the marketplace and the interstices of state and national benevolence as a complex site of contradictory impulses. Neoliberal discourses involve the production of "inclusive" lifestyles that provide opportunities for narratives of national exceptionalism based, at least in part, on the reported arrival of a new era of humane treatment for persons with disabilities (PWDs). While we neither refute nor endorse this contention of arrival at a more inclusive postmodernity, our analyses seek to explore the strange agencies that neoliberalism has set into motion under the banner of ablenationalism: first in a discussion of a backlash against the homogenizing implications of universal disability access design in cities and national monuments addressed by the contemporary European art theorist Paul Virilio, and in the complaints about paving over U.S. national parklands by American desert environmentalist Edward Abbey. Second on an international scale where international charity organizations advocate for the adoption of surgical and prosthetic interventions that shame non-industrialized nations. This shaming rhetoric emerges in relation to condemnations of a failed embrace of inclusive practices synonymous with the modernity of more advanced, post-industrial countries. Such developments unveil the ways in which disabled people are now referenced within neoliberalism as the beneficiaries of national and international systems of benevolence that require careful scrutiny by disability studies.

Chapter 2, "Educational Cripistemologies," opens with a discussion of the educational avoidance of disability studies and how a commitment to training professionals in practices of normalization (the primary product of university professionalization) preclude a more robust knowledge of crip/queer bodies from taking shape. Our examination of the inclusion of students with disabilities in the context of neoliberalism plays into wider cultural efforts to iron out differences in the heteronormative press to sameness. The resulting homogenization of "less severe" disabilities often serves as the foundation stone of efforts to secure the right for some to access public and private spaces in ways that others access them. The sacrifice of an alternatively more meaningful exploration of "the difference that disability makes," consequently, is examined as having come with unintended side effects regarding the articulation of alternatives that living with disabilities entails (Michalko 22). After all, if disability brings nothing but likeness to others into the world as its primary contribution to questions of lived embodiment, what value will it have to help us reimagine ways of artfully living less productive, less consumptive, and less exploitative lives? Among liberal pedagogical models that mask meaningful differences between bodies rather than turn the experiential value of differential embodiment into teachable moments, isn't every child effectively left behind?

Instead, we argue for the development of curricular cripistemologies (an inventive hybrid term forwarded by disability studies scholars Merri Lisa Johnson and Robert McRuer in their special guest-edited double volume of the *Journal of Literary and Cultural Disability Studies*), pedagogies that, based on twenty years of teaching projects and research initiatives pursued by the authors in tandem with our long-time Special Education colleague Linda Ware, foreground the precarious social positions of nonnormative embodiments as a foundation for instructional insight. Drawing upon Judith Halberstam's alternative deployment of constructive failure in *The Queer Art of Failure*, we argue for recognition of the crip art of failure as an alternative emergence of resistance strategies to the homogenizing dictates of neoliberal educational diversity schemes.

In Part II, "The Biopolitics of In(ter)dependent Disability Cinema," our arguments move the critique of neoliberal inclusionist politics to portrayals of nonnormative body pairings in the antiestablishment dominant cinema of John Schlesinger's *Midnight Cowboy* (1969). Here we discuss the oddball relationship that develops between a hypersexualized drifter (Joe Buck, played by Jon Voight) and an asexualized disabled con artist (Enrico "Ratzo"

Rizzo, played by Dustin Hoffman) on the streets of New York. As queer/ crip men subject to dehumanizing beliefs about socially devalued drifters like themselves, the two have to unlearn their normatively inculcated understandings of marginalized embodiments (fags, jackies, tutti-fruities, and cripples) in order to fashion an alternative ethics of interdependency. Through analysis of filmic form, we argue that the distinction between the use of flashbacks as formative to deterministic traumas of heteronormative masculinity and flash-forwards as foundational to curative futures of disability exposes two distinct neoliberal fantasyscapes represented by divergent visual verb tenses.

Alternatively, our analysis situates the majority of the film's engagement with nonnormative positivisms in the interstitial queer/crip time that exists between Joe's rejection of hustling and Rico's fantasies of the restoration of his health in the orange groves of Florida. The alternative filmic ethics of crip/queer relationships in *Midnight Cowboy* emerges as Joe and Rico fashion an interdependent lifestyle based on mutually elaborated body care rituals. By tending to the needs of each other's bodies—Rico cooks meals, cuts Joe's hair, shines his boots, and washes Joe's clothes while introducing him to the sexual subcultures of New York, and Joe carries heavy objects up the stairs, lets Rico lean on him to walk as his mobility diminishes, and purchases cough medicine with the profit he steals during a violent sexual tryst with another man—the couple institutes a crip/queer partnership more productive than any fantasized fulfillment of heteronormative embodiment offered in the film.

Chapter 4, "The Politics of Atypicality," forays into disabled persons' alternative negotiations of embodiment featured in screenings around the globe at international independent disability film festivals. Like gay and lesbian film festivals before them, disability film festivals seek to draw media representations from around the world. The space of the independent disability film festival provides an opportunity to increase public awareness of disability issues—particularly in terms of influencing the subjective domain of attitudes about disability as tragic embodiment. Such consciousness-raising efforts exist as the neoliberal explanatory rationale behind state-funded arts initiatives that provide the baseline support operationalized by disability film festivals. However, independent disability films do not (by and large) attempt to effect changes in public perceptions through standard diversity fare programming such as heroic portraits, sentimentalization, awareness campaigns, or pathos. Instead, they seek to present disability as a phenomenological intervention into normative viewing experiences. The space of the film festival consciously cultivates disability as a multiplicity of experiences impossible to reduce to a singular, universal perspective on nonnormative embodiment. In fact, audience members are encouraged to become connoisseurs of differential embodiment, a perspective that reduces disability alienation over multiple days and screenings through a developing familiarity with the myriad expressions of human variation.

Because the works screened arrive from many asymmetrical global locations, the viewings tend to achieve what David Harvey calls "political simultaneity"—a simulation of experiences from diverse cultural locations that cannot be easily assimilated into viewers' inevitably culturally centric points of view on disability (*Postmodernity* 266). The import of this series of abrupt entrances into vastly differing experiences of global disability contexts accomplishes two important effects: (1) international disability contexts are brought to public attention to thwart the silencing around disability as a politicized constituency; and (2) the screening of various international understandings of disability bring pressure on the festival's host country to more effectively address neglected contexts of exclusion, confinement, asexualization, abandonment, neglect, and misrecognition. Disability film festivals effectively lower the alienating effects of unfamiliarity by staging a pluripotent array of human differences while also using the flexibility of global information flows as an opportunity to increase awareness of the need for social change—to learn from disabled lives rather than merely accepting them in accordance with the limited principles of neoliberal inclusionism. Thus, what has been explained as a debilitating fracturing of political identity groups by internally inconsistent claims for recognition within the potentially monolithic organizing identity of "disability" has been transformed within the space of the disability film festival into a productive dynamic that we call "the politics of atypicality."

Chapter 5, "Permutations of the Species," continues this line of analysis by discussing developing traditions of independent cinematic formulas for telling stories about disabled lives. Most disability films (dominant and minority) take up a singular disabled character as protagonist with whom to cultivate audience identifications. This individuated story approach encourages experimental forms of digital storytelling that simulate subjectivities of those occupying peripheral embodiments. By employing avant-garde techniques such as audio track distortions, reversals in disability characterization techniques, jump cuts, and first-person voiceovers, independent disability cinema advances a phenomenological framework of understanding.

Independent disability cinema allows opportunities for ways of comprehending disability as developed points of view based on the creative labor of navigating worlds built for able-bodied travelers and those who more easily fit into normative aesthetic expectations of appearance, movement, and functionality. In Jacques Ranciere's words, independent disability film operates as an "aesthetic act [on] configurations of experience that create new modes of sense perception and induce novel forms of political subjectivity" (3). The array of disability portraits to which one is treated during the festivals develop something akin to a globalizing perspective on human variation, a point of view that offers viewers a "species-level" overview of global disability experience as an innovative (rather than debilitating) diversity of expressive alternative embodiments. Participants develop an understanding similar to that of a visual anthropologist collecting information on the cultural existences of participants in a mysterious, diffuse, yet globally constitutive, tribe.

Part III, "Medical Outliers: Navigating the Disability Bio(political) sphere," opens with reflections on neoliberal health care and the politics of research funding initiatives now demanded of disabled persons and their advocates. In chapter 6, "Corporeal Subcultures and the Specter of Biopolitics," we turn to an examination of virtual networks developing among disabled people advocating for more effective surgical and research investigations into rare conditions. Through a longitudinal survey of online conversations among those with esophageal atresia tracheo-fistula (EATF) and spinal motor atrophy (SMA), we analyze distinctive neoliberal pressures faced by those seeking effective health care solutions for neglected conditions. Nikolas Rose identifies "Big Pharma" (219) as the penultimate neoliberal research machine driving forward new biopolitical identities based on widening notions of "debility" (Puar, "Prognosis Time" 162). Here we discuss alternative medical subcultures seeking to improve bodily outcomes for those with neglected chronic conditions. In doing so, we witness the development of politicized subcultures using the Internet to gain attention and shape the research agendas of genetic, surgical, and pharmaceutical researchers and practitioners alike.

One important development during this nearly two-decade-long study in which we were also participants turns on disabled people's entrance into virtual domains of medical advocacy. In the cases of both EATF and SMA, disabled people commonly survive long enough to become contributors to conversations previously dominated by nondisabled parents, advocates, researchers, medical professionals, and surgeons. While discussions prior to this historical entry of disabled persons largely pertain to early diagnosis, effective surgical solutions and treatment regimes, and hopeful discourses of cure, disabled persons contributions circulate around the management of heavily stigmatized disorders in the social world. The eruption of questions of impairment in relation to the social makes the terms of survival shift toward imagining alternatively habitable futures for those with conditions formerly curtailed to infancy and childhood. In this context, these virtual advocacy networks enter openly into neoliberal funding research frays by purchasing stock in treatments (such as genetic splicing sequences) believed to be more advantageous for survival but largely neglected by research medical communities. Such entrances into neoliberal risk environments prove significantly hazardous as they entail participation in medical marketplaces of exchange value, yet the alternative is to continue a contemporary drift into negligent health care domains dominated by more lucrative disorders of debility such as cancer, autism, and Alzheimer's syndrome.

In chapter 7, "The Capacities of Incapacity in Antinormative Novels of Embodiment," we return to alternative representational systems developing in novelistic portrayals of disability during late liberalism. As a response to liberal disability representational strategies born in the wake of the civil rights era, portrayals of people with disabilities under neoliberalism have increasingly tended to approach "deviant" bodies as sites of invention rather than individuated instances of deviance, trauma, or tragedy. In opposition to rehabilitating disability on the basis of social constructivist claims that disability is in the environment and not in the person (the founding insight of the U.K. disability social and the U.S. minority models), neoliberal novels of embodiment (that which we call "the antinormative novel") explore disabilities as sites of radical human mutation wherein much of the creativity of the species lies. Here we theorize these surprising representational reversals of disabled people's embodied innovation in contemporary novelistic emplotment strategies as "the capacities of incapacity."

At the fore of this argument is the antinormative novel's challenge to those aspects of market-based fetishizations of difference that threaten to rid more radical formulations of disability of the promise they hold for fashioning alternative lives. Through examinations of antinormative novels of embodiment such as Richard Powers's *The Gold Bug Variations* (1992) and *The Echo Maker* (2007), Stanley Elkins's *The Magic Kingdom* (1985), and Mark Haddon's *The Curious Incident of the Dog in the Night-Time* (2004), we analyze ways in which disabilities are transformed into productive experiences of difference in the world. These are not politically correct romances of difference employing more positive rhetoric of disability; instead, they effectively argue that disability is better apprehended as a marker of innovation operating at the materialist edge of species innovation. Within the anti-normative novel disability becomes a way of envisioning the dynamic responses of embodiment to haphazard evolutions of corporeality, diverse genetic systems, and increasingly toxic environments.

In our afterword, "Disability as Multitude," we fill out our discussions of alternative valuation systems with a peroration on disability and its potentiality through associations with nonproductive bodies. Employing concepts of Spinoza's "radical democracy" adopted by Michael Hardt and Antonio Negri in their *Multitudes* trilogy, the afterword offers insights about ways we might refashion contemporary understandings of people with disabilities and their overriding ouster from guiding concepts of productivity in neoliberal (post-Fordist) economies. Rather than continue necessary lines of thought about the persistence of social barriers to people with disabilities achieving meaningful employment, we undertake a discussion of disability living as an ethical domain alternative to existing models of consumption. In so doing we seek to mutate the recognition of disability as a pragmatic category for engaging enactments of nationalism and normative expectations of citizenship.

We identify this imperative to conform to the demands of competitive labor markets and their attendant normative expectations of participation as a further aspect of ablenationalism. Within this politics, most people with disabilities are excluded by falling short of this participatory bottom line of citizenship, and the key guiding principles of democracy as an extension of demands of the homogenization of differences are left un(der)analyzed. When we approach disability with respect to a concept of alternative valuation rather than merely as a symptom of exclusion within late capitalism, opportunities erupt for realizing "other worlds" of possibility. In classical formulas of Marxism and liberal discourses of political economy, disability represents the existence of nonproductive bodies that cannot be successfully adapted to market-driven expectations of competitive labor. Such bodies prove needy of state and private sponsorship, marking them as superfluous to classifications of those on the outer-most fringes of neoliberal capitalism. Contrastingly, in Hardt and Negri's definition of "nonproductive bodies" we find a potentially productive alternative to body-based exclusions in identifying disability and other nonconforming populations as actively resistant to the imperatives of consumptive living (*Empire* 274). Rather than simply bemoaning a lack of inclusivity characteristic of neoliberal social orders, "nonproductive bodies" allow a more active reading based on refusals of normative modes of production that operate with respect to compulsory ablebodiedness as their unspoken foundation.

CONCLUSION: ALL "DISMODERNIST" BUT NOT ALL DISABLED

The Biopolitics of Disability offers an opportunity for scholars to pursue alternative paradigms for theorizing disability among other cross-cultural experiences of bodies identified as deviant yet now newly tolerated within neoliberalism. This book marks the important emergence of disabled subjectivities as "productively failing" in the competitive labor marketplace, standardized testing curriculums, and at the interstices of a heteronormatively driven state benevolence. Neoliberal discourses of power involve the production of "inclusive" lifestyles leading to an employment of disability in disquieting narratives of national exceptionalism. Such narratives are based on ways of giving voice to new eras characterized by humane treatments of people with disabilities and, consequently, provide a glance at the normativized disabled subject and an accompanying normalization of deviancy.

Furthermore, this normalization of some disabilities is created against other nonnormative, less easy to accommodate differences including but not exhausting differences such as neurodiversity, individuals with intellectual disabilities (particularly MR [mental retardation]), and, perhaps most importantly for our ends, those with communication- and cognition-based disabilities. This process of the normalization of disability promises a utopian future predicated on a form of ahistorical biological universalism in which we are all disabled or, at least, potentially disabled, as in the case of arguments offered by disability studies scholars such as Tom Shakespeare and Nicholas Watson's elucidation of "embodied ontology" ("Social Model" 26), Lennard Davis's "dismodernism" ("Dismodernism" 232), and James Berger's "the dys-/disarticulate" (2). Yet, while the apparent promise of this acceptance often appears all to the good—after all a little acknowledgment of shared vulnerability can only be helpful—the analyses to come explore how such contentions also undermine an ability to pay more serious attention to crip/queer populations and the alternative perspectives that their differences bring into the world.

The process of the normalization of disability developing as a presumed result of an increasing recognition among normate bodies that "we are all disabled" potentially precipitates a disastrous fall into meaningless homogenization as an antidote to bodily stigma. Such echoes of universal debility underpin calls for dismantling the social model of disability, the principle that disability is in the environment rather than the person, and approaches that critique disability as a politically suspect identity category. For Shakespeare, Watson, Davis, and Berger the idea that postmodernism entails the promise of a recognition that we are all disabled to some extent or other promotes a politically suspect inversion of human vulnerability as a defining characteristic of all bodies—disabled bodies included. In making this flattening gesture the authors place the ingenuity of living that disability involves effectively out of reach. Such contentions, we argue, are part and parcel of neoliberalism in that they undermine an ability to pay attention to unique ways in which disability leads to the evolution of alternative lifestyles, creative negotiations, and modes of existence that may go otherwise unrecognized.

Accepting the premises of "embodied ontology" in Shakespeare and Watson's case, "dismodernism" for Davis, or "the dys-/disarticulate" in Berger can be interpreted as evidence of the ablenationalism already at work. Dismodernist universalism renders the practices of nonnormative populations of disabled people peripheral to the project of living, and, without an attentiveness to the alternative intricacies of their lives, they are condemned to a visibility only within heteronormative circuits of desire (*Bending Over Backwards* 40). There is not a level playing field that all bodies occupy, and calling for a universalizing recognition of insufficiency will do little to accomplish meaningful systems change. All of these versions of disability universalism—"embodied ontology," "dismodernism," "the dys-/articulate"— effectively overshoot a subcultural formation (often the largest minority group in any population) in order to reference liberal conceptions of vulnerability as an appropriate synonym. Dismodernism further instantiates neoliberal approaches to impairment as a common disability relation without encountering the lively materiality of embodiment represented by "multihandicapped corporealities" where race, class, sexuality, and gender intersect in the risky mixings of crip/queer embodiments.

Throughout *The Biopolitics of Disability* we suggest that there is a distinction between this tendency to universalize imperfection (dismodernism) and those scholars who analyze disability embodiment as an alternative, productive basis. How does the universality of impairment scholarship (i.e., dismodernism, embodied ontology, dys-/disarticulate) not undermine the idea that the devotion to nuances of nonnormative bodies in extreme and desperate conditions results in the effacement of kinds of diverse corporeality? If we all share inefficient, discordant, and nonnormative bodies, then "the end of normalcy" seems to result in a flattening of the social/biological playing field of difference (Davis, *End of Normal* 29–30). Isn't this a form of interpretation that ultimately "negate[s] disability as meaning in its own right" (Ewart 47)? If we are all effectively "disabled," then what is to mark disability as a nuanced experiential condition?

This emphasis on a widening net of debility within neoliberalism characterizes dismodernism's penchant to operationalize increasingly amorphous concepts of "disability" to which contemporary subjects are all subject. As such disability references an expansion of pathologies to which wider populations are exposed as failed neoliberal subjects in need of market-based supplements; such developments for the theorists of dismodernism, embodied ontology, and "the dy-/disarticulate" welcomingly signal "the end of normalcy." Yet we critique dismodernist debility as a ruse of the neoliberal referencing of failed embodiments as new market niches, while the others approach disability as a new paradigm for all bodies to embrace. The dismodernist conception of debility still suggests a more agential "choice" of Althusserian interpolation within ideologies of pathology that are largely not available to disabled people whose bodies are coercively situated as deviant, nonnormative, and incapacitated. Shakespeare, Watson, Davis, and Berger all pose versions of dismodernist embodiment as a viable solution of neoliberalism in shared vulnerability. Our critiques assess the fall out from market-driven motives of debility, while dismodernist approaches argue that we no longer fetishize normalcy as desirable average. Doing so, however, reinforces a problematic "we" that discounts those with disabilities by suggesting all of us occupy failed embodiments in some way without an ability to attend to crip/queer materiality's nuances of experience. In Alison Kafer's terms, dismodernism represents the neoliberal theoretical equivalent to amputee devoteeism ("Desire and Digust" 332).

What happens to age of onset and severity if a floating concept of debility eclipses the experiential coordinates of even a "loosely applied" identity rubric of disability (that which we call in chapter 4 "the politics of atypical-ity")? Can living in proximity to prognosis bear out the same coordinates of a more engaged analysis of living with disability over a significant period of one's embodied life? As an alternative to universalist dismodernism, we would set the work of other key theoreticians in the turn-to-the-body school of disability criticism and new materialisms who make multiple appearances in this study, including Robert McRuer, Tobin Siebers, Alison Kafer, Mel Y. Chen, Rosi Braidotti, Elizabeth Grosz, and Jasbir Puar. These new material-ists of disability emphasize disability as "complex embodiment" (or what we theorize as "peripheral embodiment"). Such approaches address disability "as an epistemology that rejects the temptation to value the body as any-thing other than what it was and that embraces what the body has become and will become relative to the demands on it, whether environmental, rep-resentational, or corporeal" (Siebers, *Disability Theory* 27).

For instance, as Mike Davis makes clear in *Planet of Slums*, disabled people comprise a sizable portion of the world's most impoverished popula-tions: those who exist as most peripheral to the project of living, expendable as human waste (that which Mbembe calls the products of "necropolitics" [12]), and shunted into spaces of what Lauren Berlant identifies as "slow death" (754) at the edges of informal economies (Charlton's formulation of "peripheral everywhere" [195]); but also pursue anticonsumptive existences and artful depictions of perspectives not easily identified elsewhere. In the first critical sense, there is the global underbelly of a disability equivalent to what Nirmala Erevelles and Andrea Minear refer to as those undergoing "spirit death" with regard to the compounding factors of devalued existence where disability, race, class, sexuality, and gender collide (127). In the latter creative sense, there is a disability equivalent to what José Muñoz explores as utopian imaginings of worlds not yet realized (106). The majority of chap-ters to follow unveil worlds of disability where nonnormative positivisms unearth practices of human interdependency that might exist as ways for articulating crip/queer lives "within a constructive ethical frame that can actually be used for a map of living" within heteronormative spheres of value (Huffer 48).

The questions that guide our efforts here remain crucial for an effective opening up of disability studies discourse with respect to biopolitics: Can we keep ourselves open to the experience of nonnormativity as something other than inferiority, deviancy, and intolerable aberrancy (a mere ableist projection of the pathologizing fantasies of normativity)? Can an ethics of a failure to normalize be operationalized by crip/queer constituencies as something other than an incapacity to live as others live? How do we move forward into productive collectivities without reproducing totalizing concepts of disability identity? What are the economic and materialist stakes at risk in neoliberal efforts to normalize nonnormative bodies? Are there effective interventions available to mobilize by playing in the financially incentivized world of for-profit medicine? Can a value of subsistence serve as the only reliable barometer of success among those who are scrimping for survival despite the new rhetoric of exceptional inclusiveness offered by states to affirm their superior contemporaneity? Is there an alternative discourse of productivity available to those who exist in "nonproductive" bodies? What does resistance to neoliberal diversity feel like (even if one is quadriplegic, autistic, or otherwise mobility impaired)? It is to these questions and others that *The Biopolitics of Disability* most pressingly responds.

PART I

From Liberal Restraints to Neoliberal Inclusion

ONE

From Liberal to Neoliberal Futures of Disability

Rights-Based Inclusionism, Ablenationalism, and the Able-Disabled

This opening chapter continues a conversation begun in the introduction by examining disability's grudging admission to normative social institutions through inherently neoliberal forms of redress. We perform this analysis by mapping some key coordinates of politicized normalization strategies extant in post-Fordist capitalism largely intended to ameliorate wider historical exclusions from the body politic. In order to do so, we address four related systems of integration for disabled people that ultimately result in further degrees of marginalization for the many: 1) deinstitutionalization efforts undermined by austerity cuts to key services such as in-home personal assistance care; 2) liberal leftist backlash against the homogenizing aesthetics and ecological unfriendliness of universal design as a principle of accessibility to public spaces; 3) international disability-based claims of American exceptionalism that operate by shaming developing countries with respect to their neglectful treatment of disabled people; and 4) nationalist-inflected media portrayals of celebrity cyborgs who are provided as false evidence of the rehabilitation-military postindustrial state's inclusion commitments to providing hyper-compensatory supports for disabled people. All of these issues arise within the geopolitics of neoliberalism as a result of claims that disability integration in postindustrial countries is now complete and a preeminent sign of their successful arrival at modernity. The analyses to come refer to two key nodal points in the neoliberal management of disability: (1) "ablenationalism" with regard to the use of disability by nations and multinational corporate/charity industries as a basis for promoting American exceptionalism abroad; and (2) representational spaces of cyborgian overcompensation we call "the able-disabled" wherein excessive displays of body supplementation are trafficked globally as signs of the completion (even transcendence) of the limitations of disabled bodies. Both of these tactics prove operative within the logic of democratic rights-based models of inclusionism as they take the integration of impaired bodies (either through the granting of formerly withheld civic rights and/or prosthetic supplementation) as the foundational marker of inclusionism's critical accomplishment. The hope spurred by these misleading representational tactics signify the long overdue historical address of devalued embodiments pinning for love by nation states in which their lives have been excessively circumscribed, excluded, abused, neglected, as well as socially and materially eviscerated.

How does the effort to gain entrance to the democratic franchise of citizenship function as a tenuous tactic for accomplishing more meaningful levels of participation by disabled people? The power of this tactic, we argue, primarily rests on making disability knowable within the parameters of heteronormativity (i.e., to see disability as less differentiated from other conditions of embodiment and, therefore, within the range of the "normal" rather than deviant). Thus, the normalization of disability in the political arena has, for better and worse, shaped progressive goals with respect to the demands of neoliberalism. A weak strain of accommodation develops as a result of efforts to flatten out the dynamic materiality of disability through claims of its likeness to other forms of diverse embodiment and approximations of normalcy.

In his blog entry on *Stims, Stammers and Winks*, Zach Richter explains "Ableliberalism" as the contradictory premise that support for disability assists corporate and governmental interests but not necessarily disabled people themselves:

> When access is put into action in disability policy, its function is not actually to support disabled people but often either to make money from disabled people (and fuel the social services and healthcare industries), to make it look like the government is supporting disabled people or to normalize disabled people.

We will extend this analysis into our case studies of austerity cuts, universal accessibility backlash, and the ablenationalism to come, but for now suffice it to say that neoliberal disability couches its rhetoric of assistance in terms that mask the institutional interests it serves. Throughout these discussions we trace disability from a scapegoated and incarcerated form of difference within liberal eugenics to a limited form of inclusionism within late liberal capitalism. Our argument regarding this historical transition in the social treatment of disability centers on a shift from Fordist to post-Fordist economic contexts in the West. Nonnormative positivist methodology provides an ability to chart profound alterations in disability's social utility when economic emphases alter from a concentration on normative modes of mass production to an alternative emphasis on mass market-based consumption strategies. This ouster of disability's nonnormative materiality from normative modes of participation—that is, the nonnormative operations of those occupying peripheral embodiments—has resulted in the incapacity to recognize disability as a site of alternative value and as a potentially disruptive force within neoliberal regimes of toleration.

NEOLIBERAL BAIT-AND-SWITCH

The social model's emergence in the period of neoliberalism inevitably ties it to the very economic context in which it erupted as a critique; namely, the ways in which bodies are assessed as faulty, deviant, and socially incongruous in order to better justify their natural (and even necessary) exclusion from public participation. In forwarding this analysis social model theorists attempt to expose the inadequacies of environments (attitudinal, architectural, and aesthetic) as causative agents of disabled peoples' blocked suture into the social fabric of life. As such, the social model is itself a creature of late liberalism's strategic embrace of devalued identities and its corrective efforts to include rather than exclude what Nicole Markotic and Sally Chivers refer to as "the problem body" (1–2).

Neoliberalism continues to oversee greater and more pressing exclusions with respect to the terms undergirding opportunities for integration that then go unfunded or receive drastic cuts at a later point in time. Such austerity-based practices disguise themselves in the fog of claims to expansions in social supports due to the beneficence of the neoliberal state that are later destabilized or removed with less fanfare. As such austerity cuts often pass unnoticed as states and countries raid their healthcare budgets to shore up failing economic coffers largely available for financing military and corporate interests. Within such instances of promised supports offered then taken away, PWDs' status within neoliberalism situates them as veritable canaries in the coal mine of arbitrary, restrictive, and narrowly defined government-funded policy initiatives. Within such practices a neoliberal bait-and-switch with disabled lives is at stakes. The paradox of support for living in the community while simultaneously gutting the very social service systems needed to accomplish this kind of integration sits at the heart of the weakened strain of inclusionism extant in neoliberalism.

For example, during the years 2010 and 2011 there were protests mounted by organizations of PWDs (such as Independent Living Centers, body care workers, and disability advocacy organizations) threatened by austerity-based service reduction cuts in California. The protests took the form of civil disobedience as street art performance in the construction of a satirically titled marginalized community called "ArnieVille" (named after bodybuilder-actor-turned-governor, Arnold Schwarzenegger). Established in August and then again resurrected in October, "Arnieville" was a tent city built in order to demonstrate the precariousness in which PWDs felt they had been situated by neoliberal austerity measures. According to journalistic coverage and protestor blogs, the performance art of Arnieville sought to expose the bottom line of a disability-based neoliberal bait-and-switch: the exchange of individual liberties for state-funded services served as an untenable baseline for receiving necessary public assistance in order to live in the community of one's choosing. Such an arrangement makes one vulnerable not only to a loss of liberty by those occupying peripheral embodiments, but, ultimately, the loss of service provisions guaranteed by the neoliberal state as well.

Primarily at issue in the Arnieville protests were legislative threats to the reduction and/or elimination of in-home personal care assistance coverage (PCAs) used as the basis for disabled people's ability to escape confinement in nursing homes and other congregate carceral settings. Thus, some disabled people found themselves living in the community with the promise of state-funded PCAs only to find themselves threatened with a loss of funding for the very social service supports that made such a relocation into the public sphere possible in the first place. The potential result was deadly in that PWDs liberated from nursing homes found themselves bereft of services and, thus, on the verge of being abandoned. Re-institutionalization or homelessness became their fall back position in such a situation.

Not only did disabled people affected by budget reductions help to make surface the precariousness of support-based exchanges underwriting the fragility of neoliberal social contracts of inclusionism, but their bodies evidenced the way in which other bodies (particularly those of lower-class, racialized, and predominantly female caretakers) prove necessary to the alternative living relations of material networks. Those who protested at Arnieville turned out to be an amalgam of socially devalued embodiments—able and disabled, queer and straight, underpaid and unpaid, patients/clients and professionals/subprofessionals—and their joining of forces in social protest attested to the shared nature of precariousness that proved more wide sweeping than that of PWDs alone.

INCAPACITY: THE NEW SOCIAL STANDARD

It is in this exposé of the fragility of neoliberal governance tactics carried out by a diffuse network of skilled and semiskilled laborers in the professions of normalization (assistive technology, medicine, social work, psychology, psychiatry, and rehabilitative therapies) that disabled people assist in realizing all bodies supply the raw material upon which contemporary biopolitical systems work their productive power. To secure this point we might think of the way commercial media are dominated by selling contemporary audiences products through the heightening of awareness of proliferating zones of bodily and affective imperfection: incontinence, erectile dysfunction, migraine headaches, back pain, menstrual cramp relief, depression, acid reflux, insufficient arch support, vaginal dryness, and uterine pain during intercourse are among those conditions now referenced in a proliferating array of body ailments. Such embodied insufficiencies multiply across every surface, crevice, and cavity of the personal interior and exterior spaces of embodiment. Increasingly we come to knowledge of ourselves as embodied beings within neoliberal biopolitics primarily through understanding our bodies as containing a matrix of referenced pathologies deviating from narrow (and, ultimately, fictitious) norms of health.

Foucault's dissertation advisor, Georges Canguilhem, argued in *The Normal and the Pathological* that we only come to know embodiment through "the experience of bodily breakdown," yet the era of biopolitics has made such ways of knowing increasingly diffuse and unmoored from modernism's normal/pathological binary (209). Neoliberal biopolitics references all bodies as deficient and in need of product supplementations to treat the in-built inferiority within, a system of bodily referencing shorn of environmental causes. Contemporary bodies find themselves increasingly colonized by "Big Pharma" through a process that segments body parts into insufficiencies, ailments, and shortcomings in need of chemical and surgical interventions (Rose, *Politics of Life Itself* 219).

The historical shift from liberalism's carceral restraints on deviant bodies to neoliberalism's referencing of deficiencies across all bodies provides a key transition in historically distinct approaches to body management. Whereas liberalism recognized some bodies as normatively capacitated for a competitive labor market and other bodies as nonproductive due to their incapacitation (their defining, in-built impairment effects), neoliberalism tends to produce all bodies as languishing through excessive demands of productivity, exacerbated social anxieties, and excessive exposures to toxic environments in order to exploit new treatment markets. Whereas a prior era celebrated autonomous bodies rich in capacity, the era of biopolitics turns the corner and proliferates pathologies as opportunities for new product dissemination opportunities (that is, forms of addiction now promoted as body-altering solutions).

Incapacitated bodies are now the standard to an increasing degree, and for-profit healthcare corporations recognize them as rich veins of data for ailments largely social in their making but often realized at the level of materiality. Such interventions are delivered through the acquisition of over-the-counter medications and other forms of body-alleviating consumption. This shift to contemporary bodies as incapacitated rather than "autonomously" independent marks a massive shift in the operation of a normalizing contemporary marketplace.

Under neoliberalism the body is targeted as inherently lacking, and the pharmaceutical and medical industries promise not to remove but mask social symptoms as individualized adjustments to states of a universally beleaguered embodiment. Nowhere in this marketing scheme is there a direct address of toxic environments, workplaces, or oppressive living arrangements as the appropriate objects of critique or suspect sources of bodily debility. This loss of the exploitation of environment as causal agent brings full circle a shift in emphasis from the early eugenics period that identified urbanity as the origins of modern maladjustment and "pastoral cure" (removal to rural institutions to reestablish one's connection with nature for the rejuvenation of ailing spirits) as the appropriate intervention.

The move from liberal to neoliberal disability, then, becomes identifiable as an effect of historical forces that shift from fetishizations of full capacity to fetishizations of minor, yet prolific, incapacitations (that which Puar terms "debility" ["Coda" 149]). This ebb and flow of ideas of dysfunctional embodiment reveals the outlines of an artificially tailored infrastructure that excludes and then includes as the terms for retrofitting bodies to a new market-driven formula. Incapacity transforms into "the new normal" and, in this process, we lose an ability to recognize alternative maps for living evolved within alternative crip/queer contexts. Normalization drives the matter of corporeality underground, so to speak, in the press to flatten differences into the multicultural mosaic that continues to champion normative modes of existence while seeming to become more flexible and therefore in line with key facets of neoliberal adaptability.

NEOLIBERAL DISABILITY AND THE
ABLENATIONALISM TO COME

The era of normalization that marks a turning point in the social management of disabled people from eugenic exclusionist practices to neoliberal inclusionist approaches, turns upon the mounting cultural capital of an ever expanding "disability business" (Albrecht 82). Disability turns out to provide a key way of documenting the shift from production (Fordist) to the consumption (post-Fordist) end of capitalism's perpetual historical renewal process intended to justify its founding inequalities and wealth disparities.

The particularities of bodily accommodations necessarily send people with disabilities into circulation as *tangential consumers* of social services. Social service systems are excessively dominated by those in the controlling professions: that is, authorized disability gatekeepers that tend to approve, disapprove, and ultimately ensnare people with disabilities in the deliberations of improvement regimes implemented by experts certified in middle-class professional training disciplines such as physical therapy, social work, occupational therapy, speech therapy, special education, psychology, and psychiatry. This entry of disabled people as *tangential consumers* into market systems becomes an odd affair in that the basis of those classified as consumers usually requires at least a modicum of economic capacity to consume. Further, the managerial oriented medical and caretaking professions developed around the social ministration of disabled people's "severely" embodied lives often give way to alternative forms of minority exploitation, such as the wide-spread practice of hiring underpaid (lower than minimum wage) women of color in the United States and immigrant women from former Soviet bloc countries such as Yugoslavia and Czechoslovakia in Europe as body care workers (Kunow "Age and/as Disability").

Furthermore, and perhaps most to the purposes of understanding disability experience as a hyper-driven market subjectivity within neoliberalism is the demand to circulate as a paradigmatic patient-consumer with significant needs requiring product-based interventions. Efforts to meet expectations of individual upkeep within the era of biopolitics result in the susceptibility of crip/queer bodies to myriad bureaucratic onslaughts. Increasingly, disabled people find themselves subject to other experts' rights to determine the coordinates of one's care, support, inclusion, nonreproductive life, treatment level, and social value. Private decision-making about the nature of care is ceded to regulatory domains where payment is actually debated and negotiated among third parties (such as medical service organizations, assistive technology suppliers, home health care providers, and insurance companies). Self-advocacy policy-based initiatives implemented without an adequately remunerated labor force to implement them constitute the "best of all worlds" in this biopolitical order of things, whether in the form of "money follows the person" (as anti-institutionalization policy is sometimes referred to in the United States by disability rights communities) or recipients of Personal Independence Payments (PIP) buttressing neoliberal governance policies in the United Kingdom. The financial burden increasingly falls on disabled people to finance the terms of their own social existence.

As we discuss in chapter 6 in regard to the neoliberal calculations of single-disorder user groups, such disruptive austerity cuts in disability supports result in economic and medical dispossessions. Such dispossessions, particularly among groups seeking to secure necessary augmentative equipment and neglected treatment options, actively prevent the ability to facilitate the attainment of basic everyday needs by crip/queer bodies. Marketplace availability of prosthetic technologies and/or social service supports neither guarantee levels of access nor the emergence of utopian-oriented disabled societies under neoliberalism's rhetorical claims to the practice of new inclusivities. Instead, larger social disparities permeate the ranks of those living in peripheral embodiments. Any adequate analysis of neoliberal disability requires an account of how deteriorating social conditions are often belied by rhetorical claims to progress referenced by the new inclusion-isms. At the same time *The Biopolitics of Disability* undertakes analyses of the ways in which a more expansive concept of liberation beyond disability egalitarianism (i.e., a disability rights-based subject) might be engendered by alternatively focusing on a concept of "freedom as the ability to act and in acting to make oneself even as one is made by external forces" (Grosz, "Feminism" 142).

Consequently, whereas most twentieth-century rights-based movements have argued on behalf of access to normative social privileges by critiquing biological models of nonnormativity, disability cultures cannot effectively distance themselves from the quandary posed by a more fleshy engagement with material bodily variation. Gender, sexuality, and racial liberation movements have all pursued a rights-based rhetoric that opts to normalize differences across populations. In doing so, civil rights-grounded arguments for social inclusion based on universal human similarities have strategically promoted normatively oriented assimilationist models. Such strategies rehabilitate a portion of a minority demographic in the likeness of a dominant majority while further reifying relations of "homonormativity."

For Jasbir Puar, homonormativity includes once-marginalized members of deviant communities most capable of, or willing to further fetishize, the norms of dominant communities as a founding bulwark of their own social integration.

> Homonormativity can be read as a formation complicit with and invited into the biopolitical valorization of life in its inhabitation and reproduction of heteronormative norms ... channeled through the optics of gender and class [and we would add disability] are the attendant attributes and valuations of longevity, illness, health, environment, fertility, and so on. Through the pinning for national love, the temporality of minority model discourse is one of futurity, as endlessly deferred or deflected gratification, mirroring biopower's constant march forward, away from death, where the securitization for today funnels back through the guarantees of the quality of life for tomorrow. (*Terrorist Assemblages* 9, 27 [our insertion])

Puar's critique of minority model approaches here centers on the ways in which civil rights-based movements fail to significantly challenge the normative practices of majoritarian lifestyles that create and perpetuate inequality. In particular these strategies expose the degree to which concepts of health are linked to prevailing heteronormative choices and perpetually deferred into the future enactment of a more expansive social contract. For instance, gay marriage as a fetishization and further consolidation of heteronormative institutions of familial kinship largely available to white, middle-class, gay men or, in an even more pressing racial assimilationist model, Sikh American community efforts to publically distance themselves from deviant Muslim identities ascribed to racialized terrorists. This distancing strategy effects a form of cultural rehabilitation allowing Sikh communities in the United States to represent themselves as hardworking, patriotic, and heterosexual Americans and, by implication, dissociated from the queering forces of Islamic fundamentalism.

From this perspective, rights-based minority model approaches tend to further entrench the very institutions and value systems that marginalize them in the first place. They inevitably become complicit in the sedimentation of some populations into a zone of expendability in order to salvage an idea of a subset of enabled minority subjects as fitting into heteronormative modes of belonging. Contemporary disability rights movements have mimicked this strategy—particularly in the United States and other postindustrialized nations—by arguing that disabled people's access to normative privileges and lifestyles is dependent upon opening up public spaces (that which Hardt and Negri refer to as "the commons" [*Empire* 303]) to a wider variety of body types. So, for instance, curb cuts make wheelchair accessibility more feasible, audible signals at intersections and Braille signage better accommodate those with visual impairments, and lighting-based signaling systems in homes or hotel rooms provide those with hearing impairments the means to more adequately respond to cues in a hearing world. These are all "add-on" accommodations of a normatively exclusionary environment.

While all of these innovations of access have provided some basis for disability coexistence in public space alongside normative others, the emphasis in each of these instances does not necessarily result in a meaningful integration of alternative disability practices. Rather, accommodation provided some bodies with levels of already integrable differences into normative frameworks that did not significantly disrupt environments suited to a narrow range of abilities. We refer to this tactic of integrating a privileged minority at the expense of the further abjection of the many as ablenationalism. Ablenationalist inclusion models involve treating PWDs as exceptional bodies in ways that further valorize able-bodied norms as universally desirable and as the naturalized qualifications of fully capacitated citizenship to which others inevitably aspire.

"THEY PAVED PARADISE, PUT UP A PARKING LOT"

Some of the contradictions of neoliberal integration campaigns based on equal rights claims to live as nondisabled people live can be witnessed in anxieties expressed about retrofitting a more disability friendly infrastructure in urban and rural spaces. A nation's extension of an abstract quantity of rights to some members of a formerly marginalized group such as improved accessibility shores up its claims to the further accomplishment of its own crowning contemporaneity; in particular, the moral mission of serving even those who have been historically identified as excessively parasitic, unproductive, or excessively dependent on social resources. Yet, in seeking to meet a more flexible standard of accessibility for a greater range of functionalities, appearances, and capacities, neoliberal accessibility efforts have stirred the ire of critics, including those on the liberal Left.

For instance, in his essay "The Third Interval" the French cultural theorist and urban studies scholar Paul Virilio complains about the flattening of affective, social, artistic, and architectural landscapes (their structural normalization so to speak) based on the accessible retrofitting of urban public spaces (4). Virilio's complaints regard a nostalgia for a loss of the richness of architectural and geographical diversity evident in uneven historical overlays characteristic of nonaccessible cityscapes; concepts of universal access, he argues, are part and parcel of neoliberalism's efforts to strip-mine European cosmopolitan urbanity of the aesthetic idiosyncrasies embedded in the charms of its asymmetrical character.

As evidence, Virilio cites the universal design-based accessibility advocacy of then French president François Mitterand's argument, made throughout his administration in the late 1980s and early 1990s, that a nation's modernity is best measured by the level of accessibility it provides for its disabled and aging populations. This lowest common denominator of provision of access to a wider, and frankly more realistic, range of body, mind, and sensory types threatens to turn the idiosyncrasies of local spaces, according to Virilio, into the cultural equivalent of Walmart. By catering to people with disabilities—those who have been systematically locked out of access to public transportation and the architectural commons of shared public space due to in-built exclusionary features—the neoliberal landscape is corrupted by forces of homogeneity. In imagining disabled people as un-realistically desiring access to all places that able-bodied citizens frequent in the ways that they frequent them, Virilio makes disability over into a domesticating vector of neoliberal normalization itself.

In a similar but alternatively targeted complaint made in the direction of the receding availability of "unspoiled Nature," American environmental-ist, western cultural commentator, and southwestern desert dweller Edward Abbey argues that the despoliation of American nature has come on the heels of pressure to bow to the demands for national park accessibility as a product of neoliberal inclusionist practices. For Abbey in his best-selling book of homespun American pragmatism, *Desert Solitaire: A Season in the Wilderness* (treated by some as the contemporary equivalent of Henry David Thoreau's nineteenth-century classic, *Walden, or, Life in the Woods* [1845]), disability is best characterized by those individuals exhaustively touring the quickly diminishing remnants of the American wilderness in gas-powered transportation vehicles. As the National Park Service became increasingly privatized during Reagan era neoliberalism, people with disabilities made appearances in various polemics as those who were demanding a universalist degree of access.

In order to play this role disabled people increasingly found themselves cast as limitless consumers of the post-Fordist product of "nature"—the hording of unspoiled spaces with inaccessibility as a defining feature of a rapidly receding untainted wilderness. Abbey's arguments harken back to a Romantic aestheticization of nature available to rejuvenate the beleaguered subjectivities of industrialization's harried, claustrophobic, and toxic urban-ity. No crip/queer space of neoliberal tolerance and its attendant paving over of sacred earthen ground will threaten Abbey's modern-day desire for inac-cessibility as the defining feature of his self-imposed desert exile.

Rightly or wrongly many populations could potentially fill the role of what Abbey refers to as "that other crowd," those who had the financial means and excess leisure time to purchase gasoline-powered transportation options and "tool" around the country in the vanguard of industrial tourism. Yet PWDs are wantonly deployed in this rhetoric as paradigmatic consum-ers whose unnatural bodies drive them more often than others to the suste-nance of nature. Disability represents those who "are unwilling to crawl out of their cars" to get a direct glimpse of the unspoiled nature from which they seek rejuvenation for their excessively debilitated bodies:

This being the case, why is the Park Service generally so anxious to accommodate that other crowd, the indolent millions born on wheels and suckled on gasoline, who expect and pave highways to lead them in comfort, ease and safety into every nook and corner of the national parks? For the answer to that we must consider the character of what I call Industrial Tourism and the quality of the mechanized tourists—the Wheelchair Explorers—who are at once the consumers, the raw material and the victims of Industrial Tourism. (*Desert Solitaire* 49)

An addiction to motorized vehicles is a serious matter, and the selling off of national park lands to the highest for-profit corporate bidder further complicates the spread of neoliberal governance practices regarding the privatization of public lands. But to cast disabled people—"the Wheelchair Explorers"—in the lead role of environmental spoilers allows Abbey to play off of an emergent ablenationalism: that is, the sight of socially degraded bodies newly untethered from a prior era's carceral institutional spaces and domestic back bedrooms now threatening to overrun the nation's purest wilds. Presumably their "victimization," as Abbey puts it, involves being duped by industrial tourism into thinking that universal access and solace in nature are compatible goals.

While a vast majority of Americans drive motorized vehicles and those who visit parks do so almost exclusively by car, RV, bus, train, or plane— and most commonly some combination of these transportation options— people with disabilities have the least expansive claim to forms of unfettered consumerism based on excess mobility, particularly practices of industrial tourism that lead to the ruination of forest preserves and other natural features. In Abbey's scenario, disability enforces an inclusionary impetus resulting in the destruction of unspoiled nature for the majority of more worthy able-bodied hikers, campers, and horseback riders. Consequently, Abbey's populism arrives grounded in a thinly disguised elitism that castigates neoliberal inclusionism on behalf of catering to the needs of the exceptionally incapacitated as its model of tourist accessibility.

The critique of ablenationalism must draw upon identifications born of shared predicaments of exclusion and isolation while also allowing ways of revaluing the demographics of disability as counterinsurgent opportunities for resistance based on existences in peripheral embodiments. In part, collective disability resistance manifests as necessitated survival strategies in response to the social violence of neglect and orchestrated (largely rhetorical) campaigns of inclusionist tolerance for crip/queer people.

Whereas liberal backlashes against disability such as those pursued by Virilio and Abbey, are driven by predominantly aesthetic efforts to represent the nation as synonymous with a narrow array of acceptable, fully capacitated body types, neoliberal disability inclusionist approaches embrace bodies characterized by their possession of a fluid, adaptive ease among inflexible, human-made environments. Following Deleuze, Puar names this set of relations "assemblage," in the sense that the emphasis moves from an additive concept of devalued essences encountered in theories of intersectionality based on a loss of rights experienced by those with discrete combinations of race, gender, sexuality, class, and ability to a locus of more difficult, in fact debilitating, interchanges and inclusions (*Terrorist Assemblages* 174).[1]

Thus, while the national body of liberalism displays generic characteristics of race, gender, sexuality, class, and ability, within social and minority model contexts, disabled bodies have been located as the symptom of modernity's lowest qualification bar of citizenship, a socially produced—rather than biological—deviancy. Their incapacities render them too objectionable to be understood as unfairly barred from citizenship as opposed to justifiably relegated to special class options. In opposing this cultural relegation to expendability, recent examples of disability studies involved in "the turn to the body" wrestle with formative theoretical tendencies to write off disability as yet another constructed phenomenon while not losing track of alternative opportunities to revalue experiences of peripheral embodiment. Within these approaches are some key models for articulating disability experiences as potential escape routes out of—or, at least, as alternatives to—the fashionable linguistic and aesthetic straitjackets social constructivism has produced to date.

THE GEOPOLITICS OF ABLENATIONALISM

A status of "specialness" within neoliberalism turns out to be less than ideal as a newfound recognition since it rarely leads to significant redistributions of power, money, or liberty for most disabled people. Neoliberal modes of address afford PWDs little more than an opportunity to be referenced as newly integrated patient-consumers largely bereft of buying power. Consequently, one might be led to think that disabled populations find themselves marginalized at the outskirts of cultural power, investment, and social utility. Yet, in an alternative mode to Virilio's and Abbey's complaints about the shortcomings of a newly mobilized disabled citizenry, recent ablenationalisms have situated some mutant bodies as exceptional, even foundational to American and European efforts to reclaim a lost global status. In serving in this capacity disabled people have become effectively and normatively disabled in various localities of postindustrial nations while still struggling in a precarious economic and social environment that undermines not only their mobility but their very survivability. Likewise, we find ablenationalist claims at work in global locations outside of the disability rights homelands that gave them birth as well; ablenationalist claims are being deployed as the key argumentative foundation for underwriting charity operations in humanitarian relief efforts made on behalf of racialized disability populations abroad.

Ablenationalism cuts PWDs representationally adrift in that their images circulated in industrializing countries have been increasingly shorn from the reality of the incompleteness of the neoliberal project of integration. Disabled people now perform the nation's representational work as a symbol of expansive neoliberal inclusion efforts. In the three case studies below we mine recent disability studies work on the duplicitous operations of ablenationalist mentalities in (1) hormone trafficking for trans- and inter-sexed people across the U.S.-Mexico border, (2) cleft palate charity surgeries for low-income indigenous children in Africa, and (3) earthquake relief operations by PWDs in postindustrial countries on behalf of newly disabled people in Haiti. All of these examples deploy discourses of disability rights and inclusionism set adrift from their postindustrial economic contexts into the expansive, amorphous, and ahistorical cross-national flows of globalization. All depend upon implicit arguments of a completed integration project at home as the basis for their inclusionist international relief efforts abroad. In this environment, disability provides new pathways for the exportation of neoliberal biopolitical tactics to transcend ablenationalist imaginaries.

ABLENATIONALISM CASE STUDY NUMBER I: REGULATING MOBILIZATIONS OF GENDER

For instance, we can trace out exclusions based on bodies deemed excessively disabled while seeking out pharmaceutical interventions coming on-line across the geopolitical map of ablenationalism. Intersexed bodies deemed insufficiently gendered as male or female based on hormone level diagnostics now commonly rely on prescriptions of synthetic testosterone and other hormones. Diagnoses of hormonal "imbalance" as a symptom of excessive gender instability are based on normative quantifications of testosterone and progesterone levels in male and female bodies; essentially this institutes a hormonal dividing line of sexualized bodies. Yet availability of hormones on the market has become increasingly subject to tightening international trafficking regulations. Hormone treatment availability is effectively caught up in the heteronormative surveillance net of biopolitics that characterize the war on drugs.

In "The Substance of Borders: Transgender Politics, Mobility, and the U.S. Regulation of Testosterone," Toby Beauchamp analyzes neoliberal policy efforts to prohibit the use of hormone-altering pharmaceutics such as anabolic steroids and synthetic testosterone due to their physically disabling and "gender deforming" qualities. In doing so, Beauchamp demonstrates how disabled and transgender people threaten normative notions of gender fixity. During congressional hearings held in the early 1990s, U.S. lawmakers argued in contradictory directions that illegal hormone trafficking from Mexico moving across porous U.S. borders posed a toxic, racialized threat to American citizens. This debate occurred in spite of the fact that American hormone-manufacturing companies had opportunistically moved to Mexico and were now the primary producers of substances growing increasingly subject to governmental bans in neoliberal securitization zones.

At the same time and in a contradictory direction, stepping up policing practices of a nation's leaky boundaries could be also analyzed as an instance of American exceptionalism. Whereas "other countries" (such as "most of the world") were wantonly ignoring the dangers of steroid use for their citizens, the United States would "set an example" by more actively curbing illegal hormone trafficking of substances and simultaneously stabilizing transgender threats to heteronormative gender binaries (Beauchamp 68– 69). Neoliberalism uses arguments about buffering American populations from the threat of disability from without (Mexican trafficking in regulated hormone therapies) and within (the inappropriate mobilization of gender dysmorphias by trans-gender people). A nation secures its heteronormativity by refusing interventions that might aid gender mobilities. The result is preservation of an inelastic gender divide within heteronormativity that disguises the defining multiplicities of gender and sexuality at the expense of those operationalizing its pleuri-potent power. At the same time efforts at legislative securitization around the trafficking of hormones openly claim to protect normative citizens from the excesses of products manufactured and disseminated by the inflows and outflows of a nation's own post-NAFTA pharmaceutical industry.

ABLENATIONALISM CASE STUDY NUMBER 2:
PLASTIC SURGEONS WITHOUT BORDERS

Some of the most conspicuous forms of ablenationalist exceptionalism have emerged in international disability charity organizations seeking to export prosthetic and surgical normalization as a renewed basis for global claims to American exceptionality. Our second international example of ablenationalism analyzes the promotional intricacies of a global network of surgeons providing surgeries to correct childhood cleft palate in globally racialized countries. The workings of the international medical charity group, Smile Train, have been explored by disability studies scholars on the basis of the exportation of U.S. surgical expertise to those experiencing social death in their home countries (Jarman; Siebers, *Disability Aesthetics*; Armstrong). In particular these critiques have focused on the representational aspects of the donation marketing tactics employed by the Smile Train charity since its founding in 1999.

Tobin Siebers explains the logic of Smile Train's marketing presentation of cleft palate as one that "equates disability with loss of life, isolating the children from everyday existence and exhibiting them in a series of medical mug shots" (*Disability Aesthetics* 21). The "enfreaked" children in Smile Train's web and ad campaigns are nondescript, dislocated from specific geographies, visibly racialized, and absent of names or other individualizing markers of identification (*Disability Aesthetics* 21). By the mid-2000s Smile Train's promotions tended to portray children as mediatized bodies through comparative before and after head shots to demonstrate the "miracle" of surgical correction. While the children who receive the benefits of Smile Train's surgical treatment are described as living in abject poverty, the social contexts of these conditions are described as being alleviated, even made to disappear, after the corrective intervention's completion. Cleft palate surgeries apparently offer an effective neoliberal intervention that magically resolves stigmatized existence simultaneously at the biological and social levels.

For instance, Jarman reports that one girl with cleft palate appearing in a Smile Train ad was described as living next to a garbage dump; her father meets the family's monthly rent of $5 by scrounging through the refuse ("Resisting Good Imperialism" 113). Smile Train's lead headline portrays the necessity of the operation as one seeking "to give a desperate child not just a new smile, but a new life" (Smile Train 2012). Children with cleft palates are "often viewed as outcasts and ostracized. They will never know the simple joys we take for granted, like going to school or making friends" (Smile Train 2012). Siebers notes that the campaign naturalizes life with disability as unlivable, and argues while he is not opposed to the sharing of medical technologies between nations, his concern is primarily with the representational overlay of Smile Train's portrayals of disability. The ads naturalize the unlivable nature of lives with disabilities in order to implore potential donors to give generously and stop the "scourge" of cleft palate. To do so, Smile Train appeals mobilize donors' aesthetic repulsion toward facial asymmetry in order to gear up the urgency necessary to make a contribution toward the host organization's efforts.

Likewise, at a geopolitical level, ablenationalism relies on a binary between "giver nations" and "beneficiary nations" where the recipient is the charitable receiver of the host nation's largesse. Presumably children with cleft palates who are the recipients of Smile Train's surgical charity have been restored and, thus, fully integrated into heteronormative regimes of living from which they were previously excluded. The "simple joys" of the giver nation's surgically corrected children who get to go to school and make friends sets up a congratulatory network of American exceptionalism established in contrast to the racialized recipient nation's neglect.

The charity deliverer of corrective services positions itself as fully capable of mustering resources for its own people while securing its place as a benefactor to other, less modern (read: racialized and non-medically developed) nations. Most crucially, the process allows for the home country's assumptions about disability stigma to be dismantled and rendered a thing of the past. This process occurs despite that fact that many low income families in the U.S. cannot afford the corrective surgery for their own children. For instance, the widely disparaged, media enfreaked "Octomom," Nadya Suleman, had a child with cleft palate for whom she could not afford the surgery (Inside Edition). To accomplish this narrative rehabilitation at home, developed nations project their disability crises out onto nations of the "developing world." In doing so, a form of marketing catharsis is achieved, one that plays a dual role of projecting a version of the host nation as a generous place of medical caretakers for its own unfortunate people, and also as the fixer, at a geopolitical level, of those who lag behind "our" achievement of medical modernization.

ABLENATIONALISM CASE STUDY NUMBER 3:
DISABILITY LARGESSE IN HAITI

Alternately in tandem with Smile Train charity advocacy, we may think of ablenationalism's effects in late January 2010 as the United States, United Kingdom, and Canada shipped cast-off prosthetic items such as artificial legs and arms, wheelchairs, crutches, canes, and walkers to Haiti on behalf of the "scores of newly disabled" resulting from the collapse of structures razed by an earthquake. Standing amid the massive social and structural upheaval, CNN's Dr. Sanjay Gupta explained to audiences that the "loss of a leg" was tantamount to a "death sentence" in the decimated country. Such observations were obligatorily accompanied by offhand editorials about the insufficiency of Haiti's health care system before the earthquake. The oft-repeated tangential commentary served as a backdoor condemnation of a negligent health care infrastructure that was ultimately to blame for the number of individuals experiencing the devastation of crush wounds resulting in widespread amputations. First World Western nations would rehabilitate Haiti by sending their excess durable medical equipment to the surviving disabled victims.

In undertaking this act of international largesse, disability families, organizations, and medical goods provisioners participated in a charitable dumping of unused and unusable products into the earthquake-stricken country. The opportunity afforded by this moral mission of supplying prosthetic supplements was announced with typical media loquacity as a sign of the innate beneficence on display in wealthier countries. Their surfeit support of disabled people within their own borders would now be mobilized on behalf of another less wealthy country's newly disabled people. Nowhere was the utility of these donated prosthetic goods assessed for the demands of post-earthquake life with a disability. Wheelchairs designed for navigating paved streets in First World urban centers, prosthetic legs and arms and braces fit to other bodies, and walkers or canes made for ambulating smoothly tiled surfaces arrived in Haiti's decimated capital city of Port-au-Prince. Media hailed these gifts as the salvation of disabled lives in a country notorious for letting its disabled people languish among the premodern intricacies of its crumbling, pre-earthquake infrastructure.

But ultimately the prosthetic gifts proved less significant for the enhanced mobility they offered than for the symbolic significance they represented about disability in the host donor countries. The flood of equipment donations from disabled people and families as durable medical equipment suppliers back home represented the surfeit bounty of a greater than adequate care received by PWDs in their own lands. In turning excess equipment into the accoutrements of Haiti's regained mobility, the integration of disability was retroactively referenced as more than adequate—even a preemptively declared "mission accomplished"—within the circumference of giver nations who presumably take care of their own disabled people. The ample excess of durable medical equipment available for Haiti retroactively suggested a bounty of supports available from the issuing countries. Such symbolic overcompensation measures suggested the complete ascendancy of a more modern, Western-style, health care system in postindustrial giver nations.

This display of disability largesse is an example of the kind of American exceptionalism whereby provisions are assumed to be excessive for disabled people back home who have benefited from a surfeit of social service assistance and adaptive equipment. Nowhere did viewers hear about the teeming closets or warehouses of unused—because unuseful—adaptive aids that comprised the bulk of donations to post-earthquake Haiti. Neither was there any discussion of the difficulty of procuring useful adaptive equipment that might make the management of a life with significant disability more manageable in the donor countries from which these less usable equipment stores hailed. The inadequacies of distribution of assistive technology and equipment are erased in postindustrial anglophone countries through a sort of Malthusian denial of the rampant rejection rates characteristic of insurance industries on behalf of crip/queer bodies.

THE ABLE-DISABLED: NEOLIBERAL OVERCOMPENSATION STRATEGIES

Whereas restrictions on the trafficking of hormones across the border between the United States and Mexico, surgical repairs of cleft palate in Africa, and the offloading of excess medical devices to disabled people in Haiti cultivate the appearance of a surplus provision of services in the United States, cultural images also serve to perpetuate a false sense of completed integration cultivated by ablenationalist standards. How do media images of disabled people materialize mainstream fantasies of a beneficent, evolving marketplace within neoliberal biopolitics? How does an increasingly visible transnational trafficking in technologically enabled disability images feed the moral culpabilities of postindustrial and industrializing economies alike?

In one of the most rapacious zones of disability neoliberal market spaces—the popular sphere of product advertisements—disabled bodies are now ubiquitously referenced in commercials for myriad pharmaceuticals, prosthetically engineered bodies and minds, mutating organisms that may prove better adapted for a future world yet to come. Disabled people have become increasingly engendered by systems (and long, boring hours) of scientific observation, classification, and taxonomy, the predicative data, detail, and description amassed and leading to the micromanagement of increasingly informatic bodies. All of this data gathering attempts to render the nonnormative biological world a knowable object in the most Foucauldian sense. These particularly hyped-up, technologized, and fully rejuvenated bodies serve as cusp creatures hailing utopian worlds where access hasn't changed but bodily alteration has accomplished the necessary sleight of hand to accomplish the trick for some fortunate few.

Those of us who find ourselves living with significant levels of socially assigned aberrancy and, we might add, over extended periods of a lifespan (such as formerly informed debates over the significance of age of onset in definitional discussions of disability) have metamorphosed within this product-oriented world into the equivalent of something no longer directly kin to a giant Kafkaesque beetle. While the representational space headed by iconic disabled types such as the Elephant Man or Gregor Samsa provided the basis for late nineteenth- and early twentieth-century eugenic justifications for the imposition of social stigmas translated into internalized self-hatred, what we will call the *able-disabled*, serve as latter twentieth-century champions of social normativity now held out to a select group of upstanding disabled citizens.

For example, gracing a poster for the Emotion Pictures Disability Film Festival in 2006 in Athens, Greece, was a photograph of double-amputee turned hyperathlete, Aimee Mullins, speeding across a beach on one of her twelve pairs of artificial legs powered by resplendent coils ("My Twelve Pairs of Legs"). The image announced the arrival of yet another "new prosthetic age" originally hailed only in the 1970s fantasy space of serial television by the likes of the Bionic Man (Lee Majors) and the Bionic Woman (Lindsey Wagner). This new era of disabled athleticism—an era of buffed, muscular, yet technologically supplemented bodies—promises all of the transcendent capacity a hyperreal, medicalized culture could offer. We will unpack the creative alternative nuances of the workings and nonnormative politics of disability film festivals in chapters 4 and 5, but here we want to discuss the ablenationalist implications of hyperprostheticized bodies used as marketing ploy in this independent film festival market. Disability images circulate within neoliberal marketing networks by playing on rhetorical referencing strategies that grow increasingly common in the era of biopolitics as part of the coopting of geo-political space.

Aimee Mullins's high speed romp across the shifting sands of a southern European beach used a disabled version of the attainment of bodily prowess to rejuvenate a lower threshold of public expectation for what disabled people might accomplish. This process of normalization through the ruse of hypernormalization placed members of formerly marginalized communities in the service of modernity-seeking nations attempting to glitz up their worldwide images through a form of special inclusion (i.e., ablenationalism). The hypercapacitated body of Aimee Mullins spoke to audiences by promising that the United States did not take its minority community members for granted. They were provided with the most artful, technologized, prohibitively expensive athletic enhancements modern Western civilizations can offer; in the one case a fetishized high-tech sneaker and in the other twelve pairs of prosthetic legs that allowed her double amputee body to course smoothly over even the most unctuous of mediums such as a sandy beach with speed and dexterity.

Like Mullins, the South African double amputee-turned-paralympic (and then Olympic) athlete, Oscar Pistorius, also found himself incorporated into a narrative of overcompensation. Pistorius's prowess for running on prosthetic coils was matched only by the notoriety he gained after shooting his girlfriend, the model Reeva Steenkamp, through the door of their bathroom one night in eastern Pretoria. Like Mullins, Pistorius was commonly pictured as embodying the hypercapacity of a field-and-track machine, a postorganismic cyborg biology enabled to surpass the limits of even the most athletically capacitated among us (two-legged variety). Pistorius's scientifically engineered body coupled the tragic truncated animacy of the disabled body with the self-governing automaton-like capacity of a machine.

The tales of Mullins and Pistorius did not cohere to the traditional contours of a liberal overcoming story, one where a disabled person transcends the limitations of his tragic embodiment to attain a basic level of social participation (here the prostheticized body is hidden by a performative approximation of normalcy that can't quite successfully accomplish the level of dissimulation desired). Instead the hyperprostheticized bodies of Pistorius and Mullins are placed fully on display; the engineering feat of machinic supplementation becomes the primary object of fascination, and the viewer is left with a fetishization of technological compensation itself—not bodies extraordinary in their rescue from a disability abject, but rather a surfeit degree of compensation that suggests a wealth of supports available only to a select few: "the able-disabled." In the neoliberal narrative of *overcompensation* assistive technology is the hero and the supplemented bodies become mere vehicles for an ornate display of a conspicuous form of technological consumption. The fetishization of a machine-like capacity is both a marvel of scientific advancement and a story of ablenationalism's promise of the arrival at a surfeit supplementation and support for vulnerable bodies now complete.

Yet the lavish level of compensation for characters like Aimee Mullins and Oscar Pistorius occurs in the abstracted space of celebrity, a form of body augmentation that is completely divorced from the majority of disabled citizens lives. In the wake of the London Paralympic Games held during the UN's decade of the disabled person, Braye, Dixon, and Gibbons published a study that showed most disabled people in the United Kingdom found the athleticism of the paralympians irrelevant to their own lives as marginalized citizens ("Disability 'Rights' or 'Wrongs?'" 5). The prosthetic compensation received for these bodies had nothing to do with the everyday struggles they faced in getting a wheelchair or other medically necessary forms of supplementation. The level of multipersoned personal assistance provided to the athletes proved so excessive that many U.K. disabled people worried over the growing disconnect with their everyday lives, where personal assistance was an undercompensated luxury at best and existed always under threat of cuts by the most recent austerity measure. Finally, paralympic overcompensation stories made their own precarious lives unreal as the ablenationalist story of completed nationalist project of inclusionism relegated their own below-the-poverty-level existences a relic of a past that remained all too present.

In neoliberal narratives of overcompensation Pistorius's and Mullins's disabled bodies are not enabled as much as they enable forms of ablenationalism. In Pistorius's case his body was reinstated to its normatively upright position in the name of a remasculinized assistive technology's rescue of unproductive bodies from the scrap heap of late liberalism. Traumatically this augmentation also resulted in shooting of Pistorius's girlfriend seven times through a locked bathroom door. Apparently, the hyperprostheticized paralympian also came replete with the accoutrements of disabled masculinity's rehabilitation through militarization. Despite being armed with guns and confessing to the shooting, Pistorius was ultimately found guilty of "negligent killing" but not murder by a South African court. The excessively engineered disabled body in these instances is transformed into a machine of nationalism, one whose individual capacities via prostheticization could be catapulted to a geopolitical stage on behalf of the nation's claims to a postapartheid contemporaneity.

Disabled people watching these displays of excessive technologization from the sidelines felt quickly overshadowed by such images. One might recall the festishization of hyper-capacitated athletic bodies forwarded in Paul Gilroy's critique of the flying, jamming, and basketball shot-producing African American body of Michael Jordan. According to Gilroy, Jordan's hyperathleticized body represented the ultimate trafficking of a racialized image across the space of the Atlantic Ocean from the United States to Europe to Africa and back (*Against Race* 185). The advertising provided an ironic "positive" reversal of the devastation precipitated for Africans during the Middle Passage of the triangular slave trade. The image had little to do with the contemporary experiences of most young black men in urban centers longing to emulate the body ideals of such a media-created, hyperprostheticized, ornate sneaker-hawking celebrity. Yet the monolith of Jordan's image and the marketing empire on behalf of Nike he inspired did much to create a space where more mundane activities, such as bookishness, in the pursuits of nonnormatively athleticized racial bodies were eclipsed as worthy cultural activities.

In other words, Jordan's oiled, athletic body destroyed the legitimacy of a wider variety of black male pursuits in his tongue-lolling flight with an orange basketball to the netted rim of the basket. The multinational ascendancy of Michael Jordan became an iconic emblem of a newly rehabilitated black masculinity that normalized a version of black men made palatable for the extranormative longings of less well endowed white men, those who might have been better off studying in college or working a trade in the shadow of a more spectacular moment in racialogical salvation trafficking through the popular culture sphere of male athleticism (Gilroy, *Against Race* 63).

The representational repertoire of the 1980s and 1990s wiped out a variety of "lesser" politicized pursuits engaged by those bodies seeking to cross various abject corporeal boundaries such as access to public space and art forms claiming plural embodiments as a source of creative insight. Mullins's image in the year of 2006 was paralleled by other forms of "positive and affirming" kinds of disability representation popularly narrated in the cultural lineage of the *X-Men* (2000). The X-Men have significant—even severe—incapacities but also harbor extrahuman compensatory abilities. Compensation narratives—or, rather, schemes of stigma-destroying superpower overcompensation—rule formulas of neoliberal explanatory systems. Such systems enshrine the body that is different yet enabled enough to ask nothing of their crumbling, obstruction-ridden infrastructures, continually naturalized as environments made for most, but not by any means all, bodies. These enhanced supercrips are celebrated by post-Fordist capitalist cultures and socialist governments alike as symbols of the success of systems that further marginalize their "less able" disabled kin in the shadow of committed researchers and policy-makers conjoined to technologized creaming practices for the *able-disabled*.

CONCLUSION: "BE MORE LIKE US"

Coming on the heels of this formulation, we go on in *The Biopolitics of Disability* to analyze post-UN human rights-based optimism for the decade of disabled persons (despite the fact that the United States has still not signed on to the UN Convention's Declaration of Human Rights for Persons with Disabilities [CRPD]). This refusal to sign has come in the wake of some of the most extreme ablenationalist claims made by any nation to date. John Kerry, secretary of state for the Obama administration, argued that the U.S. Americans with Disabilities Act sets a "gold standard" for the rest of the world (*USA Today*, July 21, 2013). In the midst of largely unfounded concerns expressed by conservative groups that the CRPD would open up U.S. sovereignty to challenges of its own version of disability inclusionism by other signatory nations, liberal politicians argued that U.S. treatment of its disabled people surpassed efforts in all other nations combined. Such hyperbole resulted in unabashed claims to American exceptionalism while also sealing off U.S. disability policy from global scrutiny.

Presumably U.S. politicians would both protect the nation from exposure to other kinds of disability inclusionism practiced around the globe while also touting the nation's own accomplishments as unparalleled. Kerry's rhetoric sought to answer these concerns with the most neoliberal of criteria: "Be more like us." U.S. ablenationalist mantras argued that the answer to disability neglect was to bring other nations' disabled people up to the standard of normative acceptance already accomplished in the United States:

> In four simple words, the treaty says to other countries that don't respect the rights of disabled people: Be more like us. To countries that warehouse children with disabilities—be more like us. To countries that leave children to die because they have a disability—be more like us. To countries that force children with disabilities to abandon education—be more like us.

By advocating a global adoption of U.S. inclusionist standards politicians have argued the equivalent of a universal bootstraps narrative. Kerry's mantra of "be more like us" places disability normalization, fashioned within the limits of U.S. inclusionism, as the measure for nearly everyone else on the globe. Ablenationalist forms of abandonment and desolation are the picture Kerry draws of disability mistreatment in other places and the claim of protectionism becomes the moral barometer by which other nations fail.

While exposés of abuses experienced by disabled people in other nations are important to highlight and redress, Kerry's argument intentionally overlooks other major disability protections developed in postindustrial countries such as the United Kingdom, Canada, and Australia. Additionally, the mantra of ablenationalism also signifies retroactively to the superiority of the U.S. context in arguing the desire to achieve normalcy is the naturalized pursuit of disabled people living under "the gold standard." These ablenationalist claims haid from a nation whose unemployment record for disabled people has sat at nearly 70% throughout the era of neoliberalism; where a for-profit system of disability institutionalization has flourished and now inters more than 40,000 disabled individuals alone in the state of Florida while continuing to be beset by scandals of neglect, abuse, and euthanasia (we don't even know how many disabled people are institutionalized nationally because census reporting is not mandatory for institutions unlike prisons); where youth with disabilities are channeled into the juvenile justice system at a rate 5 times higher than other youth ("Jaw-Dropping Prison"). People with disabilities and illnesses in need of medical treatment experience widespread neglect of their health needs that often result in death in a for-profit prison-industrial complex that now boasts an unfathomable 7 million prisoners held in the country -- the U.S. incarcerates more of its people than any other nation on Earth (Meronek "Invisible Punishment"). In the wake of these staggering statistics, Kerry's dismissal of concerns about the threat of other country's scrutiny of U.S. inclusionist practices ring with the false sound of deflection of attention from scandal: as if there would be nothing for the United States to benefit from in hearing critiques from elsewhere on the globe. Finally, Kerry enunciates a form of exceptionalism for U.S. accomplishment in the world that stokes patriotic sentiments on behalf of the nation's treatment of its own disabled people.

Thus, the historical shift from liberal to neoliberal disability proves to be in full swing. Such recent historical developments require that we all put our attention to scholarship and reality testing combined with a dose of judicious caution with regards to the contemporary social situations of people with disabilities. In the pursuit of grasping ever so anxiously at the neoliberal desire to affirm the normative value of all citizens, select members of formerly fringe identities have been inserted to do the work of making heteronormative, ableist lifestyles and value choices even further naturalized.

As with Paul Gilroy's identification of the black, buffed, hyperathleticized bodies of African American athletes now commodified and traded on markets spanning the Atlantic, the newly rehabilitated, fetishized disabled body comes replete with racialized, class, gendered, and sexualized characteristics of its own—features that seem to make recent inclusionist projects a radically individualist and ever-accomplishable horizon. As a result, we pursue a rigorous study of this new transnational bolstering of crip normativities—*the able-disabled*—in order to seek out, maintain, and even challenge the transgressive alterities of former multicultural identities from which they come. In pursuit of this task, the chapters ahead undertake investigations into historically specific sites of crip/queer alternatives as manifest in the representational repertoires of the experiences of PWDs under neoliberalism.

Specifically with reference to burgeoning theories of globality (the tactics, strategies, and logistical maneuverings of multinational capitalism), we recognize as well as critique the recent global entry of disabled persons (as spoken by and for the World Bank, IMF, UN, and transnational citizen representative politics), overlapping with their traditional representation (by NGOs as well as local and national charity interest groups). The International Classification of Functioning (ICF) forms a crucial methodological and linguistic bridge between these diverse, disparate multinational organizations that oversee, channel, and mitigate disabled bodies. Thus, the price of recent efforts to fold disability into the life of the nation might prove quite steep—for those disabled subjects who aspire to find themselves comfortably ensconced among the normatively disabled while further distancing themselves from those who decline such membership. Disabled multitudes (those we revisit in the afterword of this book for their alternative promises to life as consumptive, neoliberal subjects) are actively denied entry due to the undesirability of their bodies as they seek to migrate across national borders, maneuver into professions in which they have been historically consigned to objecthood, or even qualify as truly impaired in the quest for the attentions of for-profit medical industries that certify the real terms of one's impaired status.

TWO

Curricular Cripistemologies; or, Every Child Left Behind

CAUGHT BETWEEN COMPETING MODELS

It could justifiably be argued at this point that ablenationalism does not dismantle the efficacy of the social or minority models of disability but rather demonstrates the difficulty of accomplishing the mission of integration for people with disabilities. Perhaps a better description for what is going on here is the degree to which neoliberalism holds out a false promise of inclusion; the social and minority models stress revision of tangible barriers such as accessible architecture and the modification of public transportation systems, to name just two sites of political intervention identified as critical to disability integration. To revise the environment for greater accessibility for all bodies represents the most tangible pathway to disability inclusion. Ablenationalism, rather, helps to identify the ruse of gains made by disability advocates through operationalization of a rhetoric of inclusion based upon the very aims of the disability rights movement only partially fulfilled (at best).

We would agree, at least in part, with this line of dissent, or, perhaps, accept the productive reframing of a "friendly amendment" as is common in the compromise of differences in policy circles. Yet we also want to insist that something within the social/minority models of disability is also amiss, and perhaps unwittingly fueling neoliberal strategies of inclusion on a more superficial level than has been acknowledged to date. Disability Studies has developed significant interventions for the removal of social barriers in order to achieve better integration of disabled people in public space. However, these dismantled obstacles have resulted in few employment opportunities (particularly at the professional level) for disabled people; employment has proven a Gordian knot that cannot be untied in that most statistics list disabled peoples' unemployment statistics hovering near 70% (see chart). Significantly, employment in a competitive wage labor market is one foundation stone of disabled peoples' exclusion from Capitalism (Stone 21); the other being extraction from reproductive circuits of desire (Snyder & Mitchell, *Cultural Locations* 86; Shuttlesworth, 55; Siebers, "Sexual Culture" 38). Yet, there are few significant ways in which the field can claim to have influenced the global banishment of disabled people from compensated workplace participation.

Perhaps most worrisomely, even highly funded research and policy organizations devoted to the social integration of disabled people such the American University Centers on Disabilities (AUCD) have actively resisted the most basic form of barrier removal: employing disabled people among their own management circles. While disability identities can be recognized within the limiting consumptive terms of neoliberalism as "clients," "patients," and "recipients" of services, they are walled off from the roles of knowledge-producers even among their own publicly funded networks designed on behalf of their further social integration. The only significant exception to this rule are the Centers for Independent Living (CILs) which have become the only significant employment opportunity for disabled people outside of the indentured servitude involved with the sheltered workshop system in the United States.

As disability Anthropologist, Henri-Jacques Stiker, put it nearly two decades ago, this institutional resistance to sharing the world of disability with disabled people turns on a simple fact:

> to live everyday life as an everyday thing, with and in the presence of special, specific human beings who are our disabled equals . . . is revolt because it takes back to the drawing board the whole enormous, vast, imposing specialized social organization: associations at the legislative level, public agencies at the family level. (11)

We share this sense of urgency for "taking back to the drawing board" this social service bureaucracy and would add "the educational level" to Stiker's catalogue. Nearly all contemporary "specialized social organizations" share an existence as products of neoliberal governance tactics ultimately intended to defer rather than accomplish the inclusion of disabled people. As establishments intended to manage the cultural rehabilitation of disabled peoples, they must, through achievement of their own institutional perpetuation, participate in, and even extend, the forms of devaluation they presumably combat.

In post-industrialized nations, educational institutions often serve as the professional training ground for those who administer the specialized social organizations Stiker identifies. This is in spite of the fact that institutions of higher education have historically excluded disabled people—universities, with their knowledge standardization regimens and their false premiums on instrumentalist rationalities, are some of the last places one would expect to find disabled people with their nonnormative sensory, bodily, and cognition processes. This very history of exclusion has attempted to be ameliorated by the governmental funding of mediator organizations since the late 1960s. For example the U.S.—with its volunteerist emphasis on private charitable structures to remedy deep-seated social conflicts—gave birth to Institutes on Disabilities (IODs) that comprise the Association of University Centers on Disabilities (AUCD). The IOD network, established in the late 1960s by Eunice Kennedy Shriver and other disability awareness philanthropists, was intended to integrate cognitive disability into university research agendas. Such groups argued that the establishment of IODs in every state within institutions of higher learning would bring disability to the cutting edge of integrationist innovation, policy protections, and social consciousness-raising.

This chapter will begin by examining how institutions of higher education leave every disabled person behind instead of significantly advancing politicized disability interests on three key fronts: 1) disability support services and Institutes on Disabilities have evolved under a neoliberal management system's simulacrum of disability inclusionism (the one person-at-a-time approach) while largely protecting universities from disability discrimination litigation; 2) colleges and universities have failed to successfully hire people with disabilities as equal participants in their design, research, publication, and training regimens; 3) universities with the help of disability support services offices have continued to approach disability as synonymous with impairment and the attendant lower expectations such associations entail. Instead, the overarching structure of IODs and disability support services in the academy have tended to employ under-trained, able-bodied, lower-level professionals who have little chance of bridging the gap between their clientele and institutions of higher education.

Additionally, these disability support organizations within the academy have been marginalized within universities themselves (both geographically and intellectually) as if their own institutional fates within higher education mirror those of the disabled people they serve. However, we argue that such marginalization has been ironically welcomed by community advocacy organizations because they have not wanted to be judged by the institutional standards in which they are ensconced; instead they argue to be evaluated on the "softer" standards of government-financed service or charity sectors. Alternatively, this institutional marginality within higher education institutions has allowed IODs to approach questions of their own integration of disabled people (i.e. employment) as a threat to their integrity as ablest "managerial" entities. They are the neoliberal equivalent of a disability welfare state within the academy that depreciates their clientele while promoting the basest kind of careerism among those who staff and administer them. The meaningful integration of disabled people into the AUCD can be assessed by its failure to hire disabled people at the highest levels of administration. In many ways disabled people represent the greatest threat to the well being of the network.

This threat appears whenever the prospect of hiring qualified disabled people surfaces. First, because the experience of disability destabilizes the authority of able-bodied professionals to manage and supervise the populations they are charged to "help." This undermining occurs because the "credentials" of those in their employ are based on their experience in working *with* disabled people as a substitute for the embodied experience of disability. Second, disabled peoples' marginalization in the AUCD and institutions of higher education results from a significant residue of suspicion undergirding practices of research empiricism. Namely that "shared status of devalued embodiment" with the objects one studies disqualifies the researcher on the basis of over-identification and, thus, bias the results. Empirical research on disability is historically associated with the negative valuation of disabled peoples' lives, and therefore, the undesirability of spinning "outcomes" as excessively productive disqualifies the products of disability studies-identified research from traditional standards of empiricism. Third, because disability, in serving as what Leslie Fiedler calls the "last frontier" of identity-based research, continues as one of the few areas of investigation where lived experience does not qualify as an enrichment of expertise. Social transformation, within these rationales, must exclude the contributions of individuals with disabilities who might otherwise benefit from research interventions because recipients cannot be the agents of their own social change. In all of these ways IODs, the larger AUCD network of which they are apart, and disability support service offices in the academy leave disabled people behind in higher education in the process of implementing programs of diversity-based inclusion.

NORMALIZATION AND AVOIDANCE IN THE ACADEMY

In the second half of this chapter we develop a theory of curricular cripiste-mologies in order to demonstrate how existing disability inclusionist practices in Higher Education prove purposefully insufficient; not necessarily consciously unattained, but rather an avoidable outcome that is not avoided. Avoidance, as this section header suggests, is an active outcome of work undertaken in the process of accomplishing "diversity" by, perhaps ironically, failing to achieve a meaningful degree of inclusion for historically excluded differences. It stands to rights that the efforts to include Disability Studies and disabled people at institutions of Higher Education is an awkward one—a process, we are going to argue, that is *often purposefully insufficient* due to a profound reluctance to achieve results that might prove the fleshy realization of such a mission.

This avoidance of disability in the midst of professed diversity pursuits in institutions of higher education becomes, in many ways, a given due to the academy's longstanding emphasis on producing members of a professional normative class as one key rite of passage into bourgeois (i.e. middle class managerial) lifestyles. "Professional" in the sense of legitimating expertise to enter into professional domains of oversight that often entail supervising/ managing the lives of people with disabilities; "normative" in the sense of a foundational mooring in diagnostic orientations dependent upon identifying deviance as the measurable outcome of analysis (i.e. the location of pathology as an end-in-itself). The ensuing discontents from such practices for those being diagnosed and, ultimately perhaps, those who perform the diagnosing entails the creation of a dividing line between professionals and the clients they serve; and "bourgeois" in the sense of an ability to achieve a standard of living while touting degrees of heteronormativity that distance some bodies (the diagnosed) from membership in the human community while supporting others (the diagnosers) as embodying its essence. We would submit that this professional dividing line in critical disability studies, and not more traditional binaries such as impairment/disability or disabled/able-bodied that have guided traditional disability studies, serves as a more productive scrim for pursuing critiques of avoidance in the academy.

Whether or not this capacity to produce employable professionals is expanding or diminishing does not affect the idea that normalization is the ideological rubric within which university graduates hone their saleable skills for future markets. Professional membership in what we call "the controlling professions" implicates all university graduates in recognizing diagnostic practices as the *sin quo non* of credentialing in what Richard Sennett calls "the new culture of Capitalism" (11). Our argument here is not that the project of making professionals results in the foundational problem we must tackle in the analysis of avoidance in the academy regarding the embrace of progressive disability diversity initiatives, rather it involves the transformation of the disability knowledge base in higher education. That which we theory as "curricular cripistemologies." The primary analysis of the problem we offer circulates around the fact that *the professionals the contemporary academy makes* are those invested in fashioning others as failing litmus tests of normalcy. Only to the extent that professionalization and normalization have become interchangeable at the contemporary university can we argue that one is, if not synonymous, at the root of the other.

As Lennard Davis points out, the term "normal" is relatively new; it came into the English language in its modern sense of a citizen's average or median capacity between the years 1840–1860. The practice of making a line perpendicular to another on a carpenter's square, or "constituting, conforming to, not deviating or different from, the common type or standard [in] regular usage" helps lay the groundwork for understanding how the modern university produces practitioners—particularly with respect to disability—who apply this squaring process of deviant bodies in the world outside ("Introduction" 1). This results in two overarching problems: one, that disabled people can only be objects of manipulation toward social norms of functionality, appearance, capacity, and behavior, and those who seek to apply these normative guidelines upon others do so with a great deal of institutional authority at their backs; two, the academy as the point of manufacture of these professionals of normalization proves loathe to surrender this primary duty—perhaps its most saleable commodity—on behalf of other alternatives and in recognition of other ways of being-in-the-world (dasein). The one place in which the university will grudgingly give some ground arises in the neoliberal arena of diversity initiatives.

The reason why diversity initiatives allow for what the narrative theorist Ross Chambers calls "room for maneuver" is that diversity is "the new norm" (to cite the American television series of the same name) (31). "The new norm" is a neoliberal concept linked to processes of privatization of formerly public holdings (Hardt and Negri, 301). While selling off the commons provides the most common understanding of this practice within neoliberalism, we want to speak of the nonnormative bodies that remain private tragedies while serving as reference points for the improvement of normative national health. University-made professionals of normalization keep disability a private/individuated affair by failing to attend to wider social contexts of reception for their diagnosed clients (diagnosis keeps pathology a personal matter of dysfunction because it eschews references to a wider world of systemic, social exclusion). But, at the same time, diagnosis extrapolates the diagnostic object into symptom clusters wherein the particularities of conditions are lost on behalf of consolidating generalizable medical categories of public aberrancy. Here a patient's privacy is "protected" while the disparate nature of variable bodies constituting the classification is diluted or erased all together. Thus, disabled people, for instance, often remark upon their inordinately divergent experiences of embodiment despite sharing the same diagnostic rubric with others presumably "of their kind."

What guides the training of diagnostic practitioners, at base, is an operative notion of consumer choice where the contemporary university imagines itself in response to the demands of its market base—namely potential students and their families or support networks. In order to expand its market share and appeal to a wider array of potential consumers the university presents itself as a place of tolerance, a place of flexibility (of participants, of expertise, of labor hours, and, increasingly, of part-time vs. full-time unevenly paid workers). In this sense the university becomes a place of intellectual cosmopolitanism with diagnostic authority as the shared foundation of professional identities of normalization. Diversity initiatives, in other words, expand the student market base of contemporary universities (and therefore bolster profits) while also responding to multiculturalist critiques of a historically homogenizing institutional body politic.

Now, "diversity" emerges as one of the most operative adjectives in the vocabulary of public relations firms that increasingly shape the images of universities and community colleges alike. Our filmmaker son, Cameron

Snyder-Mitchell, in his documentary film, *Branded: Are You Temple Made?*, exposes the branding process at work in institutions of higher education as one dependent on the production of an image of a cool, hip, sheik, diversity culture newly available at contemporary universities. Yet, ironically, this recent historical embrace comes replete with a limited, stylized kind of "diversity" with regard to race, class, gender, sexuality—and disability. For instance, as discussed in our previous chapter brown faces only appear on athletic courts as representatives of "the racialized body, buffed, invulnerable, and arranged suggestively with precision" (Gilroy 185); Asian women wear lab coats and peer into alchemic beakers of colored liquids to soften the rough face of white, masculinist, western empiricism; students are depicted luxuriating on grassy knolls while forms of class indenture go underground into absent discussions regarding rising student debt and the exhausting demands of juggling several part-time jobs while attending college full-time; ghosted queer lifestyles recede in a background of heterosexual couples lying with their heads in each other's laps basking on campus quads like a lyric out of The Beach Boys' "Endless Summer." Campuses are now full-blown media spectacles comprised of luxurious university lives that do not exist. Following Baudrillard, cultural critic, Michael Ventura, refers to this phenomenon as a "media event:" the digitally media(ted) space of the hyper-real where culture (lived experience) gives way to fantasy (174).

Most importantly, this artificial opulence of college lifestyle on display in higher education marketing materials is one that comes in the wake of the displacement of all evidence of the actual practice of education itself. As one Temple University professor remarks in *Branded*: "I don't see anything that I do represented here." The space of the classroom, research, and pedagogy (presumably everyday occurrences at the contemporary university) has gone subterranean in the name of this new sheik campus of affective culture on display. Universities with diversity missions now come packaged as access to lifestyles of multicultural fetishism and their public relations-derived images look increasingly like people pursuing a surfeit of leisure time activities—a variety of diverse body types enjoying media-created environments with facts such as the hole in the ozone layer, local fracking initiatives, and massive oil spills as commonplace features of spoiled worlds left far behind.

For instance at my former institution of higher education, Temple University, there was a great deal of unselfconscious congratulatory back-slapping about the fact that the institution was the "most diverse university in the country." This was neither true nor an ideal in danger of accomplishment at Temple; rather it was the ground zero of a marketing campaign that took up diversity early on (say in the late 1980s in the heyday of neoliberalism) as a path to widening its student market share. In other words, as queer Marxist theorist Kevin Floyd points out in *The Reification of Desire*, post-Fordist innovation reversed the Fordist trend of mass producing products for an average, normative everyman (white, middle class, heterosexual, male, etc.), and instead innovated by diversifying at the consumer end of the market Capitalist continuum (155). It is not merely a fact, for instance, that professions of normalization have increased (although specialization has been on the rise as a feature of neoliberalism's unfolding since World War II), but also that the kinds of people who participate in applications of social norms as their professional "objective" continue to expand. More different kinds of people now graduate from the contemporary university who know the ropes of identifying, applying, and using norms on an ever-increasing array of differently deficient people. As one professor in the Health Sciences at the University of Illinois at Chicago once stood up in a faculty meeting and baldly argued in opposition to IRB oversight restrictions: "Why can't I get unfettered access to the medical records of kids with terminal cancer? Their just going to die and we need research data most of all."

Now we're not going to prove the contention outlined here about a cynical institutionalization of diversity as a false idol of higher education. Particularly because readers employed in institutions of higher learning will be able to identify examples of "diversity" initiatives at their universities or institutions of research that employ concepts of including more different kinds of people while, in effect, resulting in the production of practitioners of normalization rather than inclusion of the bodies of nonnormative outsiders. At the same time university diversity is often about making over more different kinds of people into an approximation of norms that empty out the differences that presumably brought them to the cosmopolitan shores of the university in the first place. The production of practitioners of norms first begins as an internal process during the college-going subject's own exposure to educational normalization as a central part of their training.

Institutions, as Sarah Ahmed argues in *On Being Included: Racism and Diversity in Institutional Life* (2012), "come to have the form of a body as an effect of this work" of the institutionalization of whiteness (494). Reification of how institutional bodies 'look' is important to avoid in that institutional shapes are not given; rather they are historically inherited as patterns of recruitment, expertise, and the cultures of research. The university is effectively a product of what Lauren Berlant in her definition of sexuality refers to as "a set of patterns that align you to the world in a particular way;" universities promoted kinds of participants actively fashioned on certain types of bodies as appropriate and "natural" to its social presentation (societyandspace.com). Diversity missions, as the latest expression of this historically contingent process of environmental patterning, expand the inclusion of some nonnormative bodies, those whom we have referred to as "the able-disabled," while further solidifying those nonnormative, less easily integrable bodies marginalized by the apparent flexibility of inclusive objectives.

We agree with Ahmed's assessment regarding the naturalized fetishization of whiteness as an active outcome of historical admissions/hiring practices; but also want to modify it by arguing that such historical practices keep a university "able-bodied" and "able-minded" as well. This is only common sensical, at least from an institutional perspective, when one considers that the production of professionals of normalization would not themselves be part of the nonnormative mix over which it extends oversight. What logic would it make if those who square deviant bodies to a norm would not comply with such demands in their own bodily comportment? For example, we remember a faculty cohort in the College of Education at the University of Illinois at Chicago that would not allow a Hispanic graduate student with Cerebral Palsy to take the last required master's course in "Testing and Assessment" because, as they earnestly explained to him, "his disability might scare away students coming in to receive their own disability assessment." What university priding itself on the production of normalization professionals would not, in a collective institutional sense, abide by the terms of the squaring process it sought to sell to its students as moral, helping, corrective, professionally advantageous, potentially lucrative, and, more over, embodiment of health in the name of the national interest?

So the questions "avoidance" in the academy introduces are tricky ones in that its pursuit often excludes nonnormative bodies as much as it includes those who can be made over into available multicultural models of diversity. Particularly in the sense that diversity appears as the pursuit of one ideal— the active bringing together of collectives of difference in order to honor the creative, productive ends of multiplicity—but, in fact, often results in a sanitized, homogenized difference among those who arrive in the name of a diversity agenda. To return to disability within this argumentative frame, disability as part of diversity is akin to a weakened strain of inclusion we witness practiced at most public schools in the post-industrialized world; the kind of inclusion that begins to acknowledge disability in the rhetorical sense as serving as an aspect of diversity (alongside race, gender, sexuality, class, etc.), but rarely leading to substantive results regarding student and faculty institutional demographics or meaningful curricular transformations by the integration of critical disability studies classes. Most importantly, disabled people have found themselves at best marginally impacted by diversity/inclusion initiatives in Higher Education. At the graduate level, we would argue, there is almost no measurable impact at all.

If maintaining the institutional face as "white" has been the result of a longstanding (albeit largely unacknowledged) social process of normative hiring and recruitment practices, then maintaining the institution as "able-bodied" operates in a similar vein as a product of historical exclusions. Only in the case of disability we would argue that this maintenance of able-bodiedness has been explicit as the university historically fashions itself in the mold of what used to be called a "normal school." The normal school produces teachers as national standard-bearers of excellence, civility, health, and hygiene—the moral guardians of students who, in turn, seek to become practitioners of normalization (what cohort of students is more normed and norming than educators-in-training?).

Consequently, every student is left behind as disability remains predominantly absent in higher education. Neither the disability rights movement with its equation of barrier removal equals liberation equals civil rights, nor disability studies has made a meaningful dent in the unstated able-bodied norms that govern any of the universities at which we have been employed. Most importantly of all, we have not shaken the ground of the root cause: the unabashed commitment of universities to the reproduction of practitioners of normalization as the terms of exchange in the awarding of higher education degrees. Given higher education's emphasis on producing normalization professionals (special educators, doctors, lawyers, social workers, therapists, psychologists), disability continues to appear as antithetical to traditional diversity missions. Ultimately these missions are set in place as a buffer against public and political charges of bias, class privilege, racial homogeneity, queer challenges to heteronormativity, and a level of disability diversity that rarely extends beyond students with learning disabilities (unlike the U.K., the classification of "Leaning Disability," in the U.S. denotes mild to moderate severity of disability such as dyslexia). To counter anemic inclusion models, we must re-imagine the materiality of disability (i.e. its basis in biology) as desirable variation rather than promote normalization as a fix to professionalization, practices we might best define as the instantiation of false proximity to body norms.

While this analysis of the deferral of meaningful inclusion for disabled people exposes the difficulty of making disability integral to institutions of higher education in the remainder of this chapter we want to begin to formulate alternatives to apprehending disability as a fulcrum for deepening content and exploring nonnormative embodiment as creative alternatives to the flat horizons of normative living through the development of what we call curricular cripistemologies.[1] We begin with a brief close reading of latent disability content developed by an application of nonnormative positivist methodology to a classic secondary and postsecondary school text: Homer's *The Odyssey*. The point is to quickly demonstrate how standardized educational curricula can be deepened through what Carrie Sandahl and Robert McRuer call "cripping" heteronormative texts ("Queering the Crip" 25; *Crip Theory* 5): the ways in which cultural analysis can yield perspectives on life in socially stigmatized, yet culturally productive, embodiments. Disabled people's social marginalization occurs in tandem with their neglect in educational materials. This absence of disability discourse in increasingly standardized neoliberal educational curricula participates in the silence that accompanies the societal shame of speaking about bodies primarily understood as medicalized, singularly dysfunctional, and individuated in their impairments. This avoidance strategy occurs in spite of the institutionalization of individualized education plans (IEPs) and the adoption of inclusive education standards established by the Individuals with Disabilities Education Act (IDEA) in 1975 (Bolt, "Tackling Avoidance").

Consequently, through developing educational content, disability studies can help restore an understanding of disability as historically pervasive, transnational in scope, and culturally significant to the ways in which populations imagine themselves. As a pedagogical approach, disability studies provides ways of legitimating the lives of those occupying peripheral embodiments as offering insightful alternative modes of nonnormative being-in-the-world. These two disability-centered approaches dovetail into what we call curricular cripistemologies.

SONG OF OURSELVES: DISABILITY AS TEACHABLE MOMENT

On the last leg of his decade-long journey back to Ithaca after the Trojan War, Odysseus fails to reach his home one more time and finds himself shipwrecked on the coast of Phoenicia. The failure, ironically, provides the titular hero with an opportunity to improve disability relations in the ocean-based region. Once introduced to Phoenician culture, Odysseus quickly discovers a band of men who self-identify as a muscular tribe celebrated for their superior athleticism, skill in shipbuilding, and expertise in navigating the high seas. As a guest in King Alcinous's box he watches as the athletes engage in competitions of strength, speed, and agility with each other. At one point the participants turn to Odysseus and bait him into competing with taunts of a fear of failure; after many refusals he reluctantly joins and defeats all competitors soundly. By capitulating to these goadings about failed capacity to join the normative games of Phoenician masculinity Odysseus falls into the trap of exercising his military might. A devastating skill set he believes he has effectively left behind him in the civilization destroying wars at Troy.

This demonstration of superior athletic prowess patronizingly misidentified as fear of failure by the Phoenician athletes gives Odysseus a momentary stage. Pointedly he takes the opportunity to observe that his hosts' obsessive overvaluing of physical ability leads to more significant social elisions. The Phoenicians take for granted crip/queer talents in their midst, such as the blind poet-prophet Demodocus, a creative, multiversed, and talented performer. The singer's songs effectively operate as the equivalent of an active cultural archive that preserves Phoenician cultural history, crafts an explanatory context for their physical exploits, entertains them after the endurance required by physical competitions, soothes their ruffled masculinities, includes women as active participants in the life of the kingdom, and diversifies their ranks by making blindness into an asset they too readily depreciate. Demodocus, in other words, turns his own corporeal failings as a blind man into ways of knowing the majoritarian culture better than it knows itself.

We call this turning over of failed capacities into productive incapacities: *curricular cripistemologies*. Curricular cripistemologies offer teachable moments organized around crip/queer content that interrupt normative cultural practices. The evening's songs provide a wider range of opportunities for those who might be otherwise marginalized on the basis of socially devalued crip/queer statuses such as gender, sexuality, gender, race, and blindness. Of course, the author of *The Odyssey*, Homer, is also blind and a singer of poems. In effect, he employs Demodocus as a productively failed double; both actors use their peripheral embodiments as an opportunity to operationalize an available content-laden cripistemology. Crip/queer lyricism offers an alternative ethical value system that diverges from the normatively destructive themes of war, environmental wreckage, human depravity toward others, and brute survival.

In recognition of Odysseus's lesson to his fellow tribesman, the poet takes up his trade and sings of myth as he does on most nights following the denouement of the games. Significantly, the story he tells on this occasion involves the cuckolding of Hephaistos by Mars and Venus. Like Odysseus before him, the promise of failure places "the crook-foot god" center stage as a protagonist who bemoans his being taken advantage of by two nondisabled gods (Rose, *Staff of Oedipus* 40). Positioned at Demodocus's feet, the Phoenician athletes transform into students of their own prehistory. They find their devotion to normative athleticism seriously disrupted by a web of crip/queer content woven by a blind author (Homer), through the common disability trope of a blind poet-prophet (Demodocus), telling the story of a disabled god (Hephaestus) seeking to redress social depreciation on the basis of his differential embodiment. Mars's and Venus's desirability—associated specifically with ancient Greek bodily ideals of power and beauty—come to be outflanked by Hephaestus, a god with a disability who turns his mobility limitation into a wellspring for creativity rather than mere vulnerability to sexual deceit and able-bodied hyjinx.[2] Hephaestus uses his alternative capacity as a blacksmith to secure the couple's mutual humiliation for the amusement of others by catching them up in a specially forged net of steel from which they cannot escape. He makes a spectacle of their heteronormative antics by putting them on display for all to see in this compromising position.

The Phoenicians—and, by extension, Homer's audiences (including ourselves as contemporary readers)—experience their own ideals of capacity displaced. Rather than excessive vulnerability, crip/queer subjectivities create an alternative value system to the naturalized desirability of physical prowess, aestheticized norms of desirable body types, and subpar expectations of functionality. The upstaging of these ideals materializes a space navigated most effectively and queerly not by bodies trained and "perfected" for competition, but by the alternative cultural productivity of failed embodiments crafted by blind poets and semimobile gods.

CURRICULAR CRIPISTEMOLOGIES: INCLUSIONISM AND ITS (DIS)CONTENTS

Odysseus's experience on Phoenicia provides a historical example of the insights awaiting those who undertake pedagogical practices informed by curricular cripistemologies. *Curricular cripistemologies* involve the development of teaching pedagogies that deviate from core curricular teachings by foregrounding disability-based content. This more direct grappling with the intricacies of disability embodiment offers important social options for constructing alternative ethical frameworks for living. An alternative ethical framework results in the creation of usable maps that, from a cripistemological standpoint, are otherwise absent from standardized curricular content. One overarching goal of such content is to provide opportunities for revaluing the failures of crip/queer embodiments to fit within narrow normative frameworks. Rather we read failure to normalize as the emergence of alternative strategies of nonnormative living in order to better speak to the political dilemmas of embodied vulnerability.

The pedagogy of curricular cripistemologies depends upon the insights of human interdependency illustrated in the examples above. It is not a discourse of "specialness" wherein we learn to value disabled people as "human," or tolerate their incapacities when we discover them scraping out an existence alongside others; nor do we find the value of disability guaranteed in overcoming obstacles of social making wherein crip/queer people's incapacities are offset by the compensatory qualities of an otherwise "extraordinary body" (Thomson 5). We also refuse discovery of disability as an opportunity for political correctness wherein all bodies are valued for "diversity" in a relativistic equation of multicultural differences. Relativistic valuations of difference often lead to a process explained by queer theorist Lee Edelman as neoliberal normativity's "tenacious will to sameness by endlessly turning the Other into the image of itself" (*No Future* 59).

Instead of these various strategies for culturally rehabilitating disabled people's experiences within normative social contexts, curricular cripistemologies critically assess how communities facilitate crip/queer people's failures. Such failings result in false perceptions of absence as a naturalized condition of nonnormative existence. While social spaces superficially appear open to all who wish to navigate them, curricular cripistemologies unveil architectural, aesthetic, and moral spaces of exclusion that produce forms of abnormalcy seemingly particular to the bodies they exclude. Thus, normative assumptions encourage exclusion as inherent to the nature of those individuals who "choose" to stay home, rather than experience stigmas associated with socially imposed exclusions. In turn, the nonnormative bodies of crip/queer lives represented within curricular cripistemologies harness creative means by which to navigate alternative ways of living—in part, because they must do so to survive, but additionally, because they derive their strategies of living from the historical traces of other devalued lives (Foucault, *History of Madness* 105). Alexander G. Weheliye explains this alternative labor of survival in minority communities as "pathways to distinctive understandings of suffering that serve as the speculative blueprint for new forms of humanity, which are defined above all by overdetermined conjurings of freedom" (14).

Yet these speculative blueprints of alternative forms of humanity are openly thwarted at various turns in that there is no rehabilitative intervention that does not come replete with a strategy of making estranged bodies better fit normative expectations. In *The Reorder of Things: The University and Its Pedagogies of Minority Difference*, Roderick A. Ferguson explores the impact of educational diversity strategies of minority community cultural incorporations into public schools. Ferguson identifies late 1960s inclusionist practices as institutional ways of robbing minority students of the alternative insights they might provide to available models of living while seeming to embrace them (138–39). Similarly inclusionist practices place crip/queer bodies in the position of making normative practices more desirable: of course, they want to be like us, the story of institutional normalization goes, because our ways naturally enshrine that which all human beings desire. Opposed to this sensibility, curricular cripistemologies actively explore alternative modes of navigating the world as crip/queer embodiments. In effect, cripistemological pedagogies actively leave behind the goal of arriving at identities domesticated, smoothing away their defining differences. Such approaches to the teaching mission force an encounter with the often discomforting content of living interdependently with others.

"EVERY CHILD LEFT BEHIND," OR THE CRIP/QUEER ART OF FAILURE

Most educational tracking indicators of success point to the fact that inclusionist practices have resulted in new kinds of exclusions for crip/queer participants as opposed to integration. For example, students with intellectual disabilities receive a diploma only 36.6 percent of the time, and 22 percent drop out. The rest (59 percent) finish their schooling but receive no diploma and, over the course of their educations, spend time with nondisabled peers only in art, gym, or music (Smith, *Whatever Happened to Inclusion?* 4–5). The statistics in higher education for students with disabilities are equally troubling: in a study of degree completion and postschool success researchers found that "two-thirds of all college freshmen with disabilities fail to obtain their degree within six years of enrollment" (Gugerty). In other words, inclusionism's primary purpose of molding crip/queer bodies into tolerated neoliberal normativities scores a less than passing mark.

This chapter may be understood, then, as a companion to recent critical disability studies in education (DSE) efforts regarding the ongoing critique of an inclusionist process that *leaves all children behind*. If one can be included only by passing as nondisabled, then much of the value of crip/queer experiences evaporates in traditional pedagogical practices. In undertaking this exposure of pedagogical heteronomativity we seek to accomplish three specific tasks: (1) engage disability studies in a dialogue with Judith Halberstam's important recent work on "the queer art of failure" (147); (2) draw out how queer theorizing of the last decade can be productive for disability studies even though, as Robert McRuer and Anna Mollow point out, a more direct engagement with disability has been slow in coming within queer studies (*Sex and Disability* 3); and (3) pursue what may seem, at first, to be a counter-intuitive argument on behalf of actively promoting a certain kind of *failure* for crip/queer students in the context of curricular cripistemologies. All of these objectives combine findings from our teacher training and scholarly research projects on disability pedagogy in higher education over the past fifteen years to more effectively address shortcomings foundational to inclusionist methodologies now operative in most public schools across the nation.

To accomplish the alternative crip/queer goals of curricular cripistemologies we intend to explain why educational inclusion operates as an exclusionary undertaking in, perhaps, the most entrenched, neoliberal, and commonsense institution of all: public education. By neoliberal we mean to define education as part of an ongoing privatization scheme for selling off public institutions to for-profit interests (Hardt and Negri, *Multitudes* 302). Henry Giroux has chronicled this influx of corporate interests into schools through the arrival of product marketing campaigns of unhealthy foods in cafeterias, product tie-ins for lavish expenditures on high-end goods such as sneakers, technology-driven surveillance systems networks, and increased police presence as ever-present conduits in the school-to-prison pipeline particularly in lower-income racial communities (Disposable Youth 6-7). All of these initiatives advance the culture-wide neoliberal festishization of able-bodies that leave under-consumptive, less capacitated bodies behind.

In addition, our critique centers on inclusionism as a neoliberal gloss on diversity initiatives that get some disabled students in the door while leaving the vast majority of crip/queer students behind. Contemporary education's neoliberal practices cultivate further funding opportunities by advancing claims of successful normalization rather than drawing upon crip/queer differences as sources of alternative insight. Curricular cripistemologies, in contrast, openly advocate for the productive potential of failing normalization practices (if they were ever obtainable in the first place) because such goals entail erasing recognitions of the alternative blueprint of values, practices, and flexible living arrangements particular to crip/queer lives.

Whereas the administrative platform of former president George W. Bush pushed for U.S. educational reforms around the promotion of standardized testing that would "leave no child behind," we, in turn, present an argument for recognizing standardization of curricula as ultimately "leaving every child behind," or, at least only promoting a certain type of norm-fulfilling child in whose name most students turn up wanting. This curricular abandonment of difference in the name of assimilation occurs primarily through an incapacity (or, perhaps, unwillingness) to adapt the lessons of systemically in-built accommodations and crip/queer content designed to address the range of learning differences comprising today's classroom demographics. The neoliberal school attempts to resolve accommodating disability through downplaying rather than learning from people's differences. Through the abandonment of disability as difference, neoliberal standards guide educational reforms saturated in the questionable values of ableism, normalization, and rehabilitative masking.

Thus, what appears on the surface as disabled students' incapacity to keep up with their normative peers should be read as the exercise of an agentive form of resistance: a crip/queer art of purposeful failure to accomplish the unreal (and, perhaps, unrealizable) objectives of normalization. In *The Queer Art of Failure* Halberstam argues on behalf of a concept of "failure [that] allows us [queer people] to escape the punishing norms that discipline behavior and manage human development with the goal of delivering us from unruly childhoods to orderly and predictable adulthoods" (3). This queer studies inversion of ways to read nonnormative lives as falling below standards of heteronormative expectations allows crip/queer people to pursue other modes of existence as alternates to sanctioned social roles. These alternative strategies of living pass by largely undetected because educational assessments measure only the degree to which students clear the bar of normalization. By applying this crip/queer deployment of "failure," curricular cripistemologies undertake pedagogical practices suppressed (or, at least, devalued) within normative neoliberal educational contexts.

In adopting a strategically counterintuitive slogan such as "every student left behind," then, the cripistemological critique of inclusionism exposes the increasingly disciplinarian nature of public education's normalizing objectives. Inclusion has taught teachers a dangerous lesson in what appears to be a failed model of adaptation: crip/queer students cannot effectively compete with their nondisabled peers. The pedagogical assessment of the distance that exists between crip/queer and normatively engendered student accomplishments through standardized testing regimes is now part and parcel of their wider cultural nonnormativity. But what if a "failure to thrive" in predetermined educational roles is understood as the product of active refusals (that which Halberstam refers to as a "rejection of pragmatism" [*Queer Art* 89] and Herbert Kohl refers to as "willed not-learning" ["I Won't Learn" 134]) to "fit" disability paradigms reductively dictated by normative institutional expectations? We could take seriously the findings of DSE scholars such as Phil Smith, who points out in his book, *Whatever Happened to Inclusion?*, that education has actually lost ground in terms of including students with more significant learning needs in recent years (28).

Within this context, the objectives accomplished by public relations-driven educational "creaming practices"—those inclusionist claims to success wherein the normative accomplishments of the most "able-disabled students" eclipse the struggles of those left behind. Inclusionism, in other words, covers over an unethical promotion of the successes of the few based upon normative standards of achievement for the normative capitulations of the many. Within curricular cripistemologies disability metamorphoses from a failure of successful normalization of lesser versions of the ableist self *into* a meaningful alternative site for transforming pedagogical practices and devalued social identities. These insights come from the application of nonnormative positivist surfacings in a pedagogical project wherein productive failure sets significantly higher goals than mere tolerance within neoliberalism will generally allow.

What does curricular cripistemology look like if the subterfuge of normalcy does not dictate the socially anemic goals of inclusion—or that which Linda Ware has provocatively termed "(in)exclusion" (2)? Perhaps these reformist efforts have come on the heels of developments during the Clintonian era wherein previously inclusive legislation had to be revitalized and newly enforced. The implementation of more flexible accessibility features followed implementation of the Americans with Disabilities Act (1992) and the Individuals with Disabilities Education Act (1990). Both of these legislative reforms were necessary to update prior failures of inclusive legislation from two decades earlier, including the Education for All Handicapped Children Act (1975) and the Architectural Barriers Act (1968). These policy-based efforts to mandate the inclusion of students with disabilities under neoliberal principles of integration opened up U.S. education to those with developmental disabilities and "multihandicaps" (sometimes also including those referred to as transgender) who had been actively segregated from public education with their peers since the early 1900s and into the early 1970s. One can witness this public segregation at work in Fred Wiseman's documentary film and documentary series titled by the same name, *Multi-handicapped*, where viewers are given access to the "education" provided for deaf and/or blind individuals at the Helen Keller School for the Deaf and Blind in Talladega, Alabama. What Wiseman's films expose are the substitution of basic skills curricula in hygiene and severe sexual prohibitions in place of academic content when students with severe disabilities are concerned (Snyder and Mitchell, *Cultural Locations* 133–54).

CURRICULAR CRIPISTEMOLOGIES

In part, the results of inclusionism have been incomplete because neoliberal efforts evolve around beliefs that mainstreaming would largely require retro-fitting architectural environments in order to bring students with disabilities into buildings outfitted for their able-bodied peers: "the word 'access' . . . has been largely left out of key disability rights laws such as the ADA and when used, access has been understood in its most physical and aesthetic sense" (Richter, "Ableliberalism"). Further, the political pressures of the disability rights movements to achieve meaningful integration ultimately rely on the neoliberal approaches they presumably critique. By advocating for the right to be included alongside able-bodied peer activists in the 1980s and 1990s, the U.S. disability rights movement used a normalizing framework to give weight to their critique of exclusion. They argued that disabled people were like everyone else and wanted the right to pursue normative values in tandem with their nondisabled peers. In other words, a disability rights-based model of policy intervention relies upon assimilationist claims in order to gain access to key neoliberal institutions such as education.

As a corrective to inclusionist objectives that began wholeheartedly in the mid-1990s, scholars in DSE such as ourselves have pursued the development of a *curricular cripistemology*. Curricular cripistemologies imagine another kind of inclusion as that which entails a multitiered approach to making crip/queer lives not just integrated but *integral* to the contemporary pedagogical knowledge base (Stiker, *History of Disability* 32). As an alternative engagement with existing inclusionist methodologies that largely pursue inclusion as an outcome of assistive technology applications—the formalization of a "failed technological fix" to the integration of disabled students that we discuss below—we argue that curriculum needs to contextualize the lives of crip/queer people in order to create a context of receptivity for a more productive interaction with the embodied differences of crip/queer lives in school. A functioning curricular cripistemology entails teasing out and making visible otherwise latent crip/queer themes in educational materials as a primary ordinal in a multitiered approach. Based on our experiences in a variety of pedagogical training settings, curricular cripistemologies involve the development of a systemic, even replicable, disability pedagogy and content in combination with the active participation of crip/queer subjects.

Our collaboratively implemented projects rest largely on the findings of five key activities temporarily implemented in institutions of higher education from the mid-1990s to 2010: (1) a teacher education series sponsored by the National Endowment for the Humanities held from 2000 to 2001; (2) the development of an Interdisciplinary PhD program in disability studies from 2000 to 2009; (3) an NEH seminar for scholars in higher education held in summer 2000: (4) an NEH seminar for public middle and high school educators in summer 2003; and (5) a federal demonstration project of "national significance" on improving outcomes for students with disabilities held from 2008 to 2010. The array of educational venues within which to develop curricular cripistemologies points to a flexible alternative to the restrictive dictates of standardization. Curricular cripistemologies evolve diverse contexts for pedagogical success as well as multimodal opportunities of application for students, educators, researchers, and scholars alike.

The remainder of this chapter seeks to provide an overview of these collective pedagogical projects in DSE. Perhaps most foundational to our own crip/queer bodies of work involves promotion of curriculum-first approaches as the foundation stone of more meaningful engaged educational interactions with diversity (i.e., beyond integration). Collectively these pedagogical training applications of curricular cripistemologies provide opportunities to institutionalize options for a multitiered pedagogy based on DSE methodologies including (1) "Cripping the Curriculum" as an approach to foregrounding crip/queer histories in the transformation of curriculum; (2) "Differentiating the Nonnormative Classroom" in the classroom as a purposeful refusal to "blend" with neoliberal assimilationist approaches to tolerated minority differences; and (3) "Leaving the Technological Fix Behind," the development of alternatives to the reductionist technologization of learning as synonymous with meeting neoliberal inclusionist objectives. The multitiered nature of these approaches draw upon the productive realization of crip/queer arts of failure that reject simply "fitting in" as a worthy basis for educational projects of nonnormative positivist difference realized through applications of pedagogies informed by DSE.

Cripping the Curriculum

For the purposes of developing a curricular cripistemology, the most critical yet least well understood aspect of DSE is the reform of pedagogical content that actively absents disability from its teachings. Why is reform of curriculum the first step rather than a later evolution in making crip/queer content integral to educational lessons? To address this question we argue that curriculum reform must come first because it changes faculties' and students' facility with crip/queer "ways of knowing." Such an approach leaves normative educational goals of disability assimilation behind and espouses the implementation of curricula that forward productive alternatives provided by crip/queer cultures, histories, and art. Even the most normative curriculum offerings come replete with "fantasies of otherness and difference, alternative embodiment, group affiliations, and collective desires" (Halberstam, *Queer Art* 119). Halberstam's insights in *The Queer Art of Failure* are critical to the implementation of curricular cripistemologies as well because they provide a road map that identifies crip/queer bodies as integral to education rather than as an auxiliary student population in need of the special treatments made available by neoliberal normalization.

While the pedagogical projects cited here as the basis for our findings have occurred in diverse venues, we have consistently adopted three basic principles critical to deepening disability curricular efforts as a productive experience:

1. Our approaches can be adapted to any existing educational content because crip/queer experiences exist as a latent realization in all texts and our pedagogies are insufficiently honed to analyze them.

2. Training teachers to develop pedagogical strategies that draw out crip/queer content as an active collaboration with disabled and strongly identified disability practitioners of DSE.

3. The architectural modifications and technologically based fix-it approaches of today's inclusionism, while important, continue to perpetuate access to heteronormativity as the most worthy goal and cannot overcome deficiencies of content not reimagined to represent crip/queer experiences and histories.

Each of these principles requires a significant level of educational reinvention to implement in an impactful manner. They effectively ask contemporary educators to fail in the implementation of foundational "best practices" long believed central to pedagogical inclusionism. In achieving this failure curricular cripistemologies fashion a more rigorous educational experience for all students, including crip/queer students.

Curricular cripistemologies leave the empty goal of normalizing disabled students behind by shifting the educational emphasis with respect to crip/queer findings in four palpable ways. First, the application of disability content to existing curricular materials asks us to take experiences of embodiment seriously rather than remove ourselves to a more ethereal realm of "ableist rationality." Second, not requiring the purchase of new materials to address the insufficiencies of current texts and lesson plans avoids the oft-levied charge of too much expense as an excuse for neglecting the meaningful integration of crip/queer subjects. It also lessens the idea that purchasing more goods is an antidote to poor quality, under-engaged education. Third, the open acknowledgment of crip/queer lives as a sociological content area requires us to leave behind certain founding precepts extant in contemporary disability and gay/lesbian rights movements, namely, that crip/queer bodies are medical conditions that must be secreted to the greatest extent possible within a neoliberal moment characterized by HIPAA (Health Insurance Accountability and Portability Act) protections (the act of teaching crip/queer bodies to leave their medical histories behind). And, finally, curricular cripistemologies recognize the flexibilities of universal design for learning (UDL) in pedagogy as a means to situate crip/queer students at the foundation of our teaching methods rather than as failed exceptions to the rule; or, perhaps better yet, they are failures because they take exception to the rule of heteronormativity as the ne plus ultra of education.

Our efforts actively bring crip/queer insights as alternative curricular content to education. A key contribution of DSE has been the development of crip/queer readings performed with respect to "classic" fiction and nonfiction texts. Instances include the queer divinings of Sumerian priests regarding the productivity of harvest cycles based on interpretations of "deformed" calves' livers and aborted disabled fetuses (Mitchell, Snyder, and Albrecht, *Encyclopedia of Disability* 52); the reliance on disability-based characterizations in biblical writings (blindness, deafness, mobility impairments, madness) while other normative physical descriptors (i.e., height, weight, complexion, hair and eye color, etc.) are comparatively absent (Schipper 4); discussions of Sir Thomas Moore's crip *Utopia* (1516), where he imagines social orders predicated on the provision of adequate health care for all citizens (Dorn); exploring Darwin's arguments about "the reappearance of long-lost biologies through reversion to origins" in *Descent of Man* (109) as evidence of crip/queer evolutionary links between human ancestry and animals (Snyder and Mitchell, 2006, 13); W. E. B. Dubois's arguments in *The Souls of Black Folk* (1903) regarding the "talented tenth" and the cognitive disablement of Negro rural folk due to inadequate access to education and racial opportunity (Lukin, "Black Disability Studies" 312); the framing logic of American eugenics for interpreting Benjy's castration and institutionalization as a person with Down syndrome in William Faulkner's *The Sound and the Fury* (Bérubé xv; Snyder and Mitchell, *Cultural Locations* 168); the origins of Nazi genocide in German psychiatric institutions as documented in Hannah Arendt's *The Origins of Totalitarianism* (1951), Henry Friedlander's *The Origins of Nazi Genocide: From Euthanasia to the Final Solution* (1997), and our own documentary film on the systematic slaughter of disabled people in psychiatric institutions during World War II (*A World Without Bodies*).

This list (which could, of course, be much as long as the literary and cultural archive itself) identifies some crip/queer analyses developed by DSE scholars with respect to oft-taught writings in public education. The catalog is not exhaustive but intended as suggestive of the transhistorical, cross-cultural, and multidisciplinary reach of curricular cripistemologies. A more active relationship to latent disability content in traditional texts effectively leaves behind prior practices of pedagogical avoidance (Bolt, "Tackling Avoidance" 2011). Curricular cripistemologies make crip/queer-based content central to, rather than absented from, heteronormative pedagogies. Importantly, the goal of such teaching is not to find "positive" examples of crip/queer differences in cultural materials. Instead, we have a more far-reaching objective: curricular cripistemologies draw out a complexly nuanced human constellation of meanings for crip/queer lives akin to other marginalized histories. In particular, crip/queer experiences are those marked by what Nirmala Erevelles refers to as the "compounded interstices of multiple differences" (*Disability and Difference* 22). In other words, cripistemologies develop foundational experiences of embodiment that cannot be simplified down to the practices, modes of existence, and privileges of a narrowly conceived normality.

Differentiating the Nonnormative Classroom

In addition to curriculum-first applications, these projects all attend to the experiential proximity of crip/queer instructors delivering DSE content. Such pedagogical exchanges expose classrooms to crip/queer bodies rarely encountered in positions of educational authority. We don't make a claim for an automatic relationship between crip/queer experiences and the expertise of leading effective DSE classrooms. However, the opportunity to employ crip/queer educators plays a key role in failing the inflexible standardizations of the normatively inclusive classroom. As theorized in the literature of coming out crip/queer as a teacher, classroom discussions about bodies that do not fit into a "minoritizing logic of tolerance" (Sandahl, "Queering" 26) or are considered in proximity to institutionally fragile "strained subjectivities" (Brueggemann and Moddelmog, "Coming Out Pedagogies" 312) play a key role in developing interpretive relations to crip/queer embodiments.

This point, however, is made only while acknowledging the serious professional consequences commonly reported by crip/queer and other minority teachers in receiving disproportionately negative teaching evaluations and/or denials of tenure/promotion. The delivery of disability content as a crip/queer-identified teacher comes replete with epistemic benefits as well as epistemic risks.[3] However, our studies consistently find that the participation of crip/queer teachers lends credence (even without direct address) to the reasons why pursuing disability-based analysis proves socially necessary and educationally impactful.

While placing crip/queer instructors in front of the classroom enables one kind of educational change, the evolving participation of crip/queer students in the classroom also results in critical insights heretofore only marginally realized. If the overwhelming emphasis of today's inclusion practices on receiving a passing mark becomes synonymous with *passing* (i.e., approximations of able-bodiedness), DSE's antinormative instructional emphasis consistently results in more students coming out as crip/queer during the semester. As

Tobin Siebers explains, publically held norms of able-bodiedness require masking the disruptive visibility of disability in order to keep its shameful embodiments out of view (*Disability Theory* 97). This practice proves no less common in the normatively inclusive classroom. The approximation of able-bodiedness treats crip/queer embodiments as a matter of stealth differences at the core of passing's successful performativity. Mitigation of disability treats crip/queer bodies as levels of deviance to be avoided, or, in the parlance of curricular cripistemologies, "left behind." Their lack of acknowledgement in our presence also continues the longstanding educational complicity in under-playing the degree to which bodies differ and reveal their alternative organizations, vulnerabilities, and adaptations.

Our findings consistently show that avoiding the myriad stigmas associated with crip/queer bodies results in less desirable educational outcomes. When students spend time leaving behind crip/queer identifiers, they also find themselves implicated in the neoliberal devaluation of embodied differences. In fact, the dictates of the normative classroom draw crip/queer students into complicity with a wider social devaluation by teaching them to downplay the existence of alternative lives. The destructive requirements of leaving behind nonnormative modes of being effectively reifies the desirability of heteronomativity at the expense of the crip/queer body's consignment to what Tom Shakespeare calls "dustbins for disavowal" (284). One result is that crip/queer bodies become constitutive of heteronormativity while deflecting the pivotal role they are made to play in the false transparency of normativity. Curricular cripistemologies argue there is too much at stake in this unequal exchange of consecrated normativities and disavowed nonnormativities; thus leaving every child behind is necessary to transform existing inflexibilities extant in educational standardization. The crip/queer classroom produces a more meaningful system of differential values wherein shame about one's body as inadequate, medicalized, and pathological (the current terms of normalization within inclusionism) is abandoned. In their place curricular cripistemologies insert the creative alternatives of interdependency, that which we will theorize in chapter 4 as the politics of atypicality, and a more critical assessment of neoliberalism's founding (in)exclusions.

Consequently, curricular cripistemologies encourage the identification of personal expertise with crip/queer lives as a reservoir of knowledge. This is no shameful sequestration of knowledge gleaned from proximity to non-normativity. When the classroom conversation gives credence to the authority of crip/queer experiences, crip/queer student subjectivities gradually sense a thaw in the labor required to keep their differences at bay. Instead they begin actively cultivating personal experiences with alternative ways of being, creating fertile ground for classroom contributions.

The transformation can be profound. Students can be witnessed suddenly operationalizing ways of drawing from the authority of their experience rather than removing a formative aspect of their knowledge from conversation. In this manner crip/queer bodies shift from liabilities to be secreted away in order to become active vectors of insight from which one may engage in classroom models of collective understanding. Through such developments crip/queer subjectivities become a way of knowing the world, embodiments akin to other forms of discredited knowing such as femininity, race, ethnicity, and sexuality (yet, importantly, containing all of these differences at the intersection of what makes bodies crip/queer). The nonnormatively embodied classroom that emerges with curricular cripistemologies becomes a place in which diversity operates as a nuancing agent of the educational knowledge base.

This open exploration of subcultural differences in the nonnormative classroom provides what queer theorist David Halperin explains as "a social space for the construction of different identities, for the elaboration of various types of relationships, for the development of new cultural forms" (*How to Be Gay* 67). Likewise, curricular cripistemologies promote the classroom as a place of productive differentiation—both in relation to creating more flexibility within majoritarian norms *and* within crip/queer subcultures themselves. In Halberstam's terms the differential space of crip/queer classrooms fails to cohere into a univocal identity of difference. A curricular cripistemology, in other words, leaves no *body* behind.

Leaving the Technological Fix Behind

The passage of the 1972 consent decree in Philadelphia reaffirmed the right of all disabled children to have access to public education in the least restrictive environment. Since that time the focus of integration efforts has not been curriculum reform; rather the emphasis has targeted retrofitting inaccessible architectures and adapted learning technologies. Such interventions identify the learning environment and the learner rather than the practice of pedagogy as the desired object of change—as if a computer program will somehow magically integrate a student with a disability into a classroom that has no tradition of disability integration from which to draw.

Yet, in point of fact, we have seen little accomplishment in the cultivation of reciprocity between the experiences of disabled students, nondisabled students, and curricular content from the mere application of the magic of technology. A necessary dialectic has gone missing. The reasons for this absent conversation varies; however, the end product most consistently takes the shape of disabled students left to navigate parallel educational universes with their nondisabled counterparts. Inclusionist approaches tend to turn disability into a puzzle of accommodations and a nest of potential litigation actions to be preemptively warded off by school administrators, social workers, and SPED bureaucrats. In *Reading Resistance*, Beth Ferri and David J. Connor discuss how a case-by-case approach within SPED and resistance to implementation of the ADA inherently benefits the status quo (18). Thus, the individualized solutions offered by individualized education programs (IEPs) presumably tailored to personal disabled student needs rarely become systemic. Thus, these efforts fail to assist future generations of crip/queer students by offering them access to alternative pedagogical delivery methods such as universal design for learning (UDL) already implemented in the educational environment.

Research project funding for disability initiatives consistently underwrites the purchase of technologies such as software to buffer teachers against having to adopt more flexible strategies in their pedagogical methods. Alternatively, projects not based in the insights and practices of curricular cripistemologies leave behind false hope in technological fixes. Instead cripistemologies promote the development of content about disability as a first-order necessity. In *Crip Theory*, Robert McRuer demonstrates how reading and writing from the body helps to promote alternatives to standardized educational approaches, particularly those approaches promoted in the homogenizing goals of public school systems that emphasize finished products as synonymous with learning (168). Such approaches adapt everyone to the goal rather than attempt the diversification of true engagement based on the ways in which crip/queer lives fail to fit the oedipal mold of, say, the five-paragraph essay. Or, rather, the accomplishment of making these experiences fit the mold of standardization voids the significance accorded to what Kevin Floyd theorizes as "the social labor" of fashioning alternative subjectivities (*Reification of Desire* 75).

Almost by definition, the UDL-structured classroom promotes the unique knowledge precipitated by the ontology of diverse embodiments ("About UDL"). UDL, first and foremost, requires a systematic negotiation of needs across any assembly of student differences. Because disabled students do not necessarily know their own access requirements and university programs are often not equipped to accommodate them ahead of time, accommodations prove to be uneven implementation of inclusionism at best. The opening weeks of a UDL-structured classroom inevitably entail an active negotiation of the ways in which reading materials, classroom discussions, and visual media will be made accessible to all. Many university faculty members complain of the wasted time such strategizing entails (as we witnessed on multiple occasions in the Department of Disability and Human Development at the University of Illinois at Chicago). But commitment to UDL is seen as part of the point of a DSE-based education itself. Open discussions of multipronged access approaches bring information about disabilities into the conversation from the start as well as tutoring students in the provision of UDL-based training as a founding stone of instructional access equity.

For instance, deaf or cognitively disabled students often include assignment of a captioner who functions as a real-time stenographer of classroom conversations and lectures. While the university approaches real-time captioning as a specific accommodation for a particular kind of disabled student, the UDL classroom recognizes an opportunity to assist all participants in the rigorous engagement with academic ideas. An active exchange of ideas in the classroom often results in students losing track of the nuances of a discussion; alternatively, the sharing of real-time captioning notes online following class allows an ease of review that lessens anxiety about retention of information. When blind or visually impaired students required on site audio description of images, all students find themselves abreast of details that they might have otherwise missed. Language used in a lecture that escapes some listeners' comprehension may prompt a request to repeat the information in alternative ways. Such variations in approach to academic materials create the kind of pedagogical flexibility that seems all too missing from standard classroom environments. Rather than describe the nuances of disabled lives from afar, students often bring their own experiences to bear on what would otherwise appear as medically neutral narratives of "medical disorders." Such efforts demonstrate the ways that UDL pedagogies benefit all students, as opposed to serving as expensive interventions on behalf of a few disabled students.

As Halberstam theorizes *In a Queer Time and Place* (2005), "queer time" involves an understanding of the particular logistics that structure experiences of alternative embodiments:

> For the purpose of this book, "queer" refers to nonnormative logistics and organizations of community, sexual identity, embodiment and activity in space and time. "Queer time" is a term for those specific models of temporality that emerge within postmodernism once one leaves the temporal frames of bourgeois reproduction and family, longevity, risk/safety, and inheritance. (6)

UDL, in turn, organizes a disability time and place by shifting educational environments according to the demands of its peculiar, "nonnormative logistics." The flow of conversation inevitably slows to accommodate the accommodations, and some of the intellectual "momentum" that comes of the rapid-fire sharing of ideas may be lost. Alternatively, a more conscious setting of the pace of discussion can ultimately result in a more thoughtful array of contributions. Students in DSE adapt to an alternative information flow and, in the realization of the absence of a press of time to get ideas out, the concepts often gel into less fragmentary explanations.

A similar point might be made on behalf of a curricular cripistemology at a larger systemic level as an opportunity for the advocacy of the hiring of teachers with disabilities in school systems.[4] There has been a long-standing resistance to recognizing this argument as a valid criterion for hiring individuals as representative of a growing student population—particularly one made up of a sizable number of young people from all socioeconomic strata with disabilities including a disproportionate number of racial minorities.

Rather than excluding students from completion of curricular requirements for teacher certification based on their disability status, an informed curricular cripistemology argues for an inverse logic: the often traumatizing experience of diagnostic assessment for students with disabilities might be significantly mitigated by receiving the assessment from an adult with a disability employed by the institution making the diagnostic determination. Imagine the signal it might send to newly identified students with disabilities that a diagnosis with disability might not disqualify them from future professional employment?

Further there is a running commentary in education circles that, in jointly taught classrooms, the regular education teacher is in charge of the development of curricular materials. The teacher may introduce a section on the Spanish conquest of Mexico, for instance, and the collaborating special educator's contribution will be to hold the globe. In other words, SPED has not yet embraced the idea that special educators might make a contribution to the co-taught classroom related to the content delivered. Rather the special education teacher's expertise is exclusively located with content delivery methods (tech applications) on behalf of a couple students who might struggle with a more unilateral pedagogical approach. A serious commitment to the development of curricular cripistemologies might go some distance toward revaluing human differences as something other than embodiments that should be disguised, diminished, or hidden away as an unwanted accessory.

Why not begin training special educators in the methods of DSE as a curriculum education goal such as that featured at the Cultural Foundations of Education Program in Disability Studies at Syracuse University? What would be a more apt subject specialty than the history and culture of the disability demographic that they are specifically trained to teach? Wouldn't a background in DSE cripistemologies also serve as a source of change for non-disability-identified students in the classroom? And who better to undertake the subject expertise? In this manner, disability deepens the educational context for all learners. Its arrival as a central concern of pedagogy also performs the productive transformation of ways in which students with disabilities might imagine their own embodied experience as something from which to draw in their developing knowledge of the world.

Just as Odysseus recognizes an opportunity to identify alternative talents at work in the Phoenician community assembled for an exposure to culture-making after the games are over, so can educational systems perform a parallel act of valuing peripheral embodiments. After all, Demodocus's contribution to Phoenician culture comes not only by virtue of his own embodied experience, but also through his ability to use that experience as an entry into the exploits of even the most able-bodied participants in the audience. A true curricular cripistemology plays the entire room and promises to widen the arena of embodiment for all.

PART II

The Biopolitics of In(ter)dependent Disability Cinema

THREE

Gay Pasts and Disability Future(s) Tense
Heteronormative Trauma and Parasitism in *Midnight Cowboy*

In this section of our analyses we provide three related discussions of disability film as an alternative space for imagining peripheral embodiments within neoliberalism. Chapter 3 opens with a discussion of *Midnight Cowboy* in order to examine how disability and queer politics must deny prognostic futures of inclusion if they are based on models of integration that erase the productive alternatives made available by crip/queer lives. Chapter 4 explores the international development of disability film festivals that feature independent digital visual productions created by disability collectives across the globe. Like gay and lesbian film festivals before them, disability film festivals serve as a showcase for cross-national, biopolitical portrayals of disability as a shifting, dynamic, ever fluctuating expression of human variation and its precipitating social responses.

While the films screened often capture experiences of neglect, oppression, and violation as part of the drama of disability, the productions themselves also provide an alternative entryway into disabled people's creative negotiations of inflexible, normative cultural spaces. Further, the diversity of film festival offerings, as specifically analyzed in chapter 5, offers viewers a completely unusual vantage point akin to a global assessment of the well-being of disabled people within the larger species: "humanity." Particularly with respect to a humanity that we define within nonnormative positivisms as adaptive diversity rather than normative replication.

Taken collectively, the three chapters in Part II help us to define a *politics of atypicality* at the foundation of new collective responses to neoliberalism's horizontal inclusions. Disability cinema and the subcultural gatherings they inspire offer an understanding of political collectivity akin to the dynamics of the fracturing processes of political subject formations on the left as explicated by Ernesto Laclau and Chantal Mouffe in *Hegemony and Socialist Strategy*. Rather than forward disability as a monolithic rubric of identity, disability film festivals provide an opportunity to witness the productive fracturing of diversity cultivated within a politicized collectivity. Rather than strictly policing boundaries of what conditions count as disability, film festivals cultivate elastic definitions of disability that actively morph and stretch to encompass a wider range of human variations. Whereas most minority identities have sought to consolidate and reify social norms of belonging within normative neoliberal systems based on civil rights-based definitions (including, as discussed in chapter 1, disability rights movements), we characterize disability, on the heels of our last chapter's interaction with Halberstam's concept of the "queer art of failure," as a fortunate dishevelment of normative coherency. As a politics of atypicality disability can be most productively understood as an identity based on incoherence, one that challenges the false stability of diversity boundaries that circumscribe neoliberal minority identities while insisting on the existence of debilitated lives that are not so elastic as to make the alternative relations of crip/queer lives, acts, and values meaningless.

The challenge of the politics of atypicality becomes particularly pressing within neoliberal biopolitics, particularly in that much of disability's social oppression is based on medical classifications that overindividuate bodies within categories of pathology while turning labeled subjects into generic representations of their medicalized condition group. In resisting this expression of power enacted as identifications of deviation, the politics of atypicality substitutes an alternative grouping strategy; atypicality collects expressions of difference so diffuse, idiosyncratic, and nonreplicable that no generic figure of disability may achieve representative status. As many disability studies scholars have explained it, the choice of disability has the advantage of carrying "the drawback of generality but also the power of mass" (Price 291).

Truthfully, those active in even the most radicalized identity camps of disability often experience this failure of coherency as the collapse of a unified shared space from which to undertake collective action. Alternatively we argue that in(ter)dependent disability film festivals actively cultivate this fracturing within disability identity categories as a productive outcome of tending to a collectivity that cannot be stabilized, centralized, hierarchicalized, or organized without destroying its disruptive potential with respect to challenges of normative investments in embodiment.

As an alternative to normative regimes of inclusion, the arguments in this part on disability cinema endeavor to push through the limits of impairment to explore how disability subjectivities create new forms of embodied knowledge and collective consciousness in the midst of their social abandonment.[1] Queer and disabled people's interdependencies provide alternative ethical maps for living together outside of, even in opposition to, the dictates of normalcy. The experimental, albeit Hollywood-financed, late 1960s release of the film *Midnight Cowboy* serves as one example of the uses to which queer/crip subjectivities have been explored regarding critiques of the normative demands made upon those occupying what Foucault refers to as "peripheral sexualities."[2] The late nineteenth-century advent of "peripheral sexualities . . . entail[s] an incorporation of perversions and a new specification of individuals as . . . a type of life, a life form, and a morphology, with an indiscreet anatomy and possibly a mysterious physiology" (*History of Sexuality* 601–2).

"Peripheral sexualities," in other words, are lives designated as akin to what Alison Kafer means by evoking the category of *queer/crip*:

> What *Feminist, Queer, Crip* offers is a politics of crip futurity, an insistence on thinking these imagined futures—and hence, these lived presents—differently. Throughout the course of the book, I hold on to an idea of politics as a framework for thinking through how to get "elsewhere," to other ways of being that might be more just and sustainable. In imagining more accessible futures, I am yearning for an elsewhere— and, perhaps, an "elsewhen"—in which disability is understood otherwise: as political, as valuable, as integral. (3)

Queer/crip identities exist at the intersection of nonnormative abilities and sexualities, and, as a result, often find themselves abandoned to the fates of pathologized classifications of the socially unsalvageable. In *Midnight Cowboy* we witness the results of this cordoning off of homosexual and handicapped lives into *zones of expendability*; the enforced habitation of toxic environments as the terms of health-destroying conditions in neoliberal spaces of neglect. In order to imagine an alternative space of nonnormative living *Midnight Cowboy* offers an in-between location of interdependence that can better realize the "elsewhen" of "crip futurity" for which Kafer and ourselves long.

TOXIC SPACES OF NEOLIBERAL ABANDONMENT

Most memorably, *Midnight Cowboy*'s delineation of zones of expendability develops during the performance of a pas de deux by Joe Buck (Jon Voight) and Rico Rizzo (Dustin Hoffman) to the commercial jingle "Orange Juice on Ice, That's Nice." The couple's frenetic dance occurs as an activity to keep their bodies warm in an unheated, condemned New York City apartment building during a frigid winter. Borrowing from the symbolic conventions at work in James Baldwin's *Giovanni's Room*, *Midnight Cowboy* uses the condemned space in which Rico is squatting as a mise-en-scène for an externalization of his psychic life. They traverse a rickety exterior navigated through a hole cut in a wire fence and across the unstable surface of loose boards substituting for nonexistent sidewalk that expose the material conditions of the collapsing infrastructure—one that prosthetically metaphorizes Rico's collapsing bodily health from excessive exposure to an endangering environment. As Rico reassures Joe early on the film, the heat "don't work" but the refrigerator will keep perishables from the cockroaches for the space of a day. To emphasize the uninhabitable terrain for a mobility-impaired individual, a viewer's first visit to the apartment involves Rico leading Joe up two flights of concrete stairs littered with trash and other obstacles.

Such architecture becomes synonymous with the inaccessibility of a built and socially neglected space, one that proves hazardous to its temporary residents, rather than securing their well-being. In the apartment, walls and floors literally melt into the pastiche of worn layers of wallpaper and exposed tiers of vinyl flooring.[3] Rico's consciousness is projected onto the threadbare surfaces in the meekly hung magazine and newspaper advertisements of Florida sunshine, big bass fishing, and plump oranges arrayed around a tall glass of sweating orange juice. The images pointedly provide a meager cover for the underlying decay. In the one window over the rusting sink unrolls a sheet of greasy newspaper thinly orchestrated as a makeshift shade that only reaches half way. Provisional space abounds in these decaying zones of urban expendability, and rather than protective shelter the outside reaches inside in a mixing of toxic conditions that prove more hazardous to the inhabitants than the world from which they seek to escape excessive exposure of their bodies.

In fact, as Mel Y. Chen points out in *Animacies: Biopolitics, Racial Mattering, and Queer Affect*, what defines the social space of abjected bodies is their precarious proximity to toxic environments against which the middle and wealthy classes buffer themselves by "buying out" of excessive exposures (Chen 208). The risky, and risk-calculated, exposures to surroundings containing "bodies which are deemed 'sick' are either seen as affected by toxic elements to the point of entering disability categories or are themselves considered a polluting scourge upon human normative securities" (Chen, 212). For Chen, place often denotes social devaluation; a queer/disability Möbius strip relation to the world wherein your placement within a hazardous exposure becomes misrecognized as the hazard to which your body exposes others. The exposure rationalized by neoliberal social environments of toxicity as an acceptable zone of risk depends upon the peripheral location of risky bodies as always-already prescribed as a form of contagion from which others need shielding.

In scenes detailing the particulars of Joe's and Rico's life as urban squatters in the abandoned tenement building, *Midnight Cowboy* critically reflects on practices of social abandonment in the encroaching shadow of neoliberalism at the close of the 1960s. Neoliberalism involves forms of governance that reject the principle of governing on behalf of devalued populations (systemic provisions of government-sponsored support) through the promotion of rampant market profiteering (unregulated corporatizing) and the selling off of public spaces to private interests (the commons). By the conclusion of the film, the apartments surrounding Rico's condemned building are gradually destroyed to make way for gentrification projects and public infrastructure upgradings—Rico's tenement building is the next to go.

The specifics of this abandoned space are in many ways historically particular to the late 1960s in New York City as biopolitical power takes root as a strategy of body management within neoliberalism. The film is set prior to neoliberal forces that decimate the red-light district around Times Square led by then mayor Rudy Guiliani's efforts in the early 1990s "to clean up the city and make it more family friendly."[4] Additionally, *Midnight Cowboy*'s release coincides with the latter part of the construction of the Cross Bronx Expressway (begun in 1948 and completed in 1972); a massive freeway project built with an expressed intention of displacing more than 170,000 working-class and lower-income individuals, particularly African Americans, and members of minority communities in its construction wake (Rose, *Black Noise* 33). The expressway project knowingly hastened the forces of gentrification through the displacement of those relying on public hous- ing in impoverished neighborhoods on behalf of profit maximization for the city and real estate developers. David Harvey identifies this process of strategic redistricting of marginal citizens as the neoliberal tactic of selling public housing to for-profit industry. Harvey refers to this form of neoliberal displacement as "accumulation by dispossession" (*Imperialism* 137). Finally, *Midnight Cowboy*'s release in October 1969 straddles two important events in disability and gay history: Congress's passage of the Architectural Bar- riers Act in June 1968, which required public buildings to be handicapped accessible, and the Stonewall uprising that catalyzed the gay liberation movement in the United States only a month later (Floyd 154; D'Emilio and Freedman 274).[5]

In detailing Rico's and Joe's exposure to the environmental toxicity char- acteristic of poverty, *Midnight Cowboy* captures the difficult-to-document, death-dealing gradualism of Foucauldian biopolitics—the power to mark some populations for death (letting die) on behalf of sustaining other, more valued populations in lives of surfeit comfort whose highest function is per- haps no longer to kill, but to invest life through and through (*History of Sexuality* 139). As the queer/race theorist Jasbir Puar puts it, biopower is exercised through practices of risk calculation where profits are maximized and "health itself can then be seen as a side effect of successful normativity" ("Prognosis Time" 152). In making this argument we want to underscore a key principle of body management within neoliberalism: those who don't adequately maintain their bodies are held personally responsible for their descent into the chaos of ill health and nonwell being.

In order to examine the intersecting trajectories of newly visible public identities (homosexual and handicapped) we focus on *Midnight Cowboy*'s de- ployment of *visual verb tense* to report traumas past and future—portrayals that are historically and culturally specific to the restrictive identity param- eters placed on the queer/crip marginalities in question. It is in these spaces of abandonment that queer/crip futurity is short-circuited as a product of social neglect. Neoliberalism tends to treat all social investments that do not turn input value into output value (profits) as lesser models of failed eco- nomic and moral projects.[6] *Midnight Cowboy* provides an alternative vision by identifying the significant distance between neoliberal capitalist claims to deliver the "best of all actual worlds" and what actually exists as "bare life" in zones of expendability (Povinelli, *Economies of Abandonment* 191).

INCLUSION'S FILMIC TENSE

One of the most characteristic techniques employed in *Midnight Cowboy* is the narration of the backstories of Joe Buck and Enrico Salvatore Rizzo, respectively, in relation to filmic strategies of presentation using visual past and future tenses. Both characters are suspended in the *tense present* of expendability within poverty; their mutual experiences of desperation signify the stagnation of "slow death." Lauren Berlant explains "slow death" as "the physical wearing out of a population and the deterioration of people in the population that is very nearly a defining condition of experience and historical existence" (754). This tension is also given a *visual verb tense* specific to each character, an organizing filmic grammar, if you will, that makes Joe's queer sexuality legible in relation to a traumatic past of violence associated with rituals of heteronormative initiation, and a comedic future tense wherein fantasies of able-bodied health enable a magically cured Rico to exercise an able-bodied privilege of parasitically exploiting disabled elderly women's bank accounts in Florida.

To a significant degree, these divergent genre conventions of tragedy and comedy (repressed past and fantasy future) position queer and disabled identities in tension with each other. They occupy differing vectors on a neoliberal grid of "acceptance" toward formerly abjected bodies. For Lisa Duggan, strategies of inclusion for gay men result in a "new neoliberal sexual politics" that hinges on the possibility of a post-Stonewall moment "that does not contest dominant heteronormative assumptions and institutions, but upholds and sustains them, while promising the possibility of a demobilized gay constituency and a privatized, depoliticized gay culture anchored in domesticity and consumption" (50). For social and minority model theorists in disability studies, inclusion involves a strategy of integration through the removal of social barriers to make public space more accessible (Shakespeare, "The Social Model"216). As we have discussed in chapter 1, disability rights movements in the United States and other postindustrial countries have argued that barrier removal allows disabled people to more fully assimilate themselves into the desires, activities, institutions, and affects of their fellow able-bodied citizens. Yet, as a parallel to the arguments of queer theorists about the reductive goals of homonormativity and keeping in mind our earlier analysis of the "able-disabled," disability normalization strategies participate in a neoliberal emptying out of embodied differences. Disabled people's potential to achieve more radical transformations of heteronormative values such as autonomy, productivity, and independence get lost within the less challenging objectives of inclusion.

The neoliberal facilitation of shared public space for biological marginals, consequently, operates largely around expectations of the ability to approximate able-bodied and heteronormative capacities. Inclusionism, then, may be understood, in the words of Elizabeth Povinelli, as a process in which "the subjects of recognition (formerly abandoned social identities) [are] called to present difference (their alternative modes of living) in a form that *feels like difference* but does not permit any real difference to confront a normative world" (450–51, our italics). This kind of inclusionism creates the basis for what is effectively a neoliberal simulacrum—one that operates as an empty signifier of integration, tolerance, and American exceptionalism. Neoliberal "tolerance" effectively freezes the identity of the protagonists of *Midnight Cowboy* into normative versions of less threatening differences: thoroughly domesticated classifications of tolerated difference referenced by the domesticating labels of "homosexual" and "handicapped" (or, as Rico refers to himself, "crippled"). Asma Abbas examines this process as one of tolerated identities predetermined in advance of cultural "admission":

> The word "admission" conveys [a] mechanistic logic, where subjects and their suffering are admitted into liberalism on preset terms, and where entry into a sphere or arena requires registering at the door with an assigned role, relinquishing any matter and materiality not relevant to the operations of liberal justice (42).

In exposing the heavily policed terrain of inclusion as one of tightly defined admission criteria, the film juxtaposes the shared medical context of pathology out of which queer and disability subjectivities emerge during late liberalism.

Joe's boyhood development in all-female households position his past as latently traumatizing, an upbringing requiring professional rescue in the crucible of psychoanalytic diagnoses of deviant sexual development. In the case of homosexuality, Joe's flashbacks to his childhood become "formative events" in the sense that they could easily require the expertise of a professional listener to make them surface, to pathologize and cure them. Conversely, in the case of handicapped, the personal past is largely eradicated—no visual flashbacks for Rico are allowed during the film, only lampooning flash-forwards. Consequently, the possibility of viable crip/queer futures becomes a farce. In either case neoliberalism opens up a space of inclusion for these previously pathologized identities but only to the extent that homosexual and handicapped can be recruited to assist in further consecrating the desirability of heteronormative lifestyles.

In other words, we are arguing this is a tactic of historical exposé brought to the foreground of the film and, consequently, made available for a nonnormative positivist critique. Ultimately, assignment to domesticated neoliberal identities such as homosexual and handicapped prove out of alignment with *Midnight Cowboy's* portrayal of peripheral embodiments forging crip/queer socialities of alternative value.

BUCKING THE PAST

As Kevin Floyd argues, *Midnight Cowboy's* cinematic arrival into the space of national fantasy involves the *deterritorialization* of masculinity—"the cowboy image's largely exclusive appeal to gay men" (156). Significantly the film's ability to figure a new flexibility in masculine identity turns, to a significant extent, on the exposé of violence at the foundations of heteronormativity (156). As is evident in the early montage of Joe's memory of his sexual initiations during boyhood, the past is a mélange of abandonments at the doorstep of female relatives, exposures to the fluid sexualities frequenting his grandmother's hair salon, training in consumptive grooming strategies of body hygiene and clothing fashions, the referencing of fake cowboy histories as exteriorizations of national manifest destiny fantasies on display at local parades, and sharing the bed of his grandmother (Ruth White) as she is courted by an array of male suitors. These mixings create a pastiche of sexuality's fluidity rather than a concretized orthodoxy of heteronormative masculinity. But the film portrays the images in a jumbled series of flashbacks that encourage readings of perversity, or worse pathology, resulting from sexual confusion. Joe's sexual development is rendered as a set of montage-like cutups from which he, along with viewers, must sort and choose.

As if to underscore this cacophonous relationship to sexuality's mixings,

Joe's flashbacks culminate in a gang rape by some local town youths who capture Joe and his girlfriend, Annie (Jennifer Salt), having sex in a parked car on a country road. The spectacle of male heterosexual violence represented by the gang rape further disrupts Joe's heteronormative developmental line, as he is arrested for assaulting Annie rather than being identified as a victim of gang rape himself. As Annie is led to an ambulance on her way, presumably, to incarceration for sexual trauma in a mental institution (she is referred to throughout the film as "Crazy Annie"), she is heard fingering Joe as the perpetrator of the assault by ambiguously commenting, "He's the one. He's the only one." This singular recognition plays ambivalently in the gaps between Joe's male fantasies of himself as an exceptional lover and also as an existential implication of him in the exploitations inherent in heterosexual patriarchy.

Consequently, and in keeping with the commentary of the film's director, John Schlesinger, that he did not want to make a "gay film" but rather a film about "an oddball couple," *Midnight Cowboy* employs a psychoanalytic narrative structure implicated in the creation of pathologized peripheral sexualities (Goldstein, "Dark Horse"). This "psychoanalytic" structure privileges a past tense where sexuality is forged in the cauldron of repressed conflict and, therefore, reified in relation to its medicalized label as mental illness. It is important in the film's timeline that homosexuality, as a diagnostic pathology, would not be removed from the *Diagnostic and Statistical Manual of Mental Disorders* until four years later. Schlesinger, who was coming out to his friends as gay at the time, depicts neoliberal sexual exchange networks as saturated with violence—no "healthy" sexuality proves available for any of the characters—and the use of the disorienting flashback format operates as a visual equivalent of the return of the repressed ("Midnight Cowboy: John Schlesinger"). Heterosexuality is haunted by its formative exclusion of homosexuality and, in turn, homosexuality is positioned, in Judith Butler's terms, as "constitutive of heterosexuality" (*Bodies That Matter* 250).

To recall Halberstam's language deployed in chapter 2, Joe's flight from the violence of his own initiation into heteronormativity results in his "accomplishment" of a failed interpellation into neoliberal sexual economies of exchange. Joe's journey to New York City in order to implement his American gigolo-like sex-for-profit scheme results in multiple revelations of his own, and of his clients, debasement by violence born of the pursuit of crass monetary incentives. We can analyze the film as adopting a strategy akin to Adorno's "negative dialectics" (1970), one that tries on various explanatory frameworks of sexuality and systematically rejects them as insufficient to the task of effectively narrating the complexity of the film's queer/crip alternatives. This alternative narrative trajectory, we would argue, requires a more robust engagement with social histories of exclusion experienced by those occupying peripheral sexualities; in turn, a nonnormative positivist analysis yields what feminist theorist Lynne Huffer calls the "constructive ethical frame that can actually be used as a map for living" that queer lives entail (48). Likewise, if we invoke Halberstam's arguments of productive failure—that is, an understanding of "failure" within the realm of sexuality as nothing less than a refusal to be delivered into an orderly adult world of heteronormativity—then Joe's failure is a form of perverse success and successful perversion (*Queer Art of Failure* 11–12). We return to this line of argumentation in this chapter's concluding discussion about the potential in relationships of crip/queer interdependency.

RATSO'S (NO) FUTURE TENSE

While a voluminous archive of critical commentary exists on the figure of Joe Buck, much less theoretical commentary exists on the figure of Joe's partner, Rico "Ratso" Rizzo, particularly regarding his status as a disabled man in this "oddball couple." Like Joe, Rico experiences a traumatic past in that his father worked under the backbreaking demands of menial labor as a subway shoeshine man. Rico's father develops scoliosis and becomes, in his son's words, "hunchbacked, consumed with a hacking cough" (one that immediately recalls Rico's own "consumptive" cough and limping mobility). The father died, as Rico tells it, with so much shoe polish under his fingernails that "even a gay undertaker couldn't get it out." This "insider" knowledge or, perhaps, recourse to the stereotype of gay men's accelerated expertise around dressing corpses, displays a familiarity with neoliberal versions of homosexuality's talents. This potentially productive reading on Rico's part gets easily lost in his multiple pejorative references to "fags" throughout the film. The gay undertaker's solution, creatively enough, disguises the evidence of his father's life of manual labor by placing a pair of gloves over his hands for the funeral viewing. This act serves as a parable for neoliberal strategies of disability disguise in that nonnormative bodies interrupt sexuality in the normative field of vision—to slightly resignify the title of Jacqueline Rose's important feminist filmic work, *Sexuality in the Field of Vision*—with disability's discordant aesthetics and pathologized functionalities. Rather than displayed to celebrate a father's life of survival as a manual laborer, his depleted body is draped and placed out of view by heteronormative protocols of polite presentation.

Rico, in turn, who insists throughout the film that Joe abandon the dehumanizing nickname "Ratso" (an epithet that even astute contemporary critics of the film such as Kevin Floyd don't surrender [157]), worries that the biopolitical task of policing his own reproductive capacity involves severing the presumed hereditary lineage of disability passed from father to son. Of course, this generational linkage is nothing more than their mutual location within the body-exhausting demands of a competitive labor market. Nevertheless, Rico's self-imposed injunction requires him to not "end up a hunchback like my old man." As he tells Joe at one point, "If you think I'm *crippled*, you should have caught sight of him at the end of the day." This act of salvaging a more favorable perspective on bodily capacity comes by way of comparing his disabled body to his father's "more" incapacitated one. Such comparative tactics set Rico's ability to value his body's incapacities in a future space marked by a presumed distance from the severely disabled past of his father.

Of course, Rico can no more avoid his disability past than Joe can ditch his experience of heteronormative violence. The exposures of life within poverty result in a generational toll on health folded within the horrifying continuity of "slow death." The film critiques any eugenics-based link between Rico's father's hunchback, hacking cough, and shoe polish-encrusted fingernails as predecessor symptoms to Ratso's own impairment circumstances. Foucault's analysis of the hereditary logic of eugenics that "allows responsibility for aberrations appearing in descendants to be shifted back to previous mechanisms of reproduction in the ancestors" (*Abnormal* 315) is fully relevant here. Thus, as Joe is to homosexuality, Rico is to handicapped, two historically hemmed-in identities suggesting a transition from medical predicaments of deviance to what Agamben refers to as the "bare life" of existence for marginalized social types (Agamben 5).

However, in distinction to Joe's montage-like sequences of his traumatic sexual past, Rico's childhood trauma of disabling poverty occurs entirely in Hoffman's spoken monologues. There is no equivalent visual backstory of Rico's childhood relationship to disability in the film; Rico's hauntings are reserved, rather, for the future tense flash-forwards regarding fantasies of his nondisabled life in Miami Beach post–New York City. Most tellingly, all of Rico's flash-forwards take place in a comedic future that magically re-solves his impaired health status rendered in the glaring high-key lighting of Florida sun.[7] In these sequences Rico imagines himself to be a nondisabled gambling hustler preying on the fortunes of elderly female wheelchair users at a Miami Beach resort.

Throughout the sequence Rico appears in a polished white leisure suit as a personal assistant energetically pushing his female marks in wheelchairs to the border of a green felt gambling mat for a game of dice or bingo held at poolside. As he strides confidently beside Joe through the resort, normative-ly conventional bathing beauties in white bathing suits wave from the bal-conies and call his name longingly—"Rico." Our argument, then, in relation to the use of filmic verb tense in *Midnight Cowboy* is that as implausible as Joe's desire to prostitute himself to rich women in New York is, Rico's reha-bilitational flash-forwards locate disability sexuality in the equally implau-sible future tense of filmic cure. Fulfillment, for each character, can only be imagined in the stifling terms of profiting from the misfortunes of another, a parasitism of privilege allowed only to those who embody the normative capacities of able-bodied neoliberal identities.

While the violence of normative sexuality can be visually portrayed as a function of past-tense trauma, disability becomes a worthy neoliberal so-cial project only through an orientation to a future tense where its aesthetic, functional, and incapacitating limitations can be wished away.[8] While Rico's enactment of "slow death" in the present is utopically displaced into these futuristic fantasy sequences of healing filmed in panoramic Technicolor, his physical predicaments of immobility, hacking cough, and increasing nervosity are all displaced. This time of futurity only realized in the impossible futuristic space of cure, ironically, gives Rico license to parasitically exploit others with disabilities—a privilege in his imagination that is the exclusive province of able-bodiedness.[9] Rico's flash-forward wish fulfillments, then, depend upon an inversion of his own and other disabled people's spectralized mistreatment within late capitalism. Disability represents devalued embodiments from which others may justifiably earn the terms of their livelihoods.

AN ALLIANCE OF INTERDEPENDENCIES

In this concluding section we want to argue that the evolution of Joe and Ri-co's *interdependent relationship* in the space *between* the exploitative fantasies of sexual profitability in New York and an illusionary curative complement of vitamins C and E in Florida, offers the only viable possibility for an alternative framework of queer/disability living. A life of interdependency is organized by the two protagonists around their surrender of adherence to the values of mere tolerance accorded to peripheral embodiments within neoliberalism: Rico abandons his referencing of gay and transgender people as "tutti-fruities" and "Jackies" who populate the city's sewers, while Joe agrees to give up his attachment to calling Rico "Ratso," even while responding to Rico's discussion of reincarnation by saying, "Well, I hope I don't come back in *your* body" (1:16:05). The film creates a space formed at the boarded X on the window of Rico's condemned apartment building—each character must meaningfully reassess culturally demeaning abandonments of creatures like himself.[10]

Consequently, the film consecrates an alliance based on interdependency between queer/crip masculinities. This alternative interdependency is barely glimpsed in Rico's apartment, as if even a hint of body intimacy between the two must be screened out of view in a second-floor apartment of a condemned building with opaque windows.[11] In spite of these multiplying prohibitions, their refusal to abandon each other offers promise in the most dystopic of places. Their relationship's temporal realization is forged of economic necessity and a shared recognition of the need to redress their mutual consignment to zones of expendability. Such a project involves the creation of what Tobin Siebers refers to as a "sexual culture of Disabled People," one that actively reconstitutes desire and value between marginalized groups:

> People with disabilities share with gay men and lesbians the suspicion by the majority population that they cannot, will not, or should not contribute to the future of the human race. They will not reproduce, but if they do, the expectation is that the results will be tainted. Social stigma would have little impact on sexual behavior if it were not for the fact that ability represents the supreme measure of human choices, actions, thoughts, and values. (2012, 41)

The relationship of interdependency goes largely unacknowledged by both characters (Joe and Rico might be the last persons in the film to think of themselves as "romantic partners"). This lack of awareness of their relational pairing comes to the fore during the "Factoryesque party" when Shirley (Brenda Vacarro), who, ironically, picks up Joe for sex at her apartment, incredulously asks the pair, "Don't tell me you two are a couple?" (Schrager) Joe laughs hysterically in response and his laugh resonates on the audio track as orgy-like scenes unfold at the party. But the question is left open, ultimately reverberating in the echo as an unresolvable revelation. In turn, Rico's response is to ignore the point all together and use the opportunity to coldly calculate a deal—$20 for sex with Joe and a dollar for his cab fare home. The woman tells Rico, "Get lost, will ya," in this meager effort to take care of himself in the exchange, and Rico snappily responds, "I agree, but for that service I charge one buck taxi fare."

The irresolution of this epiphany of Joe and Rico as a couple is not played out discomfortingly; rather it gets sidelined on behalf of the press of survival through market exchange negotiations. Prior to this point in the film, homophobia and ableism surface as easy refutations between each of the two characters regarding their less than platonic dependencies. When Joe first arrives at Rico's apartment he falls fast asleep on a rickety twin bed only to wake up and discover his boots missing. When he asks wildly where his boots are, Rico calmly responds from the iris framed shadow of his head on a pillow:

> RICO: I took them off.
> JOE: What for?
> RICO: What you mean what for? So you could sleep. Christ.
> JOE: The smart thing for me to do is haul my ass out of here.
> RICO: What's the matter now?
> JOE: Well, you want me to stay here—you're after something. What are you after? You don't look like no fag.
> RICO: What's that supposed to mean?
> JOE: Well, you want me to stay here tonight. That's the idea, ain't it?
> RICO: Look, I'm not forcing you, I mean like a . . . who's forcing you?
> JOE: Oh, I'm sorry, I truly am. I must of gotten the wrong impression of you. Okay. Okay, boy.
> RICO: Look I want you to stay, all right? Look, I goddamn invited you didn't I? (52:22–59)

This series of derogatory retorts to sincere invitations and offers of mutual care continue to inform the couple's exchanges throughout the film. That's "faggot stuff" Rico tells Joe when deriding the machismo of a man walking the streets of New York in a floral cowboy suit; in turn, Joe retorts with his ultimate disability body dismissal: He's never seen Rico "change [his] underwear once the whole time I've been in New York." At this point, Rico creatively deploys his social consignment to asexuality by knowingly commenting, "I ain't got to do that in public. I ain't got no need to expose myself."

We want to argue that this mutual questioning of each other's sexual value becomes the foundation of the terms of their investment in the relationship. It allows a space in which to address the possibilities of a productively shared failure while knowingly referencing each other through the derogatory stereotypes of heteronormativity. In the displacement of an acknowledgment that both recognize the terms of the other's devaluation, the tension of their relationship exists in knowing each other's social denigration all too well and, yet, caring for each other's bodies nevertheless.

Ultimately in response to their divergent traumas of embodiment, the two characters have to reimagine themselves through a transvaluation of each other's socially marginalized embodiment. Such alternatives can be found throughout the second half of the film, for instance, in the prosthetic relationship of shoring up each other's embodied vulnerabilities. Joe serves as a leaning post for Rico on sidewalks and in stairways, while Rico cooks, maintains the household, cuts Joe's hair, shines his boots, and serves as Joe's guide into the sexual subcultures of New York. These activities underscore the intimate body care rituals each performs on behalf of the other. In addition to taking off Joe's boots so "he can sleep," Rico washes Joe's clothes when, as he tells him, the smell threatens to become a "handicap" for a stud in New York City. Joe, in turn, pawns his beloved transistor radio, shops for Rico's cough medicine, protects him from physical threats by others, and robs (perhaps kills?) a gay client in order to pay for bus tickets to Florida when Rico's health is most obviously in immediate jeopardy.

Further the two exchange information about their budgets and prospects for future success and/or failure based on pooling meager resources. In response to economic conditions, the two mutually devise ways to pursue a minimally consumptive existence within the surfeit supply of capitalist upper-class bounty; the couple lives off Campbell's soup and stolen coconuts, wearing stolen coats, among massive billboards lining the sky with messages such as "MONY" and "Steak for everybody every lunch and dinner." This elaboration of a system of mutual recognition allows each individual a fuller humanity in the eyes of the other (through Rico, Joe comes to a knowledge of the sexual subcultures of which he is a part, while Rico insists that Joe drop the pejorative label of "Ratso" and refer to him as "Rico," a foundation for a more respectful address of him as a disabled person). All of these activities threaten to unseat heteronormative systems of embodied independence, productivity, and excessive consumption as the basis for neoliberal commodifications of value.[12]

Yet this interdependent space can be sustained as political project for only a short duration due to the compounding vulnerabilities of poverty, environmental hazards, insufficient food, the laborious demands of the hustling life, and the toxic exposures of homelessness. Perhaps the most important example of this unviability comes at film's end when Rico dies just as the bus arrives at the outskirts of the promised land: Miami Beach.[13] In the waning moments of Rico's descent into slow death, Joe provides a vision of their future life that entails Joe's reentry into bourgeois homonormativity—a vision that cannot include Rico in its deep horizontal futurescape characterized by short-sleeve shirts with palm trees (Joe tells Rico that he bought him the last one in stock), freshly pressed leisure pants, and full employment in "outdoor" wage labor. In this environment the die of tragedy in *Midnight Cowboy* is cast as options for the crip/queer sociality that Joe and Rico cultivate give way to story lines of coerced reentry into heteronormative circuits of desire and the corresponding promise of no alternative inclusion for disability's "rejected body" (Wendell 11–12).

However, to take up a relationship as a cause of care for another socially devalued embodiment is to declare a degree of good to which one commits oneself. The body care that develops between Joe and Rico, while not a resolution to wider social abandonments characteristic of neoliberalism, results in a redress of their shared debasement as the terms imposed by their historical material conditions. Conditions of tense existence on the edge of late capitalism might otherwise cultivate a biopolitical response of indifference, neglect, and willingness to let die. If risk calculation is now the order of neoliberal decision-making regarding determinations of which bodies to invest, then the caretaking that takes place between Joe and Rico promotes an ethical decision to shift loyalties outside of extant neoliberal market criteria. In sum, Joe and Rico's interdependency offers a model of embodied investment in others that heteronormativity recognizes as *queer*—effeminate, disabling, and mortally wounding to fantasies of self-sufficiency in late capitalism's free market system.

NEITHER PROHIBITED NOR ALLOWED

As Elizabeth Povinelli argues, "every act of recognition creates new zones of potential life that is as yet neither prohibited nor allowed" (*Economies of*

Abandonment 98). The interdependent project unearthed by taking a non-normative positivist approach hastens these modes of recognition in order to facilitate the mutating potentials of life in the interstitial social alternative of crip/queer socialities and collective consciousness.[14] *Midnight Cowboy* demonstrates the potential value that comes of interweaving queer and crip lives together. They produce alternative values of interdependency as exceptions to the surface glosses of normalcy—modes of mutual body care where attentiveness to each other's social presentation and health becomes paramount to even a tenuous capacity to survive.[15]

These practices are forms of the collective, critical labor that comes from what José Estebon Muñoz describes as the product of *queer utopian memory*: "Memory is most certainly constructed and, more important, always political. The case I make . . . posits our remembrances and their ritualized tellings—through film, video, performance, writing, and visual culture—as having world-making potentialities" (*Cruising Utopia* 35). The "worldmaking" of disability utopian memory in film involves articulating the longing and utopian possibilities imagined by otherwise subjugated subcultures of those living in nonnormative embodiments. Lauren Berlant and Michael Warner argue that practices of alternative sociality manifest "the radical aspirations of queer [and, we would insert, disability] culture building: . . . the changed possibilities of identity, intelligibility, culture, sex, publics, that appear when the heterosexual [and able-bodied] couple is no longer the referent or the privileged example of [an impossibly enabled] sexual culture" (qtd. in Floyd 208). Many of these alternative tactics of "worldmaking" can be witnessed in the international independent film productions of disabled people to which we now turn our attention.

This satirical paper maché replica of then governor Arnold Schwarzenegger wielding an ax was made by disability anti-austerity protesters. ADAPT and other state-funded organizations opposed cuts to personal assistance services during the street performance/protest, "ArnieVille," held in Sacramento, California (2010). Courtesy of: Dan McMillan, creator of the statue.

16-18.06.2007

Diversity
unites us all

New
Benaki
Museum

ORGANISATION

SECRETARIAT GENERAL OF COMMUNICATION
SECRETARIAT GENERAL OF INFORMATION

GREEK
FILM
CENTRE

Aimee Mullins photographed by Howard Schatz © Schatz Ornstein 2000

1st INTERNATIONAL FESTIVAL

Emotion Pictures DOCUMENTARY & DISABILITY

ATHENS 2007

Front cover of the Emotion Pictures Film Festival Program featuring Aimee Mullins running across a beach on prosthetic coils. Courtesy of: Emotion Pictures: Documentary and Disability, First International Festival, Athens 2007. http://www.ameamedia.gr/en/node/67.

Opposite: Publicity still from *Midnight Cowboy* (1969): Enrico Rizzo (Dustin Hoffman) in the high-key lighting of a flash-forward sequence where he bilks disabled elderly women out of their fortunes at a Miami Beach Resort. Courtesy of: United Artists and Hellman Schlesinger Productions.

Publicity still from *Midnight Cowboy* (1969): Joe Buck (Jon Voight) and Enrico Rizzo (Dustin Hoffman) try to keep warm in a freezing cold abandoned tenement by dancing to the advertising jingle, "Orange Juice on Ice, That's Nice." Courtesy of: United Artists, an entertainment service of Transamerica Corporation.

Mat Fraser plays the narrator and protagonist of freak show histories in *Born Freak* (Paul Sapin, UK, 2004). Courtesy of http://img buddy.com/mat-fraser-actor.asp.

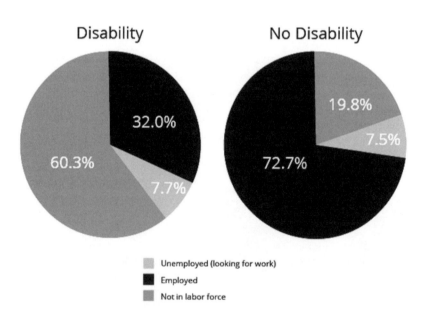

Pie chart showing 60.3% of those with disabilities who are out of the employment market all together in the U.S. Courtesy of: CEA calculations based on American Community Survey, 2010-2012.

Nightcrawler (Alan Cumming) and Ororo Munroe/Storm (Halle Berry) team up to resist the institutionalization of mutants in *X-Men II. The Art of the X2: The Collector's Edition.* New York: New Market Press, 2003: 72.

Archie preparing for an awkward standoff with his mother over disability sexuality at the ocean in Catriona MacInnes's *I'm In Away From Here* (Scotland, 2007). Courtesy of Catriona MacInnes, catrionamacinnes.com.

Crip cast from Ian Clark's *Outcasts* contemplating what to do with the able-bodied rock singer they've abducted in the car's boot (Australia, 2008). Courtesy of: Ian Clark Films.

Still of Christopher Boone orchestrating a mass of mathematical detail from the dramatic production of Mark Haddon's *The Curious Incident of the Dog in the Night-Time* (Marianne Elliot, National Theatre, 2012). Courtesy of the Broadway facebook page announcing the opening: https://www.facebook.com/CuriousBroadway/photos/a.1413191075599769.1073741828.1406251132960430/1415729722012571/?type=1&theater.

Home page of the U.K. website TOFS (Tracheo-Osophageal Fistula Support). http://
www.tofs.org.uk/home.aspx.

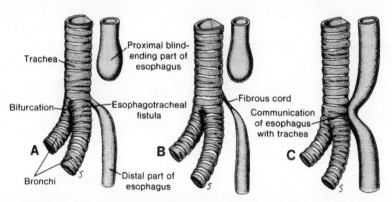

Figure 14-4. *A*, Atresia of the esophagus and esophagotracheal fistula. *B*, Atresia
of esophagus. The connection between the distal part of the esophagus and
trachea is formed by a fibrous cord. *C*, The proximal and distal parts of the
esophagus are both connected to the trachea by a narrow canal.

Medical anatomies of esophageal atresia (five common presentations of the disorder).
John Langman, M.D. Ph.D. *Medical Embryology 4th edition*. Baltimore: The Williams
& Wilkins Company, 1981, 215.

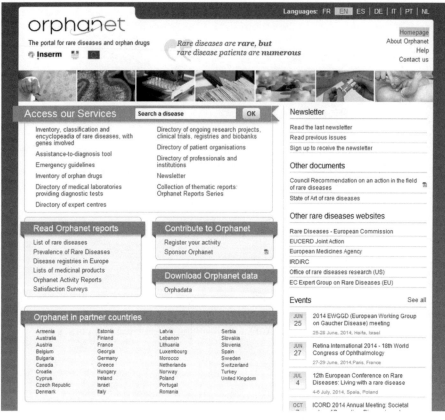

Screen shot of the orphanet homepage subtitled "Portal for rare diseases and orphan drugs." Courtesy of Orphanet. http://www.orpha.net/consor/cgi-bin/index.php.

Screen shot from George Miller's *Lorenzo's Oil:* Despite their lack of medical and scientific knowledge, Augusto (Nick Nolte) and Michaela (Susan Sarandon) resolve to learn all they can about their son' illness. Courtesy of Universal City Studios Inc., 1992.

1500+ blind students and disability activists block roads and entranceways in the capital to demand equal access to quality education and employment outside of the Prime Minister's residence in New Delhi, India, March 2, 2014. The speaker is Avinash Sahi a blind researcher from Jawahar Nehru University. Photograph courtesy of Subhash Chandra Vashishth, Advocate of the High Court of Delhi.

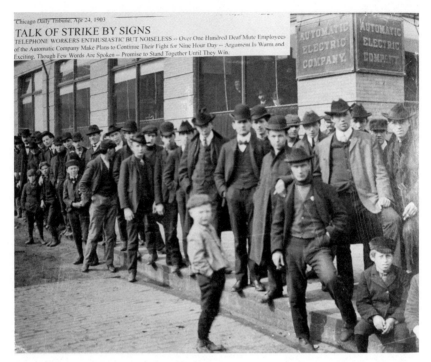

Deaf and blind workers strike outside of the Automatic Company in Chicago for equal pay (1903). Courtesy of "The Chicago History Exhibit" (curated by Sharon Snyder and David Mitchell at the National Vietnam Veterans Museum, Chicago, IL, 2006).

FOUR

The Politics of Atypicality

International Disability Film Festivals and the Productive Fracturing of Identity

Three days into the 2004 London Disability Film Festival a small, international arts community took shape. In the tradition of many disability outings, such as those depicted in popular Hollywood films such as *The Men* (1950) or *Waterdance* (1992), a group of us planned dinner at a local restaurant. Twenty-two in all, we included five wheelchair users; three Deaf persons; two with visual impairments; several with seizure-based disorders; and three with communication differences. First, we navigated London's uneven South Bank cobblestones to a nearby Pizza Express. Halting our group at the door, an employee greeted us with a double take. Next, she hollered over her shoulder to the manager: "How do we get all these disabilities in here?"

While hardly remarkable among moments encountered by disabled people who travel in groups, the question of the nature and inclusiveness of our collectivity became increasingly vexed as the festival continued. Yet unlike the ubiquity of the openly expressed consternation about assemblies of disabled people encountered in public spaces, the question came from self-identified disability community members seeking the sometimes incompatible goals of diversity and alliance. Beyond worries over the sufficiency of diversity represented in the composition of our audience, this question also extended to concern over the diversity of the representational field itself; and, ultimately, to discussions of the barriers that prohibit disenfranchised disabled people from working in all aspects of the film industry.

DEPATHOLOGIZING DISABILITY FILM FESTIVALS

This chapter discusses the rise of international independent disability film festivals as new spaces of social collectivity-making developing as a response to the homogenizing inclusionist practices extant in neoliberal biopolitics. We do not undertake a history of these festivals and their changing logics, but rather attempt to theorize aspects of their composition at a relatively nascent moment in their development. Whereas other identity movements have already witnessed a burgeoning arena of film venues that help give voice to marginalized experiences—for instance, B. Ruby Rich explains that gay and lesbian film festivals have metamorphosed from "small, self-selected audiences" to "large events . . . complete with corporate sponsors and huge audiences" (*Chick Flicks* 79)—the majority of disability film festivals are less than one decade old, enjoy no corporate sponsorship, and still draw relatively small crowds.

Within such nascent organizations, even the concept of disability collectivity proves elusive, tenuous, and fragile. Current concepts of collectivity on display at disability film festivals remain loosely tied to the goals of depathologization, or alternatively productive community iterations of disabled selves. Many films seek mainstream integration through better understanding of a single condition. However, these are quickly becoming a minor genre of independent disability film because they remain tethered to medical or rehabilitation objectives of eradication (though cure) or amelioration (through disguises of supplementation) or social acceptance (through the extension of a marginal forms of tolerance). Instead, disability film festivals have promoted films developed out of more transgressive activist sensibilities that tend to valorize oppositional identities. There is little evidence that disability collectivity has yet become marketable as an aspect of multicultural aesthetic or art house chic; there is also little desire in creating venues as spectacles for a historically overdisplayed social group.

Yet, while concepts of collective identity develop in various locations among disability community participants, disability film festivals increasingly function as influential venues for collectivity formation. Film scholar Joshua Gamson identifies this process as "organizational shaping": "*identity boundaries are shaped by and shift through organizational activity,* which itself responds to features of the institutional environment" ("Organization Shaping" 235). In this sense, disability film festivals provide alternative "contexts for reception" and operate as active filters for forging new ways of "being disabled" in the twenty-first century (White, "Queer Publicity" 73).

Additionally, unlike other minority groups, disability movements (including the independent international film festivals they help spawn) have to reimagine exclusionary public spaces including alternative theater seating layouts, presentation formats, and projection techniques. Transformation of the environment has always served as a key feature of politicized disability rights movements; even a marginally integrated collectivity cannot take shape if bodies that define the collective find themselves physically excluded from sites of political fomentation. Film festivals also transform public arenas and, ultimately, help to revise the cultural infrastructure of accessibility for all bodies with respect to which disability collective identities take shape.

In order to understand the nature of disability film festivals as organizational entities and to comprehend the ways in which new in(ter)dependent disability films challenge normative, ableist representations of crip/queer lives, this chapter employs a nonnormative positivist methodology to move between descriptions of festival operations and close readings of exemplary independent disability film productions. We employ an anecdotal structure based on our attendance at a variety of disability film festivals around the world between the years of 1995 and 2010. In doing so, we follow in the tradition of key feminist and queer commentators—such as B. Ruby Rich (1998) and Patricia White (1999)—who have taken up specific film festival contexts as a dynamic site where distinctive features of subcultural life come into being. As one of the few public spaces within which to actively fashion alternative crip/queer identities, film festivals challenge internal and external orthodoxies that tend to quickly sediment within politicized identity groups. They not only serve the important function of historical recovery, they also seek out a variety of perspectives on the meaning of disability from older and younger generations of disabled people and nondisabled participants alike.

In this manner, and as we conclude in this chapter, disability film festivals actively disrupt static boundaries of increasingly orthodox disability rights-based identity movements—even with respect to disabled people's concepts of their own collective makeup. The multiple ways of viewing disability made available to audiences participating in disability film festivals play a key role in what we call the politics of atypicality—the refusal to remain within the strict boundaries of medically and socially prescribed categories of sameness. Those diagnosed with cerebral palsy (CP), for instance, are *not like each other* in that bodies adapt to and navigate their own environments in myriad ways. Yet at the same time individuals with CP also experience overlapping experiences of oppression as their bodies violate normative expectations of appearance, functionality, and communication.

In refuting investments in fashioning likenesses of nonnormative embodiment (i.e., static identity classifications based on universalizing diagnostic criteria) disability film festivals actively renew themselves and the audiences in attendance. As the compilation of a range of independent efforts to revise formulas of embodied, cognitive, and sensory differences, disability film festivals avoid the pitfalls of more stagnant efforts to simply substitute dominant devaluing characteristics with what some disability scholars refer to as "positive" representations (Longmore, "Screening Stereotypes" 37; Dwoskin, "Whose Film?" 214). Disability film festivals often screen products that violate concepts of political correctness. However, it is in this release from the strictures of inflexible biopolitical contexts that independent disability films upset rigid boundaries that continue to separate "abnormal" from "normal." Disability cannot be, ultimately, an identity that actively polices its own borders; instead, independent disability film strives to recognize disability as an integral—as opposed to merely integrated—aspect of human embodiment.

COLLECTIVITY OF THE INCARCERATED

Much like a prior generation's promotion of women's film festivals and the current international explosion of gay and lesbian film festivals (White, *Chick Flicks* 74), independent disability film festivals have gone worldwide. Programming in multinational, cosmopolitan urban centers such as Sydney, London, Moscow, Berlin, San Francisco, Toronto, Melbourne, Calgary, and Chicago, disability film festivals have focused social debate on the cross-cultural exclusions faced by disabled constituencies. They provide vantage points from which to contemplate differences across geographical, social, medical, experiential, and disciplinary lines.

Because disability cinema itself strives to bring stigmatized bodies into contact with other nonnormative embodiments, film forums have had to interrogate their own programming and access practices based on normative programming and participation regimens. Consequently, and unlike other minority film festival formations, disability film festivals move beyond the consideration of alternative content. They also have to reimagine largely taken-for-granted normative modes of festival space, presentation, and commerce in such a way that allows the widest diversity of bodies to participate. Today's disability film festivals provide environments where a variety of accommodations can be found on display. Sign language interpreters, augmented hearing systems, real-time captioning, audio description, integrated wheelchair seating, personal assistants, lights-on safe space screening rooms, language translation, and increasingly strict demands that filmmakers caption their films, all serve as innovations of a wider range of public access features. Whereas even the most progressive theaters, for instance, may advertise particular showings accessible to deaf patrons or advertise that augmented hearing systems may be available upon request, few provide audio description for visually impaired participants. At disability film festivals, all access features remain available for viewers without the necessity of making a special request or attending a ghettoized screening session. The goal, in line with disability accessibility strategies promoted in chapter 2 by the development of curricular cripistemologies, is to institutionalize an array of systemically in-built access pathways in order to allow the greatest number of people in peripheral embodiments to participate.

The prevailing lack of accessible infrastructure in public spaces develops in the wake of the cultural aftermath left behind as a result of the entertainment industry's exclusions of disabled people from mainstream participation. Lack of accessibility left disabled people literally on the outside looking in or, perhaps even more common, stranded at the marquee without options. Even when accessibility features were provided, one could often find them only in segregated locations or during "special" accessibility performances for the disabled. Historically, separate locations for individuals with physical, sensory, and cognitive differences have provided accessible infrastructures in exchange for their residents' wider liberties. Nonetheless, those who inhabit them have sometimes transformed segregated experiences into sites for collective undertaking. What looks like segregation from the outside may look like collective participatory formats to those segregated within. In other words, while disabled people do not forge coalitions among each other "naturally," the historical confinement of some often results in productive alliances. Thus, collective cultural creativity erupts in spite of the organization of spaces commonly designed to thwart such goals.

In line with our findings in crip/queer interstices of heteronormative narrative options in *Midnight Cowboy*, some of the most telling examples of collectivity forged in segregation occur in recent mainstream disability cinema. We now have a variety of award-winning cinematic narratives—one could call them a disability tradition awaiting discovery—where undesired segregation results in resistance-based activities of world-making (Muñoz 805). Although those living in peripheral embodiments end up sharing these "special" locations against their will, the ironic continuity of segregation results in bonding on the basis of recognizing a shared predicament: a dynamic collective formulated around the exchange of insights generated by lives in "rejected bodies" (Wendell 1996).

Those who have sought to tell this story have engaged narrative forms that often unfold in the following manner: individuals classified as deviant find themselves isolated from mainstream cultures with others who share little in common beyond an exiled predicament. This historical situation forges identities that are not automatically chosen but rather negotiated out of necessity by those who share a common fate in set aside zones of expendability. Thus, disability collectivity does not evolve out of shared diagnostic categories of being (although single-condition self-help groups certainly exist, as we discuss later on in chapter 6); instead, they result from common encounters with discrimination, exclusion, and experiences of alterity (peripheral embodiments) that systematically prohibit disabled people from meaningful social participation.

Segregating situations, for instance, might throw together people with epilepsy and those who are deaf and/or blind, as is the case in U.S. documentary filmmaker Fred Wiseman's films about the Helen Keller Institute for the Deaf-Blind in Talladega, Alabama titled collectively *Multi-handicapped* (1986); or, perhaps, in spite of the reliance on formulas of the able-disabled there are moments in the Hollywood film *X2: X-Men United* (2003) where mutant bodies find themselves isolated in an institution on the basis of divergent "special" powers. In each of these cases, segregation turns isolation into an object of analysis among disabled people. Thus, in *X2*, when Nightcrawler (Alan Cumming) asks Storm (Halle Barry) about rationales behind the long-standing practice of isolating mutants, Storm knowingly advises: "They're afraid of us." Storm's comment instructs the new recruit that the mutants' segregation is not of their own making. Because mutants have come to inspire fear, misunderstanding, and repulsion in the nonmutant population, segregation operates as a form of mainstream inoculation against the threat of a marginalized other.

X2's insights result from the contemplative space that segregation ironically produces among incarcerated subjects. Storm becomes a cultural critic of confinement practices by necessity. Her character maps the field of segregation in order to master its operation, rationale, and structure. Likewise, Storm solidifies a bond with Nightcrawler at this moment of generational sharing; their community becomes a by-product of an imposed condition that necessitates analysis of wider cultural behaviors from which to grow cautious and even escape.

Once segregation results in an unintended community of identifications, persons segregated on the basis of disability aesthetics—that which Tobin Siebers explains as "the way some bodies make other bodies feel when in their presence" (*Disability Aesthetics* 1)—cause discomfort for others who often participate in the creation of a politics. Widespread segregation practices have shifted toward the allowance of a neoliberal tolerance to be felt across nonsegregated populations. This neoliberal acceptance comes in the historical relocation of disabled people to institutions that create social structures which remain incapable of providing shared cultural spaces they are presumably established to rectify. However, publics and nations have not had to engage with disability in any way other than through the anemic forms of recognition cultivated by ablenationalist rhetorical practices, particularly when disabled persons continue to be legally isolated in many countries.

At the same time, individuals trapped within institutional structures become increasingly nonadept at navigating extrainstitutional locations. Thus, for instance in the film *Rain Man* (1988), the autistic character of Raymond (like Rico, also played by Dustin Hoffman) finds the world outside his regulated institutional life uninhabitable. The film's story argues that Raymond cannot return to the community because his disability prevents him from successful integration. We would argue that, at the least, Raymond's true incapacity has been produced by the experience of institutionalization itself. One's daily regimen becomes determined to such an extent that adequately managing a life beyond institutional walls must be shown to be impossible so that extraordinary limits on mobility can be justified as "care."

Even an apparently emancipating institutional drama such as *Girl, Interrupted* (1999) revalidates the necessity of confinement. In the film, incarcerated women develop bonds during illegal gatherings in the underground tunnels below their lock-down ward. These planned insurgencies transform the underground space into an alternative cultural location beyond the walls—both literally and figuratively—of the disciplinary society above. Yet similarly to *Rain Man, Girl, Interrupted* persists in affirming that institutional life is necessary unless inmates singularly manage to "free" themselves of their "afflictions" by taking responsibility for their own ill health. In the latter case, mobility is withheld until subjects grow docile and, in the words of Jamaican-American writer Michelle Cliff, "tame their wildness" in their acceptance of the necessity of their confinement.[1] Hence film offers scenes wherein institutions become opportunities for alternative disability community formations—those founded on the necessity to escape cultural locations that literally represent their devalued social status. However, the ultimate political potential of alliance must be ultimately surrendered for the sake of rationalizing the continuation of confinement practices for "those who need it."

In addition to unintended collectivity, institutionalized bodies come to feel some comfort with the intricacies of embodied difference. Familiarity with difference develops among disabled people that more mobile citizens are less likely to share. However, the development of knowledge about the plurality found in peripheral embodiments is often lost or denied as residents "mature" beyond their segregated confines. Newly discharged individuals, largely bereft of institutional communities, grow ashamed about solidarities they previously shared under segregation. Widespread public disavowal of disability translates to elected forms of alienation from other disabled people. As a result, narratives recently authored from politicized disability perspectives, both in print and image, work to reverse expectations about one's shameful life as a subject enduring segregation in late liberalism, as well as bear witness to the necessary politics of reclaiming alliances with the community one may seem to have "outgrown," or even escaped. The contours of this shared storyline should be credited as the product of disabled people's coming of age as a cultural force.

DISABILITY FILM FESTIVALS: THE PROMISE AND PROBLEM OF POLITICAL SIMULTANEITY

Reclaiming alliances with other identities based on devaluations of peripheral embodiments represents one key way in which independent disability film radicalizes concepts of normalcy within neoliberalism. Festivals featuring disability provide communal opportunities to, in Simi Linton's words, "claim disability" (vii) from what Tom Shakespeare has referred to as "dustbins for disavowal" (283). This critical undertaking occurs on a variety of levels: aesthetic, social, and political. In part film festivals achieve goals of social transformation through opportunities for prolonged exposure of audiences to bodies with which they may feel uncomfortable simply passing on the street. For instance, in Paul Sapin's documentary film *Born Freak* (2002), audiences spend nearly an hour with the narrator, Mat Fraser, who is a child of the Thalidomide generation. As Mat leads us through his struggles to be a respected actor, through the history of the freak show, and into a contemporary moment where prurient viewing practices live on, audiences grow, if not comfortable with, at least less alienated from his body. This strategy of intimacy and prolonged exposure to disabled bodies, communication modes, perceptual capacities, and appearances reduce feelings of estrangement from disabled people's differences. As Patricia White explains this process in gay and lesbian film festivals, "Modes of spectatorship specific to festivals' multiple publics and histories compete and are transformed" (76).

Since shared experiences of devaluation, segregation in claustrophobic spaces, and the need to enunciate a politics of disenfranchisement provide the raw material out of which politicized minority constituencies are fashioned, a global mosaic of disability perspectives represents one of the best promises for cross-national disability politics.[2] In fact, in keeping with our arguments about the failing utility of the social model of disability in chapter 1, the array of offerings in independent disability film may be said to have already exceeded contemporary social models of disability pursued in the academy and within disability activist movements. Thus, one answer to the question—"How do we get all these disabilities in here?"—is that the virtual nature of disability cinema allows a shared space to serve as a more flexible nexus for enunciating a politics that challenges in-built exclusions based on time, transport, presentation format, and space. Such flexibility results in part from the fact that, like their other minority festival predecessors, disability film festivals are to some degree autonomous from those they represent (Gamson, "Organization Shaping" 235).

As a reflection of this partial autonomy of composition, tastes and interests, new disability independent cinema ranges across all genres. These works commonly draw upon well-worn popular and professional training film formulas that collectively misrepresent disability as personal tragedy, bodies in need of cure or repair, unseemly human dependency, and/or abominations to be banished from the contexts of polite society. In their place, recent disability productions operate as opportunities to overturn debasing forms of disability-based image consumption. While most analyses of minority film festivals today worry over the influence of economic cooptation or what Patricia White refers to as the formation of a "'community' . . . identified with a market segment" (*Chick Flicks* 75), disability film festivals, like those who produce the films, have not yet significantly wrestled with the effects of excess capital influx. This is because they have neither garnered corporate sponsors nor depend upon mainstream audience appeal to support their efforts.

At this time disability filmmakers and festival organizers operate in a relatively constructive (albeit underfinanced) historical moment when they may pursue subject matter that might otherwise easily offend in more well-traveled public venues. The products do not package their social perspectives in slick media veneers; instead they tend to occupy the farthest economic crannies of the independent film market. Filmic rules governing the portrayal of disability suddenly seem held in abeyance and a relatively untrammeled representational niche opens. Additionally, much of the flexibility in presentation comes from the production of an international independent film market where divergent cultures and contexts form the backdrop for independent disability cinematic plots.

Disability film festivals are relatively eclectic affairs. For instance, a festival participant can view a film about a U.S. figural artist with spina bifida, then watch a documentary about Deaf artisans manufacturing a bell in St. Petersburg, while later attending a panel on digital film produced in the breakaway Soviet republics of Georgia and Chechnya. Such a cross-cultural leap within the space of a few hours presents both problem and promise for international disability film festivals in particular and disability studies in general. We have arrived at a historical moment so characterized by the instantaneous transmission of digital information that our ability to effectively generalize across cultural lines is increasingly tested. This is in spite of the fact that we have a need for globally based disability movements that can extrapolate from political efforts enunciated within specific cultural locales. Disability film festivals and conferences as new collective spaces, in other words, position themselves at the intersection of one of the most fraught gaps in contemporary experience. The Canadian philosopher of globalization David Harvey refers to this situation as "political simultaneity" (*Postmodernity* 263).

For Harvey political simultaneity defines efforts to reconcile the "perspective of place with the shifting perspectives of relative space" (*Postmodernity* 262). Situations born in the midst of extreme cultural specificity arrive on our monitors and screens almost instantaneously in real time. These images traverse vast geographical distances with their cultural differences intact; as a result, the shared spaces of their reception become both an opportunity and an obstacle: an opportunity in that representation literally brings home experiences of places and geographical events formally less available, and an obstacle because audience interpretational abilities are taxed as cultural differences intensify. Thus, while most contemporary theorists have followed Derrida in the contemplation of speed as the quintessential postmodern dilemma, Harvey shows how space transforms subjective experience as well.

This modern ability to traverse space rapidly inaugurates a crisis of representation (not to mention geopolitical practices and neoliberal monetary networks without borders). Yet grappling with this experience is not a new one. For Harvey, modernist artists took up the question of how one best captures this simultaneity of experience. In *The Sound and the Fury* (1929), William Faulkner wondered how the novel could entertain the simultaneous observations of three brothers—one a person with Down syndrome, one a morbid romantic longing for the reinstitution of Victorian chivalric codes, and the third a rabid eugenicist—all gazing up a tree at their sister's undergarments as she calls out a play-by-play of their grandmother's funeral from which they have been banned. In order to approximate these synchronous events, Faulkner turned to the newest narrative techniques in film (i.e., three-pronged editing) for his multiperspectival crosscutting narrative technique. Additionally, in the opening chapter Faulkner employs a cognitively disabled subjectivity coupled with the evolving storytelling techniques of cinematic art as a combinatory style of narrative innovation. In part, because disabled subjectivities have been cordoned out of bounds, their privileging in community-based artworks represents a unique social vantage point (this point is further developed in the following chapter).

Likewise, during the naturalist and modernist eras of literary experimentation, nations began referencing each other with respect to the implementation of increasingly restrictive disability policies as the primary eugenics period came to a crescendo. Comparative statistical studies of feeblemindedness in European and North American countries began; marriage laws and institutionalization practices crisscrossed the Atlantic to be adopted in nearly every eugenics nation; sterilization practices were literally lifted, translated, and implemented from one country to another; and influential eugenics practitioners from one nation were feted and awarded honorary degrees in another.[3] This cross-cultural importation fueled the eugenics movement as one of the first international collaborative sciences.

Consequently, geography, which had previously hampered the fluidity of social responses to disability from passing across national borders, was now largely surpassed as an impediment to traffic in disability containment strategies. The irony of this historical situation is that as policies around disabled people's mobility became increasingly restrictive and permanent institutionalization developed as a reality for expanding numbers of "subnormal" people, traffic in eugenics ideology expanded and became increasingly mobile. The rapid export of concepts and policies can be lethal in this sense, and Harvey's analysis helps us contemplate ways that the experience of political simultaneity is not a simple matter of productive fluidity within neoliberalism.

Perhaps it's not surprising, then, that disability film has gained an explicit advantage in the last decade during a veritable renaissance in digital arts. Disability digital arts involve the low-budget production of cinematic narratives in digital video formats by independent disability-based organizations and individuals. Due to the pressures of competitive markets to produce high-quality, yet increasingly affordable imaging equipment (handheld video cameras, nonanalog editing software, high-resolution videotape, digital cameras with video capacities, flip phones, etc.) disabled people and their underfinanced social organizations are now taking to the streets in order to record their stories. Such opportunities essentially place the means of production within the reach of a historical group that has been traditionally excluded from modes of self-representation.

Unlike other art forms such as theater, performance art, stand-up comedy, and live readings that require the physical presence of artists to deliver their cultural product, disability digital art travels in a rectangular box without a personal assistant! At the November 2004 Moscow Disability Film Festival, for instance, the economic impoverishment of the breakaway republics made physical attendance at the festival prohibitive for filmmakers and disability actors/activists alike. At the same time, a largely disenfranchised disability community in the host city found themselves attending a festival for free, watching the productions of those with disabilities now inhabiting the "outlands" of former Soviet Union society. Thus, film festivals represent a vital site of cultural exchange between participants while public transportation remains inaccessible both economically and physically.

If the experience of simultaneity collapses distance through the advent of technologies that accelerate speed and condense space, then participation rituals of viewing shift as well. The ability to gain access to perspectives from a variety of locales allows an unprecedented opportunity to contrast disability social formations. In the short French film *Sang Froid / Cold Blood* (2002), for example, one views deaf people cast as animalistic predators chasing a hysterical able-bodied human prey. The pursuit takes place in a haunted, snow-covered rural terrain among trees, scrub pines, and nocturnal creatures. Ultimately the would-be victim flees to a church that rises like a mirage on top of a hill in the Nordic landscape. He enters the religious sanctuary, bars the door, and flees behind a life-size crucifix for protection from this unholy, Deaf, vampire-like gang. However, his sought-for refuge behind well-worn religious icons results in an ironic inversion as the crucified Christ leaves his station on the cross and devours the comfort-seeker in front of his presumed predators. The film transforms deaf actors from gothic carnivores into harmless, even empathic, witnesses of this gruesome plot twist (thus they share an affinity with the film's equally surprised audiences).

Such moments of identification in disability film begin to unwind the Gordian knot of personal alienation among those communicating within distinct linguistic universes. Distance collapses, a common plot formula turns on its head, and the religious setting becomes lethal rather than protective of those seeking refuge beneath its paternalistic veneer. Deafness is effectively decriminalized in the process. The violence comes unexpectedly from a religious icon of self-sacrifice (i.e., Christ died for our sins), and the deaf onlookers bless themselves and look on with a degree of horror, pathos, and thankfulness that they have avoided such a fate.

In addition, film's ability to quickly cultivate self-recognition with others on the basis of a stigmatized condition provides a challenge to the pathologizing dictates of European religious frameworks that represent deaf people as "demoniacs" (Bragg, "Mute God" 166). While the contexts linking disability to sin may be distinct (*Sang Froid* offers a Christian, Nordic, rural, European landscape as its setting), they begin to achieve a form of universality among those marginalized throughout the world on the basis of their use of alternative communication systems. Historical efforts to discount sign language as a legitimate language, and therefore discount deaf people's cultural production and minority group status, result in an inverse diagnostic scenario where nonoral communication strategies become the communicative context. Accordingly, deaf audience members find themselves as the addressees of a medium that has only grudgingly accommodated them through the sporadic adoption of captioning.

Likewise, in African American filmmaker Oriana Bolden's short film, *goodnight, liberation* (2003), we watch another alternative narrative formula unveiling itself. For Bolden, whose condition at the time of the film has no formal medical classification, the documentary form serves to dispel an absence of recognition for her non-apparent disability. While the refutation of medical labels has served as common cause among disability communities, *goodnight, liberation* performs its critique with reference to a political activist context. Whereas much independent disability cinema aims its analysis at ablest beliefs and policies (i.e. at those existing outside disability experience), *goodnight, liberation* addresses an "insider" network of political participants within the subcultural category of those in peripheral embodiments. On one account, the film provides an opportunity for those among the peripherally embodied to compare their own experiences with stigma across pathologized racial, gendered, class, and disabled bodies. The film cultivates an argument that unveils the economic imperatives that mobilize the need for insurance coverage, medical treatment, and prosthetic/chemical supplementation.

Bolden situates her audience as fellow disability, queer, race, and antidiscrimination activists whose political commitments may ultimately obscure the investments of those like herself who are precluded from normative modes of political participation by their bodies. The structural inaccessibility of health care and affordable medication channels her political activism in much different directions. In one scene, she leaves her house to attend a political rally only to be turned back by another bout of acute stomach upset. From this point the film jump-cuts to a nude image of herself in the mirror. The filmmaker videotapes her own body as an explanation as to why her physical political participation is not possible. However, while this level of private exposé should prove revelatory of embodied secrets, the viewer is left with no new information with which to pursue a more informed diagnostic angle. The eight-minute video becomes her unexpected contribution to a politics that would otherwise march on without her by counting her as physically absent and bereft of the political commitments necessary to social justice work.

Such use of independent disability cinema's address of historically underrepresented audiences cultivates a highly differentiated effect: it situates the activist context itself as influenced by disability experience while also using the film to encourage solidarity on behalf of nonnormative embodiments. Independent disability film itself, within this scenario, becomes an alternative form of political participation. Thus, Bolden pursues her activism within a wider ableist arena while simultaneously attending to the exclusions that prove endemic to disability rights-based activist movements themselves.

In films such as *goodnight, liberation* the unity of experience among disabled people resulting from shared identification in restrictive environments finds itself identified for different ends. Whereas an inflexible social context that excludes the inhabitants of peripheral embodiments from participation continues to serve as a force of cohesion, disability cinema exposes the insufficiencies of leftist contexts as well—especially those that reproduce the very hierarchies they presumably contest. If, according to the theory of impairment effects, we find ourselves limited with respect to the form of our activist participation (as we all inevitably do), then this context itself can function in an oppressive manner.

In fact, films such as *goodnight, liberation* help to demonstrate the degree to which an exclusive focus on discriminatory ableist social contexts continues to situate an able-bodied audience as presumed normative viewers. The address of multiple, intersecting activist contexts—gender, lesbian, racial, class, disability—as necessary sites of intervention turns those constituencies into legitimate locations for the cultivation of new political cinema; and yet, in doing so, they foreground their own activist efforts in the process of giving disability a privileged foreground. Biopolitical demands upon the body now become a factor in the forms of expression that one's activism might take. Disability is no longer situated as a "separate" movement from other activist contexts but becomes part and parcel of wider resistance movements.

Such developments, we would argue, need to be theorized in order to counter concerns about political fracturing that have beset other identity groups as well. B. Rudy Rich argues film festivals often promote dissatisfaction among their participants because "audiences don't want disruption. They don't want 'difference.' Instead they hunger for sameness, replication, reflection" (*Chick Flicks* 82). If, as Harvey points out, the experience of postmodern simultaneity threatens to undermine larger collective efforts of resistance in the name of single-group identity politics, then adding disability to the mix of activist contexts disrupts expectations of sameness even in organizations showcasing difference. To cite a movement protesting antiexclusionist contexts for being exclusionary themselves is "fightin' words" in some political domains. Is disability the identity movement doomed to break the camel's back of identity politics, as some leftist critics have charged? Because disability inserts a material contingency into social movements—including its own—does such an operation necessarily undermine the push to place oppression within a purely social context?

These are critical questions that all disability film festivals and the screening of disability films in other activist contexts inevitably introduce. The issue now "plaguing" various social movements—and we want to argue this must be recognized as an alternative strength within crip/queer collectivities—is the degree to which we can search for unity across differences without jettisoning their content-specific cargo. Is the postmodern project of observing differences still feasible while also orchestrating effective political resistance across social movements? How can disability differences that exist across bodies as well as political contexts serve as a catalyst for renewal—particularly within the new analytical space created by international independent disability film festivals?

THE POLITICS OF ATYPICALS

Signs of the difficulty of achieving inclusion while also orchestrating a meaningful collective identity continue to manifest themselves at disability film festivals. Near the end of a panel on disability filmmaking and politics at the 2005 London Film Festival, one audience participant argued that the film festival was "oppressive" because it failed to "represent neuroatypical people in its cross-disability sweep." At this particular moment the question was posed within the following contexts: first, the panel itself consisted of a person of color with a visual impairment, a well-known disability studies theorist and filmmaker who uses a wheelchair, the main festival organizer, who uses a cane and adapted shoes, and a community activist who also makes films, sings disability folk songs, and employs actors with cognitive disabilities from a local day center in northwest England. The gender makeup of the panel included two men and two women with ages spanning from thirty-two to fifty-one years.

The panel itself had been situated at the end of four days of a global, multicultural disability film festival.[4] Like most disability events the festival, quite ironically, had become a marathon of participation that ran from noon to 10:00 p.m. every day. A quick sampling of the film festival's programming identifies entries from an array of global locales including, but not limited to, Australia, Canada, the United States, England, France, the Balkans, India,

Mexico, Finland, and Spain. Not all the films were captioned, but all were audio described. In addition, the festival attended to cross-disability issues including Down syndrome, deafness, visual impairment, ventilator users, racial minorities with disabilities, "mental retardation," polio and postpolio, leprosy, congenital impairments of various kinds, postthalidomide individuals, short stature, and psychiatric survivors, to name a few. In other words, not standard diversity fare even for your basic neoliberal disability-is-diversity event.

This overview of the context within which the question erupted is provided not in order to invalidate the questioner, but rather to demonstrate the degree to which efforts to attain meaningful diversity inevitably conjure up dissent on the basis of inadequate representation. One may make observations about disability film festivals that are similar to those Eric O. Clarke makes about gay and lesbian film festivals: "While the celebratory tone of narratives about lesbian and gay inclusion in the public sphere seems at first glance warranted, such narratives fail to ask how this inclusion is defined and on what terms it is granted" ("Queer Publicity" 84). In many ways festivals that advertise one of their primary virtues as a weakened strain of neoliberal disability inclusion encourage dissent around the very situation they set out to correct. In fact, the more the identified event consciously tries to achieve diversity, the more likely a charge of underrepresentation surfaces.

Coming on the heels of the complaint about neuroatypical people's absence, a deaf woman stood up and signed her retort to the panel that deaf people represented a linguistic minority distinct from disabled people. One of the female panelists addressed the advent of disabled women's separatist groups in the United Kingdom as a corrective to the patriarchal-identified organizational structure of most disability collectives. One person of color with a disability commented on the paucity of racial minority representatives at the festival and charged the Afro-British moderator with succumbing to tokenism. Finally, the film festival organizer tried to reconvene the festival's efforts at solidarity by arguing that his goal was to achieve a continuity of political expression. Diversity, indeed.

Now recounting such moments when this kind of factionalism threatened politicized identity-based gatherings has become almost commonplace in analyses of identity-based film festivals (White, "Queer Publicity" 75; Rich, *Chick Flicks* 5; Rich, "Collision" 80; Clarke, "Queer Publicity" 84). Nevertheless, the request for representation of neuroatypical people that set off this train of comments was both accurate and necessary, particularly given that some of those most susceptible to discrimination within and without disability subcultural contexts gather under this rubric. Neuroatypicals endure a multipronged oppression in that they often lack a visible marker that makes them recognizable as "disabled" (as did the speaker in this instance), while also experiencing conditions that effectively undermine their ability to function within inflexible norms of behavior in public contexts governed by the logic of biopolitics. Further, neuroatypical people find themselves subject to myths of hypercapacities (for example, autistic savants) featured in mainstream fantasies such as *Rain Man*. In *Rain Man* audiences discover a title character presumably capable of excelling at the nuances of casino gambling (such as card counting) while failing to qualify for life outside the walls of the institution.

A divide-and-conquer mentality among contemporary intraidentity group interests often erupts as a result of the weight given to representational inclusiveness. For instance, during a screening of the aforementioned British satire, *Killer Cure*, at the Picture This Film Festival in Calgary, people with physical and cognitive disabilities are pitted against a psychopathic killer who would certainly prove a candidate for psychiatric diagnosis. The film depends upon such divisions in order to champion identifications with one group at the expense of another. Perhaps a Lacanian analysis would argue the inevitability of such substitutions. However, in a disability context, this political strategy produces the potential for further alienation among constituencies who might otherwise find common cause.

In this manner, inclusionist approaches tend to take participants beyond coherent alliances while seeming to encourage them. A more inclusive politics become tenuous at best, and even independent disability film can play to requests for solidarity that threaten to keep other identities firmly entrenched within depreciated conditions. In other words, within neoliberal inclusionist environments all identity groups participate—knowingly or not—in market systems that celebrate differences while sometimes doing little more than fetishizing them. As long as the divisions hold and remain relatively inelastic the market can appear "tolerant" while exploiting differences as product. For theorists like David Harvey the fractures that erupted at the London Disability Film Festival prove symptoms of a tendency toward postmodern nihilism. While he celebrates correctives to historical materialist analyses of excluded constituencies, he also critiques the inevitable disaffiliations promoted by multicultural agendas promoting forms of group narcissism.

However, in spite of these continuing developments, our final argument here runs askew to Harvey's analysis. We want to recognize the competing claims of various identities parading beneath a "unifying" identity rubric—in this case disability—as necessary to the vitality of disability collectivities. Rather than lament further demands for representational accommodation by those identifying as neuroatypical, for instance, the disability movement is dependent upon them for its own productive *functional incoherency*. Because disability movements have typically begun as resistance efforts to outstrip the validity of medical diagnoses as overly general, stigmatizing, and, in most cases inaccurate to the actual experience of disability, part of the effectiveness of politicized disability efforts has been the refusal of any simple coherency within diagnostic categories. Disability studies scholars argue against the ease of medically classifying differences together. Because of medical efforts to pin down and dispense with some bodies, a commitment to incoherency becomes a necessary premise for any rights-based disability politics of identity. This commitment grounds its claim upon the seemingly paradoxical premise that nontypicality unites us amid an array of professional and social efforts to lump us together in shared stigma.

Thus, we would argue that the incoherency of disability identifies common contexts of social disenfranchisement while allowing peripheral embodiments within the movement to multiply and exert—even highlight—the irreducible particularities of nonnormative bodies. To borrow another of Harvey's phrases—"simultaneity of heterogeneity"—disability movements have been founded on the expression of discontinuity while existing in shared spaces of artificial coherency imposed from the outside. Seclusion seeks coherency amid a sea of differences, and the imposition of this discomforting likeness becomes the site of our political action.

Near the conclusion of British filmmaker Martin Taylor's short video *Berocca* (2005), a father with cerebral palsy arrives at a beach on the island continent's edge. With him is his son, whom he has adopted or kidnapped from a state-supplied surrogate foster family. The father of the foster family runs a corrupt pharmaceutical business but retains custody of the boy because the film's adult male protagonist's disability and unmarried status presumably make him unfit for performing the tasks of parenting. The two have spent the day driving across the English countryside and undergoing a variety of experiences that seek to reconnect two socially alienated people together. The differences between the two characters prove intense: the father's neurological differences contrasting with the son's intensity of introspection and muteness (some reviews of the film diagnose the boy as autistic). In partnering such atypical characters the story undermines more homogenizing neoliberal arguments of filiation based on bonds of familial likeness, patriarchal kinship, genetic dispositions, and so on. The two experience each other's lives as differences that cannot be easily accommodated within their own frames of reference.

Ultimately the film winds down to an enigmatic final scene where the boy walks off into the sea (to his death?) while the father struggles to get his wheelchair out of the car in a desperate but ill-fated attempt to save him. The time it takes to extract the father's mobility device from the car makes him too late to effect any rescue of the boy. The two figures have merely come together for a time against the norms of their community (one that includes other disabled people) and then inevitably drift away from each other, pursuing their own paths of interest. Their relationship is not based upon the eclipse of one another's differences but an intensity of identification across individualities.

We end by offering this film as an important example of the ways in which disability must sustain a politics of mutuality while attending to differences that cannot be so easily subsumed under the logic of a unifying identity category. In fact, the intensity and disruptive nature of such differences need to be theorized as the mechanism through which the movement achieves its most valuable nonnormative transformation of neoliberal inclusionist practices. Disability movements have grown suspicious of a logic that simply assures audiences that disabled people are just people with differences (the ruse of neoliberal inclusion practices discussed in the introduction and chapter 1). Such is the case for other minority film festivals as well: "In its quest to secure inclusion, mainstream lesbian and gay politics in the United States has sought to reassure straight Americans that lesbians and gay men are 'just like everyone else,' and in this sense it seems to have restricted itself to a phantom normalcy" (Clarke, "Queer Publicity" 84). This phantom normalcy will certainly not suffice for disability communities founded on the critique of normalcy as a false standard of human value.

Each absence of difference in our representational repertoires provides the opportunity to renew this commitment as a rejection of neoliberal static being on behalf of crip/queer becomings. Such an identity embodies the "truth" of various lives in that, like other dynamic subcultural collectivities, disability is not ultimate arrival at an ontological essence but rather a sign of the fluctuating coordinates of embodiment deferred, deviating, and never complete. Disability, in this sense, is more akin to the multigenerational construction of a cathedral, one sporting adaptations, improvements, and alterations and yet never staving off the degradation of time, environment, and social exposure. In Raymond Carver's famous short story titled "Cathedral," a sighted man falters at explaining the organization, aesthetic, and architecture of a cathedral on television to a blind ex-lover of his wife who comes to visit:

> I stared some more at the cathedral before the picture flipped off into the countryside. There was no use. I turned to the blind man and said, "To begin with, they're very tall." I was looking around the room for clues. "They reach way up. Up and up. Toward the sky. They're so big, some of them, they have to have these supports. To help hold them up, so to speak. These supports are called buttresses. They remind me of viaducts, for some reason. But maybe you don't know viaducts, either? Sometimes the cathedrals have devils and such carved into the front. Sometimes lords and ladies. Don't ask me why this is," I said.

Like the cathedral's multitiered structure the narrator piles up details in a ramshackle series of connectives. Ultimately, they form a chaotic enjambment of unrelated materials and metaphors that don't give the sense of a coherent monolith but rather a hodgepodge array of features tossed together. While the oral explanation fails of words to describe the polyglot nature of the edifice, the blind man's desire to visualize the structure forces the protagonist's greater intimacy. At this point he instructs his sighted guide to get a paper and pencil and draw the cathedral. The blind man follows the illustration by holding gently to the pencil and then touches the lines on the page. Thus, it is the collaborative nature of their struggle to make the cathedral's structure materialize that brings its messy contours into greater proximity. Not a denial of its idiosyncrasies but rather a dual engagement with its undulating surfaces and supporting bulwarks. Such are the contours of a true politics of atypicality.

In the next chapter we chart further alternative insights of this politics in a series of close readings of the narrative and technical tactics adopted by independent disability cinema productions. In juxtaposing these analyses of narrative film approaches, we intend to deepen an understanding of subcultural media navigations of those occupying peripheral embodiments beyond the superficial offerings of neoliberalism and ablenationalism.

FIVE

Permutations of the Species

Independent Disability Cinema and the Critique of Ablenationalism

CONTEMPORARY DISABILITY FILMS AND FILM FESTIVALS

While chapter 4 details developments within the organizational and administrative structure of disability film festivals, chapter 5 arranges its analysis around the experimental content of independent disability film plots and technical explorations. In particular we seek to examine the rise of "ablenationalism" as both a conduit for, and in direct tension with, the politics of atypicality. Increasingly film festival conveners find themselves negotiating a delicate line in order to achieve their goals of revaluing life in peripheral embodiments as an expressed outcome of their programming agendas.

Seeds of this analysis first took hold during a screening of the short film *I'm in away from Here* (Catriona MacInnes, U.K., 2007), at the November 2009 "The Way We Live Now" International Short Film Festival in Munich, Germany.[1] The film begins with a man masturbating on a public beach. He is interrupted by an older woman who calls his name out as if in a desperate attempt to find him and, thus, restrain this onanistic pursuit of sexual pleasure. As the film progresses, more information arrives: the man, Archie, is identified as neuroatypical and on the autistic spectrum. The woman turns out to be his mother. But at the start, we don't know exactly how to place Archie in a cultural or geographical sense. We neither know why he chooses to masturbate in this particular place, nor why the woman is trying to gain his

attention. The audience awakens with Archie, suddenly and without warn-
ing. Signaled by distortions on the audio and video tracks, the world crashes
in upon viewers as well as the protagonist; we cannot interpret the story
amid these sensorial intrusions coming from every direction. Parental stalk-
ing, efforts at surveillance, and wide-ranging social prohibitions on crip/
queer sexuality collide and create a paranoid atmosphere. The audience feels
caught out with the protagonist for some illicit crossing of normative conventions, but the reason for the punitive circumstance remains ambiguous.
The film ultimately leaves Archie and the audience immersed in an experience that belongs to neither, an enigmatic story marked by a shared inability
to keep the interruptions at bay.

To begin in medias res is nothing new for experimental independent film.
Both popular and avant-garde film movements have provided abrupt entry
into film's narrative spaces for decades. Here, though, it takes on additional
significance as part of the upending of many of the normatively comfortable viewing coordinates that come not only with contemporary independent disability film narratives, but also with their places of exhibition—that
which we explored in the previous chapter as the independent disability film
festival circuit. Both the films and the festivals challenge expectations and
understandings of normative narratives, spaces, and people. Independent
disability cinema provides a public space within which to raise issues related
to the place of disabled people during a period of expansive globalization
and mediatization. They also provide opportunities for the readjustment of
perspectives on disabled subjectivities and on the normative systems of classification that assign pathologizing definitions and categories to peripheral
embodiments.

When we speak of independent disability films, we refer to predominantly video-based works created on low budgets (less than US$100,000
but in many cases below US$10,000) and without the backing of a multi-
national corporate commercial mainstream U.S. film industry. Independent
videos derive largely from local community contexts but speak globally to
people with disabilities living around the world. There is an assumption of
some degree of overlap between local contexts of stigma, isolation, and social placements that inhibit mobility, civic participation, and sexual expression. As discussed in our application of David Harvey's theory of "political
simultaneity" in the previous chapter, the intersections of the local and the
global usher in complexities around definitions and categorizations as well
as cultural rituals of reception. Independent disability cinema productions

are typically funded by arts-based governmental organizations supporting the promotion of national identity unification projects abroad; yet these films represent the stories of those typically omitted from national narratives of ability in the country in which they are made. One of our main goals here is to understand the seemingly paradoxical nature of these competing impulses. This examination will chart how ablenationalism constrains the degree to which crip/queer bodies can be integrated into imaginaries of the body, while also analyzing how developing forms of neoliberal tolerance open a limited creative space for filmic challenges to the embodied dictates of national belonging.

This defining "peripherality" extends to the aesthetic realm, as many independent disability films are nonnarrative, eschewing conventions of exposition, conflict, and denouement. The style is more akin to the literary genre commonly referred to as "slice of life"—a brief examination of different variants of embodied life come into contact with the benign social management schemes characteristic of neoliberalism. This tendency toward a refusal of conventional narrative arcs might be understood as the film equivalent of what queer studies theorist Lee Edelman calls "no future" and what disability studies theorist Ann Kafer refers to as a "politics of crip futurity" (No Future 11; Feminist Queer Crip 3). Like "nonreproductive" queer and transgendered bodies, people with disabilities find themselves denied ways to narrate viable futures for themselves, and thus independent disability cinema allows an exploration of alternative modes of transmission and expression of nonnormative modes of being.

Likewise, crip/queer lives pursuing options of sexuality collide with prohibitions against intimate contact. Whereas queer sexualities experience the censorship of nonreproductive sexual practices, crip sexualities engender more wide-sweeping fears about any engagements in reproductive sexuality whatsoever—specifically, the emergence of historically and culturally specific fears surrounding the genetic transmission of lives commonly considered unviable. As Michel Desjardins argues, the sexuality of people labeled intellectually disabled has been systemically repressed within Western societies since the rise of the Industrial Revolution and the bourgeois moral order (69). While queer lifestyles conjure protests about inappropriate sexual object choices, crip lifestyles cause objections to any sexual object choice at all. The prohibition against expressions of disability sexuality are foundational and the anxiety on display at the opening of I'm in Away from Here sets the tone for misplaced paranoia about the well-being of crip/queer bodies such those diagnosed on the autistic spectrum. In contrast, a nonnormative positivist emphasis facilitates movements toward making illicit sexualities a matter of cultural resistance and alternative appropriations of heteronormative prohibitions.

Because traditional storytelling mediums such as film have proven largely disinterested in imagining productive life stories for disabled people where the demographic population is projected into successful futures, independent disability film responds by narrating the results of socially truncated options within the strict confines of a truncated form: the film short. In a great number of independent disability films, social roles are reversed and disabled people perform acts of "counterdominantnarratives" commonly associated with the activities of politicized minority groups (Rose 61). The films also emphasize a stake in a universalizing humanity shared by disabled people that tend to reify dominant assumptions about disability inhumanity. These complexities are born of the complexities of a pervasive liberal humanism as solution to forms of neoliberal toleration. As such, independent disability films provide alternatives that often prove ineffective within existing cultural contexts of inclusive politics.

For instance, in the short film *Yolk* (Stephan Lance, Australia, 2008), an adolescent girl with Down syndrome is forced to return a copy of *The Joy of Sex*, one she has stolen from the local bookmobile, after her mother discovers it hidden between her mattress and box spring. The imperative of a "nonreproductive" life for disabled women is crystallized in the scene of returning the source of a culturally forbidden knowledge to a mobile library. Yet the daughter belies her obedience to the mother's dictates by hiding the book beneath her farmer's bib as she exits the bookmobile. The bell to her experience as a sexual being cannot be unrung, however, and the film leads us to witness the overhead shot of an intellectually disabled girl's *jouissance* in the soft-focus fantasy sequence that follows. The young woman is captured by an overhead tracking shot splayed akimbo with a neighborhood boy on a lush green Australian hillside in the woods where they have secretly met previously. Both figures hold expressions of postcoital bliss on their faces in entering experiences of sexuality prohibited to people with intellectual disabilities by heteronormative circuits of desire. Perhaps, ironically, these countercultural sexual acts of resistance often entail pursuing normative practices denied to those in nonnormative bodies.

These films tend not to receive local theatrical release, but instead share a distribution network of independent disability film festivals held in major metropolitan centers such as London (London Disability Arts Festival, www.disabilityartsonline.org.uk/ldaf-film). Another instance of the redress of sexual prohibitions by heteronormative social conventions occurs in the disability film *Outcasts* (Ian Clark, U.K., 2008), wherein a disabled woman joins forces with three other disabled characters to kidnap a charity-minded able-bodied entertainer—a hypersexualized Mick Jagger–like rock singer—dressed in a cheap sequined shirt and touring patient rooms at a hospital. Instead of acquiescing to the untenable results of consignment to an asexual future, two members of a disabled foursome abduct the singer, stow him in the trunk of their car, and meet the other members of their group at a prearranged liminal space on the edge of some untended cornfields with an ominous nuclear power plant poised in the background.

The kidnapped figure represents the equivalent of a captive audience—a debased sexualized attraction admired within the narrow aesthetic interests of a homogenizing middle-class pop culture. The rock singer's captive presence makes him available for active ideological and aesthetic reprogramming regarding demeaning views on disability. In staging this absurd situation the film asks audiences to contemplate a coercive seduction fantasy, briefly played out on film, wherein disabled people insist on their attractiveness and successfully argue on behalf of their own worthiness for love. The film turns the tables on the rejected body's exclusion from romantic entanglement by challenging an iconic representative of normative sexual culture. The dark humor of forcibly absconding with a figure of debased mainstream sexual desire provides the disabled cast with a momentary outlet for expressing their own sexual frustrations and progressivist social fantasies. In the process, their surreal scheme insists on the legitimacy of its result if only able-bodied culture would give it a go.

Other festival venues include:

- Melbourne (The Other Film Festival, www.otherfilmfestival.com), Moscow (Breaking Barriers, festival-eng.perspektiva-inva.ru)
- Munich (The Way We Live International Short Film Festival, www.abm-medien.de)
- Berkeley (Superfest International Disability Film Festival, www.culturedisabilitytalent.org/index.html)
- Athens (Emotion Pictures, www.ameamedia.gr/)
- Calgary (Picture This: www.ptff.org/ptff_main/2011-festival.html)
- Helsinki (Kynnyskino Disability Film Festival, www.kynnys.fi/kynnys/english.html)

Each screening location operates as a cosmopolitan gathering point for showcasing independent works about the struggles, triumphs, exclusions, successes, and everyday living experiences of disabled people. The films offer aesthetic interventions, challenging narrative standards, and normative film conventions such as continuity editing, while deprivileging normative body movements and appearance through the casting of disabled people in the roles of characters with disabilities. Key filmmaking practices are sent into hiding and, in so doing, are exposed as the conventions of a normative visual media artifice.

The events and characters now appearing on screens at disability film festivals chart reactions to the historical "reentry" of disabled people into neoliberal normative social orders that are specific to their respective nations, in the wake of histories of formalized exclusion from the most rudimentary aspects of human community. These films (and festivals) begin to defy entrenched attitudes toward people with disabilities as non(productive) citizens, and to challenge host governments to create more flexible policies and access to infrastructure for all. The festival screenings themselves may provide such impetus, not only on-, but also offscreen, as venues must be made physically accessible to all attendees. Even the timing of events is relevant, as programmers account for the numerous difficulties faced by people with disabilities in everyday travel. Accommodations of crip time becomes of paramount importance.

In effect, the main function of independent disability cinema, a term that embraces both the films and the conditions of viewing, lies in critiquing the exclusionary social orders that we have called ablenationalism. Applications of ablenationalism involve the implementation of national normativities that work to police the local boundaries of physical, cognitive, sensory, and aesthetic foundations of embodiment. Normative values grounded in a narrow concept of bodily acceptability produce disabled bodies as exceptionally deviant. By default, the various national concepts of body norms are often complicit with "ableist" sensibilities that cherish the "abled" body as normal and advance this norm as a precondition for social inclusion and acceptable citizenship.

Disability film festivals counter this foundational exclusion at the heart of national formulas of belonging; they engage alternative ways of "being disabled" as an antidote to histories of social rejection by inflexible and unaccommodating norms. This is achieved by showcasing independent films and promoting stories that feature nonnormative bodies, capacities, sensory experiences, and subjectivities. The experience of independent disability film is one seeking to counter the euphemistic tactics of ablenationalism through offerings that involve immersion and alternative exposures to atypical lives.

MULTIPLE SUBJECTIVITIES ON SCREEN: *JAK TO JEST BYC MOJA MATKA*

As an example of the immersion and exposure to atypical lives that independent disability films offer, the short film *What It Is Like To Be My Mother* (Norah McGettigan, Poland, 2007) evolves around the encounter of a nondisabled daughter with her mother, who has recently undergone a double amputation. When shown in the context of a disability film festival, it offers an opportunity for reflexive exploration of multiple, conflicting expectations and identities advanced by ablenationalist sensibilities. The film uses a family drama to stage a now common political conflict about the necessity of policing the borders of disability representation between disabled people and nondisabled image-makers. At the same time, it raises questions about the nature of disabled community, where kinship and difference merge. The search for commonalities is often fraught, particularly given the competing demands of access and limited resources.

In the opening scene we learn that the daughter has made a film about her mother's struggle to "regain independence," and the video has been selected for screening at a disability arts and film festival. The mother, who is introduced lying on her back working with weights on a padded therapy table, expresses disapproval of the daughter's desire to show the film at the festival because the would-be filmmaker "doesn't have a disability" and therefore cannot represent her effectively. What can such filmic display accomplish? Once the daughter convinces her mother that the film festival screening could be a positive move toward a future career, the mother agrees to attend and even to make an appearance on stage prior to the screening. After being introduced by the festival host, the mother moves to center stage and insists on making a dangerous transition from her wheelchair to a precarious standing position on crutches hovering above the audience. The festival participants clap following the mother's banal, yet successful effort to stand on prosthetic legs. Holding their attention, she tells them to give her daughter a hand now, in case they end up not liking the movie. The event turns into a humiliating experience for the daughter.

During the screening the mother grows increasingly upset and rolls out of the theater before the film concludes. In the following scene, she wheels herself stubbornly in the rain while the family's cab driver follows behind. Later, mother and daughter are reunited in the vehicle; the mother grudgingly admits that the daughter has made a "good film," while the daughter grumpily refuses to return the mother's hug. Ultimately, the daughter demonstrates indifference to the mother's sense of violation by resting on the laurels of film festival acclaim and replacing one kind of recognition (parental) for another (artistic). This scene depicts more than the micropolitics of a family: it calls forth the larger political context of disability cinema with the potential for social rejection experienced by both subjects and filmmakers.

Initially, the daughter's intention to have the film shown at the festival appears potentially exploitative. Later on, however, when they get to the festival, the mother engages in attention-seeking behavior, undermining her daughter's aspirations to be taken seriously as a filmmaker. While, at the onset, the mother suspected her image may be exploited, toward the end of the film the daughter is put off by her mother's attention-grabbing behavior at the festival. The two individual stories that evolve here reflect the various agendas, benefits, and downfalls of film and festival display. Likewise, the audience's allegiances shift from one character to the other as the film asks the viewers to contemplate whether direct identification is a precondition to the creation of a successful portrayal of disability. It also asks an even more difficult question: Whether an artistically worthy film should be shown without the consent of the disabled subject being filmed.

To highlight this point, the film stages an interview sequence showing the filmmaker/ daughter awkwardly asking the subject/mother: "Did your disability impact on your life?"

Besides taking an amateur interlocutor's approach at asking impossibly open-ended questions, the daughter's query is laden with assumptions about asexuality, unemployability, incapacity to parent, and failure to maintain the interests of a lover. The below-the-knee double amputee mother pauses before answering with a cool retort: "I used to buy shoes—now I buy gloves."

What It Is Like to Be My Mother examines critical questions about film images of disabled bodies and narrative re-creations of lives lived with disability as retold by filmmakers. Questions of objectification proliferate as able-bodied image-makers and disabled individuals are on display for the festival audience, receiving accolades, awards, and moments of glory, but much of it feels as if it is at the expense of a further degree of public objectification. At the same time, *What It Is Like to Be My Mother* purposefully avoids delivering an answer to its titular thesis. A more accurate title might be "What is it like to be the daughter of a disabled mother?" or, better yet, "How my mom's disability looks from the perspective of an able-bodied daughter seeking to adjust to her alternative embodiment." The innovation of the film is in its argument that there is no such thing as an authentic subjectivity of disability. The daughter imposes her version of what it is like to be a disabled mom, while the mother's participation in the filmmaking process proves fully performative in its own right. Ultimately, *What It Is Like to Be My Mother* contemplates how film belies the illusion of direct access to disability experience, and depends on bodily spectacle as well as an attendant level of personal violation for its power.

CHALLENGING DEFINITIONS

The oscillation between exploitation and objectification, and between acceptance and rejection, illustrates many of the tensions around identity production in disability film festivals. As discussed above, the films are often produced in a national context but aimed at transnational audiences. Yet each stop offers a moment to intervene into the local discourse that establishes these exclusionary power relations (which manifest themselves in other discourses, whether legal, political, or cultural). Perhaps most notable, though, is the way that disability challenges identity-based projects by calling attention to the permeability and mutability of identity.

The alternative universes showcased at disability film festivals strain the boundaries of commonly worn conventions of disability representation. The film works to foreground the fact that disability film is filtered through the point of view of able-bodied narrators; of protagonists equivalent to those whom the African American filmmaker Spike Lee calls "gatekeepers" in reference to white characters who draw predominantly white audiences into racial community experiences of national norms (*Do the Right Thing* 32). Independent disability film festivals upset the sanctity of the able body's right not to share public space with crip/queer ones; the festivals parade a pastiche of oddities as foundational to the social and material dynamics of disabled bodies in tension with social norms. Disability itself provides challenges to identity production since it implies a medical condition, confers a legal status, and describes a state of being. The festivals accept—and even promote—this complexity that challenges neoliberal political efforts to forward a less challenging social message about experiences of disability, such as disabled people are just like everyone else. Rather, disability film festivals share a new materialist model of disability that is an identity of difference based on shared experiences of exclusion and the intricacies of nonnormative embodiments.

Yet while exclusionary experiences of stigma-based rejection are common, disability film festivals show disability as a strategy of referencing identity in the absence of a coherent and universally shared experience of embodiment. This strategy questions containment of any sort, fighting against the forms of identity-building that contribute to exploitation and exclusion. They are not to be counted among the various social missions of fixing and stasis "wishing to contain the messiness of identity within formulaic grids" such as diagnosis, special education, rehabilitation, and prosthetic supplementation (Puar, *Terrorist Assemblages* 212). The curated programs offer a tactical deployment of body chaos and demand critical engagement from a range of audiences, including policymakers, employers, government officials, teachers, parents, therapists, medical personnel, and commercial business operators. The films require accommodating the arrival of new generations of politicized disabled people in public and private spaces.

Disability film festival programming embraces a collective identity of distinct experiences. The festivals gather together a variety of human differences and place them on display in nonsequential and/or nonthematic relation to each other. The screenings tend to avoid grouping films according to conditions, parallel kinds of discrimination, or other organizing principles, since the act of categorizing disabilities represents a form of oppression in and of itself. Without this conscious orchestration of films into normative narrative groupings of disability as deviance, festival audiences become connoisseurs of human variation—essentially viewing aficionados of diverse embodiments. They dabble in the persistent nuances of biological differences, social constructions, and mutating screen presences. They are not meant to become therapeutic or diagnostic experts, cultivating skills to manage these unruly bodies.

The festival circuit offers a tactical vantage point that is not easily duplicated in other contexts, particularly insofar as the venues sweep up a wide net of new video productions from around the globe and stage them for simultaneous consumption over a condensed period of several days. The cumulative programming effect results in an opportunity for audiences to assess the range of experiences across the world, and pick out possible trends. With its orchestrated influx of international filmmakers, actors, experts, producers, and activists, the disability film festival gives voice to otherwise estranged artistic and documentary points of view, and highlights the situation of an alienated people navigating disabilities in a variety of barrier-ridden social milieus. As such, disability film festivals provide us with a useful barometer for understanding the degree to which disability rights, identity, and representational strategies are transforming (or not) our understanding of people with disabilities.

The festival circuit—by definition—recognizes disability as a contextual phenomenon of ever-mutating proportions. Disability film festivals are consciously created contexts that bring together surveys of disability that are carried out within various national borders; without this evolving global context of reference, close readings of individual films have relatively little to tell us about the nature, reception, and impetus for the creation of alternative cinema. The multiplicity of screening venues at the festivals enables an important context for understanding disabled concerns "at large."

The films themselves become essential agents in this definitional process, not only as sites for determining trends and issues, but as a key way in which disabled people might be able to communicate through the physical barriers of mass transit inaccessibility, intensive immigration restrictions, and poverty. Disability films transcend barriers toward acquiring the degree of extranational mobility that is often denied people with disabilities in immigration scenarios and to achieving improvements in access. Consequently, the array of offerings at independent disability film festivals provides an overview of the global "health" of disabled populations as they navigate increasingly diffuse, and largely inhospitable, social networks.

Moreover, these challenges to the system, these bodies on the periphery of acceptable embodiments, may offer something else: a chance to reconsider all forms of social identity, and not merely nonnormative formations on the fringe of ablenationalist inclusion. Crip/queer people represent boundary creatures at a contemporary historical juncture akin to the sea serpents, the dragons, and the "deformed" native beings seen at the edges of world maps in the context of early colonial cartographies. Whereas these extrahuman figures previously marked unexplored geographies of the primitive, disability film festivals recognize the margins of the species as the locations of what discredited evolutionary biologist Richard Goldschmidt once referred to as "hopeful monsters" (205–6), a case of rapid evolutionary change in individual organisms that holds promise for the longevity of the species as a whole.

Thinking in terms of evolutionary biology, we approach disability film festivals as sites for change on a massive geological scale. The festivals offer meeting places that reveal national constructions of disability and call attention to the dynamic cultural contexts that shape geopolitical concepts of disability as difference. The diversity of disability on view exhausts any pretension to an overarching human "'commonality." No longer inevitable and enduring, these formations are inherently mutable and contingent. The festival puts social norms under scrutiny because the diversity of disability on view here exhausts any pretension to an overarching consistency, symmetry, or normative functionality of human embodiment. The disability film festival does not advocate neoliberal inclusionist clichés such as "We are all alike," although a few frequenters of these festivals are still prone to making such universalizing claims. Rather, international independent disability cinema expands our knowledge of human difference in seeking to document experiences of embodiment that, by definition, cannot be exhausted.

Not only are individual disability predicaments not well understood (as festival programmers are fond of saying, "you've seen one disability, you've seen *one* disability"), but disability filmmakers venture out into the peripheries of the peripheral embodiments represented by their subjects. Within such an effort to gather up those on the margins of the margins, cultural norms become recognized for what they really are: inelastic standards of homogeneity incapable of accommodating a wide array of human diversity.

Disability film festivals, as gatherings that function both onscreen and off, allow for radical collective reflection. The collection of films screened revels in displays of peripheral embodiments to the point that identity-making practices are what come under scrutiny. We are not claiming that film festivals produce the change to which their individually showcased products aspire, but as programs and meeting places, they draw up the permutations of a species (i.e., people with disabilities inhabiting crip/queer bodies) into one net and lay them out for reflection on the nature of the year's "catch." How plentiful is the species? How successful the survival campaign? How great or insubstantial the migration? In what environments does cohabitation prove most viable? How much innovation can be detected? What corners of the species are most endangered? From where do the greatest threats derive? What is the firmest evidence for adaptation?

Such a project is akin to the efforts of photographer Auguste Sanders, as portrayed in Richard Powers's novel *Three Farmers on Their Way to a Dance* (1992), in his failed fin de siècle project to collect all physiognomic facial types of the American people. Film festival audiences serve as amateur investigators of the exclusions and alternative navigations that persist across cultural contexts. Even as film offers the inclusive medium capable of representing unfamiliar bodies, while attending festivals still proves inaccessible to many disabled persons, communication across disparate cultural contexts remains a necessary objective for producing greater levels of interaction with crip/queer materialities through cinematic narrative.

CINEMATIC INTERDEPENDENCIES: THE COST OF LIVING

Actual attendance at these film festivals is rarely the point (although they all undertake Herculean marketing struggles to get their local clientele to participate). Filmmakers, producers, actors, and invested individuals populate the majority of the festival's audience and seek each other's assistance in deepening their own art, as well as securing the birth of a next generation of disability filmmakers, commentators, and participants. With this relatively specialized audience in tow, film festival conveners actively orchestrate a choir of voices regarding disability and, in doing so, expose relatively nondisseminated work projects to a wider, international, film art audience. Participants bargain and trade film works with the intentions of bringing the products of others' video labor back to their home countries for future screenings and further conversations. Disability is conceived largely as an opportunity to stage otherwise muted cultural conversations about the value of greater intimacy with human diversity.

Improvement of conditions for people with disabilities in the host country of the festival is more rare than real. In some rare cases, however, film festivals succeed in bringing about change. Such was the case with the 2007 "Emotion Pictures!" film festival held in Athens, Greece (www.ameamedia. gr), where, following a series of protests, local disabled student organizations received assurances from the minister of cultural affairs that a dedicated disability programming channel would be made available nationwide. In most places annual events fizzle from lack of funding and/or tensions that accompany the strain of attaining the ideals of the politics of atypicality before such measurable and tangible social effects can be realized.

Yet, in many ways, the results of political praxis remain beside the point. Independent disability film festivals stage their projects as a necessary coping device of subcultural resistance to the homogenizing dictates of national normativities and the attendant expressions of ablenationalism. Disability film products are not David against Goliath—but rather more akin to David in a wrestling match to the death bereft of even a slingshot. The more modest goal of the disability film festival is to generate a discourse on film about the meaning of disability as if it were "up for grabs," which it is, and independent disability filmmakers seek to push the saltationist transition on embodiment as definitively mutating and ever dynamic. Disability film festivals enable a critical space that opens up disability to the true multiplicity of its expression across the species. Rather than being treated as exemplifying unviable lives, disability at the disability film festival records the messy networks of human materiality as they interact with technological spaces such as human-made environments, prosthetics, media-made contexts, and nature. The point of gathering together so many diverse examples of human differences is the creation of a catalog of multiplicities that threaten to fray the already decaying fabric of narrow human norms made acceptable by neoliberal inclusionism.

Disability film festivals document individual space lived expansively within the limited national spaces of tightly constrained social mobilities offered within contemporary ablenationalisms; disability studies scholar Celeste Langan calls this tactic of finding ways to move within socially delimited space "mobility disability" (459). For instance, in the award-winning film *Body and Soul: Diane and Kathy* (Alice Elliot, United States, 2007), one of the disabled protagonists is seriously wounded by an inattentive train conductor who drives her wheelchair into a wall while attempting to assist her boarding. Ironically, the two disabled women are on their way to protest the incarceration of fellow disabled citizens in state-funded institutions. As a result of the injury suffered, the two women find themselves spending the rest of the film immobilized within their own house and responding to the medical mismanagement of the victim's broken hip. Throughout independent disability films we witness the efforts of loose confederations of "families" (biological or chosen) akin to the conscious development of the value of interdependency between Diane and Kathy. Similarly, independent disability films document the choices of disabled individuals and their advocates as they elect to untether themselves from complex medical equipment requiring their permanent isolation in hospitals and clinics, and where trained professionals suited to operating such apparatus have inflexibly congregated.

Documenting such health-based decision-making allows audiences to imagine disability unleashed from isolated corners of existence, and brings about some temporal relief. Such films follow the precarious entry of people with disabilities and their advocates into the risks of a life lived as nonnormative by those who insist upon an active relationship to other others, an elected habitation of those who exemplify the permutations of the species that will not be closeted in laboratory specimen jars akin to a previous century's curiosity closet.

The productions of disabled people shift audience angles, perspectives, and relationships to peripheral embodiments by using crip/queer bodies as new modalities of social practice. In the U.K. mixed-ability dance film *The Cost of the Living*, David (Eddie Kay), a double amputee character, dances with an able-bodied woman. The camera is positioned in a cutout in the dance floor and audience vantage shifts to a floor-level vantage point; the characters' movements mimic the ways in which alternative bodies move, and, in turn, wait for each partner's previous move to complete as they propel each other's body into a further level of the performance. The dance is witnessed at a window of the studio by Eddie (David Toole), a queer man with Tourette's syndrome. Consequently, the disability universe of *The Cost of Living* is transformed into what may be characterized as the crip/queer space of nonnormative interdependencies: the space of divergences and convergences among multiple differences of embodiment, cognition, and sensory interaction.

While each film discussed wrestles with its own particular reifications of ablenationalist practices and beliefs, its own ensnarement within neoliberal orders of reproductive sameness, the ensemble of films available for viewing across the space of multiday international film festivals significantly pluralizes encounters with human variations. They tend toward a diminishment of audience alienation with embodied differences while avoiding the alternative problem of flattening the field with platitudes of claims to universally shared identities in disability. We suggest, in drawing upon these multivalent media portrayals of disability in various global locations, that the exploration of subjectivities wrought within neoliberalism unveils alternative possibilities for an ethics of living interdependently with others developed within disability subcultures.

Such plumbings of experiential navigations involve the opening up of formerly prohibited interactions based on sexuality, body care, arts/cultural programming, shared access to public and private spaces, intrusions upon bodies, and the ambivalences of disability inclusion projects. In each of the examples provided, disability "failures" to meet ableist expectations result in inversions that challenge the assumed positivity of heteronormative practices, beliefs, and capacities provisioned for able bodies.

PART III

Medical Outliers
Navigating the Disability Bio(political) Sphere

SIX

Corporeal Subcultures and the Specter of Biopolitics

> —It is conventional to call "monster" any blending of dissonant elements ...
> I call "monster" every original inexhaustible beauty. (Alfred Jarry. quoted in
> Hebdige 102).

CLOSED SYSTEMS AND THE IN(TER)DEPENDENCIES THEY NECESSITATE

In Part II our analyses focused on the film productions and screening venues of independent and mainstream dominant cinema to demonstrate some collaborative axes of representation undertaken by those inhabiting other peripheral embodiments. In this third part we pursue some further avenues for the exploration of nonnormative alternatives available in the subcultural perspectives unfolding on social media and developing within contexts of neoliberal biopolitics. Whereas the previous sections focus on disability education, film, and arts community productions, this chapter moves outward into the domains of medicine, literature, and political economy through engagements with contemporary dilemmas of health care and the rise of consumer-run virtual networks.

Namely, the activities under scrutiny here are (1) those practiced by crip/queer participants on social media forums among single condition user groups; (2) late twentieth-century antinormative novels of embodiment that turn on revelations of disability as unexpected creative capacity in order to expose cultural investments in normative conceptions of aesthetics, cognition, and functionality; and (3) the radical underpinnings of disability at the foundation of Hardt and Negri's concept of multitudes (the spontaneous eruptions of global networks of resistance to late capitalist forms of exploitation) in the afterword. Our closing remarks regard the potentiality of approaching disability as "nonproductive labor"—an alternative to capitalist overdeterminations of the ability to sell one's labor power on the market as the nexus of productivity, and thus, a normative baseline of human value. Further they chart avoidance of crip/queer people living under the radar of late capitalism and struggling against consignments to consumer-directed identities.

In some respects we might think of these domains of bounded disability participation as akin to other semi-permeable universes such as the Biosphere 2 (Biosphere 1 is the planet Earth). Biosphere 2 was a project undertaken in fall 1991 to create a completely controlled, "natural" environment within one contained structure in the desert of Arizona (Winerip, "A Second Act"). The biosphere is a 3.14 acre all-glass arboretum-like Earth systems scientific research center intended to operate as an enclosed ecological space. The structure was built in the town of Oracle and was intended to make the interdependencies of life systems available to researchers for study and measurement ("Biosphere 2").

Two different human research groups inhabited the biosphere during mission 1 from 1988 to 1991 and mission 2 from 1993 to 1995 ("Biosphere 2"). The first mission was characterized by animosities that developed between two divided encampments based on arguments over methodological research practices (Winerip, "A Second Act"). The second mission was prematurely aborted when financial disputes over the management of the environment and the mounting costs of the experiment led to mission 2's premature abandonment ("Biosphere 2"). While the experiment was largely undertaken to understand the interdependencies of hermetically sealed off ecosystems, the invention of something akin to a human-scale control group, the work came to reveal the antinomies cultivated by human actors operating under a twenty-four-hour surveillance camera more akin to the contemporary reality show "Big Brother" than a display of scientific exercise of dominion over nature.

Perhaps, ironically, the fate of the naturally simulated interdependencies of ecosystems in the biosphere gave way, after its sale to Columbia University, to a test tank for observing the destructive effects of greenhouse gasses and global warming trends ("Biosphere 2"). All of these intensities operate in the bio(political)sphere for people with disabilities under neoliberalism. Disabled people represent excessively supervised, researched populations prone to being positioned as canaries in the coal mine of environmental and social exposures. Mel Y. Chen writes in her book *Animacies* that disabled people share intensive affinities with other marginalized populations (largely people of color) "shaped by what or who counts as human, and what or who does not" (30).

In this section we want to underscore how the toxic environments of for-profit health care research networks participate in this neoliberal social annexation of those peripheral embodiments. Such research networks promote normalization schemes based on the emptying out of disability-based differences and active exclusions from competitive labor environments. Nearly all efforts in the domain of for-profit medicine serve as components of the bio(political)sphere of disability influencing global interactions among marginalized forms of citizenship. If biopolitics is most distinctively characterized by Foucault's formulation in *The History of Sexuality* as "the right of death and power over life" (157), then these collaborative disability domains are seeking to survive experiments of exclusionary (sometimes death-making) environments manufactured for the maintenance of some privileged lives over others—those who embody lives that cannot be effectively accommodated within the human-made toxicity (of attitudes, structures, environments, and practices) of the neoliberal built biopolitical sphere.

In particular we analyze how the rarity of some impairments that require extraordinary medical care (such as multiple surgeries to reconstruct unviable organs) fail to galvanize enough promise as lucrative interventions for medical practitioners, pharmaceutical research corporations, and health care systems alike. In neoliberal for-profit medicine a premium is placed upon the numbers of people who might benefit from a particular treatment regimen in the risk calculations of viability for future medical research, the procurement of financial backing for the development of treatment technologies and protocols, and the training of sufficient expertise in medicine to improve viability for those in peripheral embodiments. In these economically generated measures of who is worth saving, one is left with the immoral quandaries of which bodies should receive treatment and which ones should not. Often lack of treatment results from the fact that no research organization has identified a sufficient market-based demand for promoting profit-based research and development (R & D) explorations. Those who exist under the classification of "letting die" have been increasingly subject to participating in the economic press of funding generation schemes to underwrite necessary treatment, pleading with surgeons and researchers to undertake skills training in necessary interventions, and, most recently, purchasing in the neoliberal for-profit medical markets to underwrite potential "cures," treatments, and medications.

THE SHADOWY ENCROACHMENTS OF IMPAIRMENT

This book began with an explication of the key idea that disability studies as a field of inquiry has broadly come to agreement on issues of impairment. Whether through the assignment of interventions to embodied incapacities and inadequacies writ large, or by the application of "medical model" diagnoses of pathologized states, impairment is left on the other side of a boundary. This strategic walling off of impairment from scholarly examination in disability studies has been largely accomplished through the excise of medical terminology. For instance, Leeds University's internationally influential journal *Disability and Society* has a language policy now undergoing its third editorial board revision ("Editorial on Language Policy"). Just the fact that the language policy has already been revised three times in the relatively short life of the journal says something about the contingent nature of language and those bodies it intends to reference. The current "Editorial on Language Policy" explains that submissions organized around concepts of "impairment" run the risk of offensiveness if steeped in the empiricism of medical language: "Firstly, we will not publish articles containing offensive language, even if these words are based on medical or diagnostic classification" ("Editorial on Language Policy"). By taking this position, *Disability and Society* openly installs a filtering mechanism on articles as preemptive qualification of its criteria for publication consideration.[1]

Tom Shakespeare points out that even the distinction between "people with disabilities" (a predominantly U.S. vocabulary) and "disabled people" (the U.K. preferred term) has increasingly become a language litmus test in the application of a "strong social model" assessment of progressive disability research (6). The prohibition on medical and "medicalized" language also factors into canon building, or, perhaps even more effectively, the parsing down of the field to one key book. As one of the field's key contributors claims, all one needs for disability studies to occur is one book, like Mao's little red book, Mike Oliver's *The Politics of Disablement* (Barnes 580). Consequently, one scholar's formulations of social disablement help to maintain a degree of coherence for a discipline that also becomes a matter of identity-exclusions. Witness, for instance, Jenny Morris's influential *Pride against Prejudice*, which adds women into the mix of identity-based inclusive orthodoxies disability studies must promote as a totalizing solution to a socially produced exclusivity.

Nonetheless, disability studies scholarship continues to tug at the impaired body/social model divide for more than a decade now (Thomas, *Female Forms*, 1999; Shildrick, *Leaky Bodies*, 1999; Finkelstein, "Social Model Repossessed," 2001; Shildrick, *Embodying the Monster*, 2002; McRuer, *Crip Theory*, 2010; Mitchell and Snyder, *Narrative Prosthesis*, 2000; Snyder and Mitchell, *Cultural Locations*, 2006; Shildrick, *Dangerous Discourses*, 2012; McRuer and Mollow, *Sex and Disability*, 2012; Kafer, *Feminist Queer Crip*, 2013). Importantly, disability studies still probes the ways that "medical discourse" sediments stigma through the institution of impairing categories; but new work also shows how medicine can neither grasp the social predicaments of disabled persons nor nuance its own universalist account of conditions sufficiently. Myriad forays into the minefield of medical language continue to occur in order to better assess its elisions, inaccuracies, and conscious exclusions. While editing the five-volume international *Encyclopedia of Disability* the editorial team purposefully sought out scholars diagnosed with particular conditions to write entries that might best explain their bodily presentation in the world (Albrecht et al.). In many instances such "treatments" served as correctives to the extant medical catalog in that authors sought to be attentive to the misprisions of medicine and to the relative lack of overlap most disabled people experience even when sharing a diagnostic label.

Or, if medicine, indeed, does understand many major "vital" issues (as bioethics puts it) confronted by disabled people such as access to "skilled nursing" at home (i.e., attendant care), and/or "assistive tech" (i.e., ways to navigate marginally accessible environments), it is limited in the kinds of interventions it can undertake to correct such exclusions. Altering bodies rather than environments operates as the only point of entry in what we referred to in chapter 1 as "professions of control." Witness the disastrous Ashley X case in the northwest state of Washington, where surgeons used techniques that stunted the development of secondary sexual characteristics in order to compensate for the difficulties of moving and caring for the growing body of a disabled girl with invasive surgeries. And this form of disastrous intervention, of course, was implemented with full approval of the hospital's institutional review board and bioethics review board (Kafer, *Feminist Queer Crip* 49).

Where contemporary scholarship discusses reappropriation of the terms of oppression, or trades in artful means for evading pervasive structures of stigma, some disability studies "body talk" (including our own work in this mix) dares to name diagnoses or conditions as something other than forms of medical false consciousness. One key goal of critical materialist analyses is to research the histories and experiences that attend diagnostic etiologies in order to create pragmatic knowledge in methods that often arrive at one's bedside under emergency conditions, much akin to psychiatric survivor movements from the sixties (Lewis 124, Price 299).

Perhaps it is time to return to the scholarly suppressed topic of impairment in parallel to what Robert McRuer pointedly asks of the limits of disability identity models: "Can we at this point begin to trace the limits of the 'new group awareness' [i.e., disability identity politics], especially as that awareness is not simply dismissed but taken seriously, noticed, and utilized by state and market? How does 'the group' grapple with those figures who do not, or cannot, or will never 'constitute themselves as a minority identity?'" ("Disability Nationalism" 172). In making this pointed commentary McRuer asks us to grow more skeptical about the omissions, exclusions, and ways in which we normalize disability in a neoliberal market that fetishizes some differences while continuing to spurn an array of other ways of being in peripheral embodiments. As we've attempted to demonstrate throughout *The Biopolitics of Disability*, the effort to take seriously the situation of disability as subject to historical shifts is to assist in the work of imagining new normative concepts of difference operating in schemes of American exceptionalism (i.e., ablenationalism) around the globe. For instance, McRuer's recent essay coauthored with Julie Passanante Elman on "the gift of mobility" provides an important example of U.S. missionary wheelchair groups who cite technological abundance as a hallmark of American health care supports and, at the same time, support socially regressive campaigns against the legality of gay relations in non-Western contexts.

In this chapter we would like to risk a further extension of nonnormative positivist methodology through undertaking an analysis of groups that might openly eschew the moniker of "disability" in the name of single-impairment constituencies. We will refer to these communities that largely enact their efforts through social media worlds of non-disability-identified communications as patient expert groups (or PEGs). PEGs provide an important example of that which we historicized in chapter 1 as neoliberal identity efforts that result, in part, from the shift in early twentieth-century conceptions of congenital defects burdensome upon social resources (eugenics) to a demographic-based belief in populations as potentially rich veins of wealth and health (biopolitics). While this historical dynamic may at first seem to underwrite a dramatic improvement (and we don't wish to rule this out), our concern here will be with the ways in which recent web feedback loops serve to fashion medical subjectivities particular to new arenas of for-profit medicine in an age of biopolitics.

SINGLE-CONDITION USER GROUPS

In *The Politics of Life Itself*, Nikolas Rose defines biopolitics as "concerned with our growing capacities to control, manage, engineer, reshape, and modulate the very vital capacities of human beings as living creatures" (3). PEGs play a key role in the cultivation of health-care-related interactive systems in that they encourage discourse across social, national, and professional lines of knowledge. On these websites one is likely to read comments made by a range of participants such as parents, advocates, physicians, researchers, industry entrepreneurs, social organizers, and, increasingly, people occupying the peripheral embodiments in question. While the latter participants are still underrepresented within these web-based groups, they make an increased presence in the discourse that comprises PEG conversations.

The disruption that inevitably attends the entry of people with impairments into their treatment discussion groups proves significant. Particularly in that these "open forums" have carried on for so long without them. In most cases the crip/queer bodies discussed are too young at the initiation of exchanges concerning the particularities of their nonnormative anatomies and the inadequacy of treatment regimes necessary to their survival. Thus, the primary conversants have been parents, advocates, state-appointed guardians, physicians, nurses, and other professionals in medical, pharmaceutical, and disability research fields. The specific vectors of this virtual demographic profoundly shape the on-line conversations that occur.

Consequently, the arrival of new generations of adults who have survived these diagnostically hazardous conditions increasingly strains the conversation by complicating both the propensity toward overly sentimental, pathos-ridden ideas of caregivers and the unduly traumatic—often life-threatening—ideas of medical personnel alike. In fact, one of the interesting aspects of studying PEG conversations is the ways in a more productive, nonnormative concept of disability emerges and catalyzes change in multiple directions. People with impairments are in some ways more likely to be lurkers on PEG blog sites where parents, caregivers, physicians, and researchers trade information about experiences with complex (often rare) disorders. The social network groups continue to imagine their audiences as possessing primarily essentialized Western normative identities such as Caucasian, First World, heterosexual, contingently middle-class parents who have recently given birth to children with rare anomalous body types. Who wouldn't want to listen in on a conversation about their bodies between those with so much invested in them? And yet embodiment itself is its own knowledge system, and the entrance of adult viewpoints from survivors changes the terms from one of bodies without subjectivities to those seeking to actively fashion subjectivities on behalf of others like and unlike themselves. Importantly, PEG discussion groups move conversations from more static concepts of impairment and appropriate surgical/chemical/curative interventions (an admittedly urgent topic in most of these scenarios) to an investigation of nonnormative ways of being in the world with disability. It is in this way that PEGs often lead to the fashioning of an alternative crip/queer politics worthy of note for disability studies.

A FEW WORDS ABOUT METHODOLOGY

In the interests of full disclosure let us explain that we have enrolled and participated in several PEGs since the mid-1990s, when our daughter, Emma, was born with esophageal atresia (EA/TEF is the primary PEG group we will be discussing as our lead case study in this chapter). The offshoot of efforts to effectively treat her primary condition (EATF) surgically likely resulted in her development of cerebral palsy and blindness. Since that initial enrollment, which coincided with the group's first newsletter, we have read more than six thousand web entries from more than four thousand people. Of those postings, a few dozen have been contributed by individuals who self-identify as post-esophageal atresia (i.e., living with the condition themselves). An equal amount of time has been spent perusing and contributing to EA/TEF's sister site in the U.K. called TOFS—esophageal is spelled with an "o" rather than an "e" in the U.K. The name also refers to the science fiction context represented by green-skinned humanoids from the planet Tof in *Star Wars*.

Over the duration of their development the sites have gone from snail mail newsletters to email exchange groups to formal listserv communities with rigorous intake methods and multiple forums into which one may drill down through a deepening archive of discussion holdings, commentaries, and subject areas (both professional and nonprofessional). The PEGs certainly give tangible proof to Nikolas Rose's contention that as medical citizens within neoliberal biopolitics we are expected to take active control of our health management regimes to a greater extent than in any time in history (154). This active control taking health represents the double-edged sword of biopolitics and results in the desperate necessity of participating in funding initiatives on behalf of physicians and researchers to provide the missing profit motive for future investigations of potential medical treatments for members of rare condition groups.

IS THERE AN OPPRESSION TO HAVING TO MANAGE YOUR BIOLOGY?

A substantive portion of Rose's research in *The Politics of Life Itself* involves an assessment of the activities of patient organizations such those discussed here. By and large, Rose finds such gatherings regrettably "amateurish" in that they control the activities of professional and policy experts by calling attention—and, therefore, resources—to the abandoned shores of their impairment group's need for expert health care provision. His analysis, to some extent, resonates with the misgivings of liberal mindsets bemoaning the loss of neutral governmental institutions to special interest groups. Special interests or not, such activities attempt to place even the rarest disorders on the map of biomedicine's active concerns—Rose's term for profit-based intervention efforts led by Big Pharma ever in search of new conditions to conquer or, at least, mask with ever proliferating medications (often failed drugs developed on behalf of some other disorder group now seeking legal remuneration—more on this development at chapter's end).

Just a few cautionary words about long-standing disability studies concerns: within contexts such as PEGs, where medical information is traded in significant quantities, promotion of "cures" is, at times, uncomfortably rampant. However, the forums tend to operate as a kind of historical anachronism; some persist from an earlier, more "naive" medicalized era of disability despite the fact that few believe in the promise of rewriting the biological basis of nonnormate organisms to any substantive degree any more. There is a palpable diminishment of hope in cures-to-come despite the persistence of discussions that involve the advent of potential miracle cures in the near future. One gets the sense that cure-based talk has become a strategy of PEGs to keep medical practitioners invested in the logic of medical break-through and the potential of innovating signature treatments for rare conditions. PEGs strategically deploy "cure talk" in order to keep physicians and researchers engaged and online, so to speak. Significantly, that which Rose bemoans most fiercely is a historical shift that now makes everyone responsible for one's own biological well-being in a way that had not been previously recognized.

However, we would argue that this is exactly where generations of disabled people have found themselves for decades: that is, in an active relation to the management of their bodies and the attendant social expectations of body management regimes that follow. If Rose behaves nostalgically for an era that was less so for a majority of people, then he primarily avows the privilege of avoiding this relation to one's body as the foundational experience of normative embodiment (in other words this prior disinterest is an expression of the privilege of ableism itself). In this sense Rose's concern is primarily with the arrival of a new, expansive continuum threatening to erupt between and across bodies based on new marketing opportunities to consume products geared to alleviate symptoms compelling the attentions of the individuals they afflict. We share this concern but not the suddenness and "amateur" participation that Rose laments.

Consequently, our goal here is less "pessimistic" than Rose's with regard to the role of PEGs (although we spend some time discussing their inevitable limitations) in that they may assist new disability materialisms in realizing a desirable yet, at least to this point in time, largely elusive objective in disability studies proper: namely that bodies exist on a continuum of variation with each other and that it is an act of culture that divides them into categories of privileged likeness and marginalized pathology. Such arguments develop in the work of Lennard Davis with regards to "dismodernism" and Nichols Watson and Tom Shakespeare's arguments regarding the need for a new model of embodied ontology (*Bending Over Backwards* 232; "Social Model" 27). As explained earlier we disagree with positions advanced by Davis, Watson, Shakespeare, and others that argue for a more general recognition that "we are all disabled" as a substantive solution to the marginalization of people with disabilities. In further explaining this

disagreement here it helps us to analyze the developments in historical discourses characteristic of PEG exchanges within neoliberalism's prolific and
proliferating cyber treatment for-profit networks.

Likewise, we also want to interrogate the premises of medical universalism that continues to regressively seek out strict parameters with respect
to disorder classifications while producing concepts of disability that are
ahistorical and not culturally specific. We believe that PEGs attack this
ruse of professional rationality through their emphasis on multiplicity of
experience amid disorder—the individuated nature of each person's experience of "impairment effects" (i.e., difficult bodily, cognitive, and sensory
topographies)—although we would argue that the net result is inevitably
a problem of excess individuation (allow us to return to this topic near our
conclusion). We conclude with a discussion of an as yet unrecognized potential of collaborative research interventions pursued by PEGs in what we
refer to in chapter 4 as "the politics of atypicality."

PATIENT EXPERT GROUPS: RECONSTRUCTING THE MEDICAL FEEDBACK LOOP

In keeping with our mutually constitutive theme in *The Biopolitics of Disability* of feedback loops between disability and neoliberalism, our study takes
up questions of the neoliberal state and its relation to an increasingly anarchic medical market. In doing so, we assess the growing influence exerted
by PEGs on the direction of research and the resourcing of socially based
supports. Finally, we seek to grapple with those who exist on the fringes of
recognizing themselves as belonging to the marginal identity group marked
as *disability*. Specifically we probe developments in the two-decade or longer
formation of single-condition user groups on the Web as they further nuance medical concepts of bodies different from normative concepts of embodiment. In articulating this formulation of difference PEGs participate
in the creation of discursive communities that often keep those occupying
peripheral embodiments from disastrous surgeries or opportunistically ig-
norant of available technologies.

As identified earlier, our primary case studies include two particular social media groups formed around the biopolitical transfer of information regarding surgical interventions and maintenance for those born with unique
organ forms and missing internal parts. These discussions are examined

largely with respect to discussions about the digestive system among those who participate in the group, EA/TEF (based in the United States) and the U.K. group that names itself TOFS. Both groups have participated in the policy-influencing practices of medically based web groups seeking to promote the training of physicians in corrective surgeries and directing research funds toward potential genetic interventions such as gene replacement or combinatory genetic coding interventions. Esophageal atresia and other birth syndromes of the thirty-fourth day of cell division all stubbornly lack, at least if one is a genetic counselor, evidence of genetic transmission or any consistent code across subjects. Likely this "failure of cell division is caused by exposure to environmental toxins (such as lead, mercury, or pesticide run-off). Some have survived across history with marvelous surgeries (performed on internally "monstrous" bodies) such as a piece of colon or a plastic tube that can be healed into place and adopted as a surrogate conduit for the missing segment of an esophageal organ. One man on the U.K. listserv writes that he was fed by a g-tube directly into his stomach until the age of twelve, when he had a surgery that inserted a piece of colon from his throat to his stomach. He is now in his forties and when he eats he pushes food items down with his fingers if he needs to, because the mechanism lies close to his skin. In another instance a U.S. woman writes that she tries to treat her need for yearly esophageal dilations like going to the grocery store—a level of routinization that would only arrive as adult survivors came online and discussed their lives on the forum. In both cases adult survivors of EA/TEF or TOFS explain the management of anomalous bodies as individual predicaments of the postsurgery altered body. Consequently, these are not disability identifications in the usual sense, but rather exchanges among those who identity as persons with surgically adapted impairments.

This is not to say that EA/TEF is not a highly morbid condition. The one longitudinal study completed most recently and conducted in Finland found that there is approximately a 50 percent survival rate to the present. The study measured outcomes since the late 1960s when several kinds of esophageal prosthetic organs were becoming surgically standardized in surgical repair approaches. As surgeries performed by technical experimenters, the follow-up to any kind of filling the gap grows tedious and is left to the medically adapted subject, personal support networks, and less experienced medical practitioners outside of the key surgical power centers that specialize in such interventions.

This is one of the main reasons why PEGs have developed in such burgeoning numbers over the past two decades. As a result of these listservs, impairment-specific subjects can now chart their common predicaments in postsurgery altered bodies. Many participants list as many as forty to seventy dilations. Dilations involve a delicate process of widening the reconstructed esophageal organ at a site of stricture with various kinds of bougies or balloon dilators under anesthesia. Obviously such excessive reliance on emergency room visits, typically conducted under urgent situations of food impaction, makes post-EA/TEF creatures into extraordinary medical specimens in need of urgent surgical management throughout their lives.[2] The originators of these postsurgical lives are the surgeons, only a few recognized for hundreds of accomplished connected tissue interventions, and each comes replete with a personalized school of corrective techniques (the "Foker Technique" being most notable). A handful of surgeons are sought after from Leibniz to Madagascar, and often travel to various global outposts to share techniques. They travel to patients who are on g-tubes in many different settings where active secretion management with twenty-four-hour suctioning takes them to the edge of viability.

We might argue that such medical missionary-like efforts continue to promote First World solutions in Third World contexts—a kind of medical colonialism and failure to attend to the specificities of local contexts could be charged in this case. Yet, in a strange twist, we find that non–First World interventions—that is, those practiced for the convenience of medical industry calculations of cost efficiency and not on behalf of the viability of the patient beyond the acute medical period—have followed physicians back to resource strained health care systems in the United States and U.K. In the case of EA/TEF, for example, a procedure called a "stomach pull-up" is designed to pull the stomach into the chest cavity to bypass the lower esophagus. A surgeon who recommends a more patient-innovative approach of "growing the ends together" comments wryly, "You got a third world repair in a first world clinic." Reportedly, the stomach pull-up repair is less labor intensive for physicians, all relatively speaking, but "experimental" in regard to lifespan: the guiding assumption is that connecting esophageal tissue to itself by placing it under traction for several months while the ends grow together and, eventually, overlap is the best surgical solution. This intervention is known as the "Foker Technique" and is practiced as the only acceptable surgical intervention to correct EATF at hospitals such as the EAT program at Boston Children's Hospital. (The National Center for Esophageal Atresia repair can be found at http://www.childrenshospital.org/clinicalservices/Site2807/mainpageS2807P16.htm).

Because the intervention and maintenance of these conditions proves so complex, the EA/TEF and TOFs organizations provide support for those undergoing treatment; medical and social advice for survival with surgically altered anatomies; clinical and experiential bases for comparison of post-surgical viability; stresses on individual/survivor psychologies as secondary conditions to be recognized and treated/managed; ways in which others have successfully networked support on behalf of funding and assistance in their home communities; putting brakes on procedures and techniques that are now widely recognized as unsuccessful in treating the anomalous anatomies characteristic of those occupying peripheral embodiments, as well as appropriate foods and eating techniques for those with impaired motility. In other words, the EA/TEF and TOFS networks have become their own medical sites of expertise guiding patients, parents, and other invested individuals in advice largely unavailable at their local hospitals or neighborhood medical clinics. Within neoliberal for-profit medicine, surgeries for repairing rare disorders are increasingly becoming signature events wherein a hospital practices one particular intervention even as the evidence mounts that such repairs are often incommensurable with quality of life or organismic survivability.

MEDICAL SUBCULTURES AND NEED FOR STRUCTURES OF COHERENCE

In these ways, then, TOFS and EA/TEF actively advocate within medical and policy systems for a dampening of acceptable expendability factors related to the disease. PEGs represent neoliberal survivor groups seeking to assist others in the avoidance of threats not only by collecting group information on surgical corrections but through operating as a subculture seeking to establish their own histories, myths, and structures of coherence. Each member intake involves schooling in the ways in which various individuals and groups have managed their own bodies with altered medical anatomies. The primary danger in failing to gain access to appropriate corrective measures—outside of inadequately trained surgeons—involves entering a vortex of ahistoricity regarding acceptable surgical solutions and postsurgical navigations of normative social orders. In this void the EA/TEF body is fully subject to the limits of medical knowledge and the ideology informing medical options provided in any given nation, region, or community.

A common communication arriving on the website involves the setting of a mother (often sans father) crying at her child's bedside and blogging about how she has been given an ultimatum that, by morning, she must decide what surgical procedure to undertake. Within two hours seventeen responses are posted, promoting best options for surgical choices and some added details not mentioned in the "doctors' comments," particularly regarding prognosis in postsurgical life. The EA/TEF social media world operates as a virtual advocacy network, rapidly filling in visitors on the merits and demerits of various treatment approaches, likely outcomes, and futurity. In other words, the blog sites are populated by "biopolitical" creatures through and through, without the funds, numbers, organizational efforts, or collective political clout akin to earlier grassroots HIV advocacy communities seeking to direct the most effective, radical care routines. They recognize themselves, instead, as competing for resources and attention in the larger sphere of health care systems while offering community recognition at the individual level. Sometimes this grassroots intervention effort merely includes broadcasting highly unique, uniquely strange, formulas for thinking about urgent medical dilemmas across global boundaries.

Because they are quasi-medicalized, the listservs require preregistration as part of the intake method wherein those who seek to join reveal a detailed, intensive medical history characteristic of the disorder group. The intake involves an "amateur" (i.e., not officially sanctioned) version of the longitudinal study in that it seeks to gather information about the condition group one individual at a time while operating across the semipermeable national boundaries characteristic of neoliberalism. The collection effort now spans a history of nearly four decades and codes data systematically in order to offset the failure of medical collection systems (the original surgical techniques were developed in the 1950s for esophageal cancer survivors and those who had ingested bleach and other toxic substances that destroyed esophageal tissue lining). This effort provides opportunities to identify patterns—such as the critical coupling of Nissen fundoplications with esophageal correction techniques to dissipate painful reflux—that serve the group as it actively fashions a medical history no one else is documenting.

Like other subcultures the PEGs do not necessarily challenge medical orthodoxies of treatment regimes; they are not overtly political animals in this sense. Instead they work at the personal narrative level actively fashioning attitudes of acceptance in their sharing of information for individuals who find themselves occupying relatively inflexible medical and social systems. They do not, for instance, denigrate particular kinds of surgeries overtly (this is more likely accomplished offsite across exchanges of personal emails). Instead, individuals who have had the surgery in question talk about their lives, the obstacles encountered, the medical procedures undertaken, what worked and what didn't, and the highly individualized techniques for managing their postcorrective bodies. The PEG commentaries "massage" data, in other words, on behalf of incoming participants in order to direct a quick, yet nuanced understanding of medical and nonmedical options. Such contrasts and comparisons are widely unavailable within neoliberal medical domains pushing marquee interventions on behalf of larger profit-taking goals.

Because the stakes are so high, the prevalence of the condition often misidentified as relatively small in numbers (this is not the case due to the fact that incidence of this likely environmental mutation is identified on the TOFS site occurs in 1 in 3,500 births), and the corrective techniques hoarded in a handful of medical power centers largely in the United States, the U.K., and France. One finds a universe operating on these website discussions comprised predominantly of surgeon animals, caretakers, and survivor creatures. The surgeons actively troll in order to seek out life forms for which they can take responsibility while also padding hospital coffers based on exorbitantly expensive intervention regimes; and survivor creatures that feel the originality of actively maintaining their singular embodiment status as a kind of unrecognized labor in active mutation management schemes. Whereas most surgeon animals seek out the opportunity to perform these high-risk/high-prestige surgeries, adequate follow-up care is difficult to come by. The social media landscapes created by EA/TEF and TOFS provide a regimen of living—not with anomaly—but, rather, with medically altered bodies.

EA/TEF: THE ARTIFICIAL JOIN OF THE SOCIAL AND THE BIOLOGICAL

The EATF/TOFs groups have grown so expansive in their mediation efforts to connect policymakers, medical professionals, chemical entrepreneurs, people with pre- and postaltered bodies, and parents and caregivers, they now hold international conferences where stakeholders meet up and discuss their experiences. The TOFS group had a meet-up in October 2010, for instance, that included, for the first time, presentations by people with medically altered bodies that have survived into adulthood. The EA/TEF group held its first international collective meeting in Paris during May 2010. At the EA/TEF gathering all stakeholders in attendance were included in the social networking part of the meeting and in the medical panel discussions as audience members, but primary speaking roles were largely reserved for the professional practitioners—particularly the surgeons discussing their corrective intervention techniques and histories. The gatherings are explicitly identified as necessary for the prolongation of variable human lives represented by medically defined and socially misunderstood bodies.

Whereas most subcultures have been described as traveling the circuit from resistance to incorporation, PEGs tend to invert this formula by going from participants and promoters of dominant industries such as charity and medicine to internal destabilizers of these systems (Hebdige 130). PEGs ultimately become critics of less successful treatment regimes and lead a wave of skepticism that ultimately gets incorporated into new research models challenging some aspects of the medical status quo. They also become equivalents to breakaway republics as they provide alternative forums for critiquing the inadequacies of host organizations such as the Muscular Dystrophy Association (MDA) or hospitals specializing in less viable surgical corrections. They percolate resistance from a standpoint of the incorporated by cultivating forms of information dissemination that trouble biopolitical normative acceptance of mortality rates as a natural outgrowth of the will to correct. Likewise, the formula for information-based exchanges shifts. Whereas the majority of PEGs began by promoting the feasibility of interventions and the necessity of seeing value in complex medically mediated lives, they have increasingly become arbiters of quality of life with regard to one intervention over another. PEGs discover themselves providing support for new consumers (largely parents but increasingly surgical survivors) by negotiating histories of techniques and avenues for extracting resource pools that remain largely hidden.

What is particularly unique about the operations of these PEGs—they are atypical of other similar social media formations—is that they have all bypassed, to one degree or another, national charity systems by going "international" and collecting together demographic information on single members of the disorder group at a global scale. This massive medical enrollment effort has been undertaken to enhance the visibility of rare disease populations—that is, to gain the numbers necessary to influence government policy and research laboratories to direct resources on behalf of a viable medical market constituency. Perhaps the most worrisome feature of neoliberal healthcare orders is not that one must manage a medicalized subjectivity, as Rose argues, but rather that one must compete to make a disorder group appear visible (and therefore fundable) in order to be worthy of an intervention that may keep one alive. In other words, PEGs, in the most pointed neoliberal sense, understand that the endgame is the necessity of fashioning themselves into a demand-based market for potential treatments. The absence of such treatments is the direct outgrowth of an earlier history of eugenics-based practices where EA/TEF and other digestive anomalies (such as colonic blockages) were considered medical interventions unworthy because they often occur in tandem with other highly stigmatized differences such as Down syndrome (Bérubé 52).

Perhaps even more significantly, in making the case for the evaluative weighing of surgical interventions and follow-up care routines, PEGs have infiltrated the perspectives of caretakers and adults with rare disorders into the professional ruminations of medical practitioners and research domains. It is now almost a commonplace that surgeons tip their surgical caps to the superior knowledge of the disorder held by parents, caretakers, and increasingly, the patients themselves. What prompts this more person-centered landscape to take shape is the ways in which rare disorders command the necessity for narratives of individual creativity and productive management of conditions little known to most medical professionals beyond stainless steel-lined surgical walls. While each disorder congregates around a few specialists skilled enough in treating and advising others on appropriate medical decision-making, participants present themselves as amateur, yet knowledgeable, practitioners of a life. While medical experts have evolved a limited set of interventions that work (and advise members as to those that do not), PEGs excel in the nuances of particular strategies to live with anomalous bodies in the world regardless of correction method and associated complications. They operate in ways akin to support networks for transgender individuals or those in psychiatric survivor groups in that a vast array options are open and open support is key to group participation because postsurgical life is difficult enough no matter what route one undertakes to get there (Butler 6, Lewis 121–122).

The goals here are multifaceted in that the groups have advocated for a variety of initiatives over the past decade including (1) standards of care to lessen the rampant nature of medical experimentation bequeathed from previous ages when no interventions were yet available; (2) a developed second-opinion network where those in search of treatments may tell their stories of medical mayhem and postsurgical questioning and/or the solicitation of pragmatic advice—usually responses pile up within a matter of hours from professionals and nonprofessionals alike; (3) an aggressive advocacy network that tells people where to go and what to do in order to realize their own and their loved one's sustainability; (4) active advocacy roles involve PEGs in policy debates wherein governments are directed toward funding groups and methods that prove most promising in the eyes of those impacted by the condition; finally, (5) entrepreneurial ventures by PEGs that involve pooling limited financial resources to purchase stock in genetic engineering therapies and therapeutic correction techniques in which they have a financial, medical, and developmental stake. In this way PEGs keep some of the credit and profit for their informal, unauthorized expertise for the articulation of treatment regimes particular to impairments of a peculiarly complex order such as EA/TEF.

Increasingly PEGs have established themselves in roles as unremunerated, yet increasingly effective, external assessment organizations who critique the degree of success achieved by private and publicly financed operations claiming to benefit the target population. They critique inappropriately pathologizing language employed by charities and medical practioners alike, and assess whether multi-billion-dollar middle-man organizations provide a meaningful level of support to the active upkeep of anomalous lives. For instance, MDA finds itself opening and closing down portals because PEG participants insist on disclosing the meager nature of the organization's allotment of individual support ($500/year toward supplies and repairs of assistive technology per person) for those it claims to help.[3] In these ways impairment correction, maintenance, and social viability all serve as the springboards for highly politicized organizations disclaiming their politics in the name of celebrating the value of devoting resources to an ever increasing pool of variable human lives now referred to as the bearers of "rare diseases" (more on this in a moment during our closing reflections).

Lives lived for years within the intensive apparatus and protocols of highly technological medical systems are not akin to concepts of "bare life" wherein one is subject to the vulnerabilities of inadequate material resources and excessive exposure. Instead we might think of these addendums to neoliberal forms of life as third-party payer consumers—that is, those who wield few monetary resources of their own but exist in a bureaucratic limbo between the high-stakes negotiations of profit-oriented medical, technological, pharmaceutical, and insurance markets. They are bodies turned into anomalous biologies qualified (and de-qualified) as available for lucrative research-based markets and medical intervention efforts without an identifiable capacity for direct consumption purchasable by those requiring the services. In other words, as we analyzed in chapter 1 regarding disabled people as medical consumers who lack purchasing power, the membership of the PEGs is an entirely new order of life within neoliberal, late capitalist health care orders.

MISUNDERSTOOD BODIES

Bodies that come into being in the time of neoliberalism are, by definition, historicized materialities marked by changing intervention techniques and experimentation-now-turned-misunderstood-anomaly. The active management of insufficient surgeries has developed into an inexhaustible thread of suggestions for surviving, first, the condition and, later, the correction. People with colonic interpositions, stomach pull-ups, or primary anastomoses performed without prerepair traction to encourage tissue growth write in to discuss their personal methods for moving food through tortuous esophagi with significantly impaired motility.

All of this activity in the informal domains of medical informatics is a signpost for neoliberal assumptions involving the privatization of health care as states slough off more nationalizing social options onto privatized medical initiatives while simultaneously increasing governmental research investments. As a result, PEGs form at the intersection of the historical failure of charity markets to adequately distribute funding to their namesake constituencies and late capitalist medicine on the lookout for profitable bodies in need of high-upkeep regimens. The EA/TEF PEGs have evolved from formerly impossible interventions to bodies representing competitive opportunities for expansive insurance revenues. As such, these particular neoliberal anomalous bodies (and those made responsible for caring for them) now find themselves in a position of having to actively manage their own pursuits of well-being as an entrepreneurial enterprise as well as performing the life-sustaining tactics of everyday living.

PEGs participate, albeit reluctantly at first, in this historical outcome (this is part of the problem) by participating in medical research initiatives as cultural locations of disability that have become increasingly available to experimental research and treatment groups. One can find PEG discussions wherein individuals are encouraged to take up their own local charity campaign efforts to accomplish a desirable surgical intervention or gain access to an expensive piece of assistive technology not covered by their insurance, or they are led to pursue active counting efforts regarding real-time condition holders around the world that might add up to enough mass to galvanize future research and the often overlooked training efforts subtended by technical innovation practices.

One visible outcome of massification initiatives involves the medical collection effort managed in Paris by the French Ministry of Health and INSERM (a Parisian medical research organization) called, appropriately, Orphanet. Orphanet is a database of rare diseases and orphan drugs seeking to connect amorphous biological conditions with pharmaceutical and genetic treatments in need of suitable bodies with which to interact. The site's authors identify rare diseases as those biological phenomena impacting 1 in 2,000 biologies or less with regard to prevalence (EA/TEF is listed as one of them despite exceeding the maximum quantity demarcation of rare conditions by 1,500 births). Orphan drugs are those medicines granted status as potentially therapeutic for the treatment of rare diseases before they have been tested in humans. Currently, thirty-six countries participate and nearly six thousand rare diseases are identified and described on the site. Articles are written in English and translated across six languages.

The stated goal of the project is "to gather, manage, and increase surveillance" of rare diseases that are underresourced as health concerns in Europe and around the world. Users of the site include professionals (who account for half of an average of 500,000 hits per month), patients and families (who account for another third of all hits), and journalists, policymakers, teachers, students, and other interested persons. The database is primarily situated in a pathology-oriented context in that it includes encyclopedic entries about rare diseases as expressions of congenital malformation, clinical treatment domains, research trials, and as having failed to obtain a match with an orphan drug. Approximately one-sixth of the site includes social-supports-based information such as connecting interested surfers of Orphanet with patient support groups or PEGs and local advocacy initiatives in participant countries.

While there is much to say about this development, let us quickly explain that Orphanet operates as a rather deadpan, electronic, systemic, and interactive neoliberal organism wherein one can gain access to a great deal of information about relatively singular conditions (what the website refers to as "rare diseases (orphans)"). The taxonomy mission on display through Orphanet strains any user's sense of a coherent, operative concept of pathology as a guiding rubric of rationally organized variant biologies. In fact, what one comes away with is the productively failing concept of normative biology; alternative bodies are all we have and Orphanet may prove productive in failing as a last-ditch attempt to work the binary of the normal and pathological into a working dichotomy. Pathology is simply growing too nuanced, multivalent, and divergent to operate as the alternative to a universally undifferentiated norm.

SPECIFYING DEBILITY IN THE SPACE OF ANONYMITY

While one could argue that even in their emphasis upon variation within the condition group PEGs are, by their chosen singularity, overindividuated and therefore opposed to the foundational disability studies emphasis on those bound by shared stigma rather than individuated anomaly. Yet what these collective longitudinal gathering efforts show is that wherein identity-based collectivities inevitably sort themselves around essentializing criteria of bounded belonging, the bringing of new bodies into being entails, perhaps, an even more expansive potential. In her book *Mad for Foucault: Rethinking the Foundations of Queer Theory*, Lynne Huffer argues in favor of a more radical Foucauldian objective in our formulations on the politics of subjectivization. Rather than inserting new, progressive norms in place of old norms, as is the inevitable objective of neoliberal identity-based politics, Huffer urges queer theorists to follow a more Deleuzian reading of Foucault in efforts to destabilize the concept of norms all together: "Specifically, the Deleuzian rethinking of the subject in Foucault involves a radical intervention into the logic of inside and outside—me and not-me, subject and object—that normally guides us in our conception of ourselves as entities in a world" (30). Whereas the ostensible objective of PEGs and Orphanet is to individuate each rare disease classification (and each rare disease holder) within its own medical and social specificity, the obverse result is taking shape: a movement into a form of particularity that creates an ever cascading plethora of bodies, types, kinds, and experiences.

Rather than isolate voices in their narrative particularity, these efforts result in losing voices into the ether of the infinite variations comprising human embodiment. This consequent chaos has a productive potential, however, in that it serves as a force that can undo norms rather than simply expand them. Huffer explains that radical politics hinges upon an arrival at anonymity rather than the specialization of identity as a point from which

> to think of the queer [or disabled] subject as an atmosphere . . . to move the subject away from himself (or his dialectical negation) toward the place of anonymity that is the promise of the subject's undoing. This promise of anonymity is, again, a historical problem. "In the past, the problem for the one who wrote was to pull himself out of the anonymity of all; in our time, it is to erase one's own name, to come to lodge one's voice in the great anonymous murmur of discourses which are pronounced." That move toward anonymity—the disappearance of the subject—constitutes for Foucault a move away from rationalist judgment toward the coextensive multiplication of forms of existence. (117)

Huffer's important argument here is not to be mistaken for a rights-based universalizing homogenization of identity subjects as in Davis's formulation of "dismodernism." Instead she aims to cultivate higher order recognition at the level of the social wherein mutability becomes an order to reckoning with human animals as indeterminate forms of becoming. The "disappearance of the subject" in this particularly Foucauldian turn results in a step away from the sedimented layers of historical othering attendant in concepts of identity as excessive deviance from normative universals. Thus, rather than the anonymity of the rights-based subject as growing more and more akin to its normative able-bodied other, a nonnormative positivist understanding of crip/queer bodies would entail further levels of differentiation while simultaneously producing a greater respect for variation as synonymous with unfolding understandings of embodiment.

Orphanet's increasingly global incorporation effort on behalf of rare disease types, research laboratories, orphan drug companies, and patient expert groups might be described in these very terms as the lodging of "one's voice in the great anonymous murmur of discourses which are pronounced." It is the digitized encyclopedic movement toward a space of anonymity wherein the result is the counterintuitive objective of single-condition group collection efforts. Rather than resolution into further specification and pathological differentiation, the expansion and consequent massification of PEGS and other medicalized collectivities threatens to make notions of identity in shared stigma implode as a viable collective foundation for more bounded identity-based efforts.

Instead, the neoliberal "grasping of life at its biological roots" (Hardt and Negri, *Empire* 29) brings forth so much awareness of "debility" that disability itself no longer holds as a coherent placement of those members of the excessively stigmatized. As Orphanet pursues its medical collection efforts on behalf of singular condition groups, normative medical registers of pathology strain under the proliferation of so many multiplicities of ab-normalcy (or, what we might some day call *being*). This, as we find in queer theorist Lee Edelman's critique of liberalism in *No Future*, is an appropriate escape hatch for the empty premise of neoliberal inclusion, one in which the endless elasticity of minority models merely proposes to expand and make more tolerant existing norms rather than undoing them all together. This is a true politics of atypicality.

CONCLUSION: DESUBJECTIVATION AND THE PENDING COLLAPSE OF NORMATIVE BIOLOGY

We want to end on a point of culture: PEGs are increasingly providing van-tage points on what we might consider a primary goal of queer studies, as enunciated by Michael Warner, and needs to increasingly become recog-nized as a principle for disability studies: "bringing new bodies into being" through revelations of ways to creatively navigate an inaccessible world with a significantly stigmatized body (Warner, *Trouble with Normal* 12). Today, popular press magazines such as *New Mobility* show us neoliberal dead-ends of designer marketing of food tubes, mickeys, joysticks, and catheters as a new freedom for wheelchair lifestylers—fantasy and hypocrisy for crip/queer survivors.

In conclusion, there are at least three ways of understanding the out-put of PEGs as collaborative disability navigations of neoliberal health care disparities to this point in time: (1) as subcultural formations that are loosely affiliated networks of participants who share a relation to bodies so anomalous that the discussion of their complexities can be understood as "resistant" just by bringing a knowledge of more difference into the world (i.e., "bringing new bodies into being"); (2) as countercultural formations in that they consciously destabilize medical orthodoxies of classification sys-tems and turn normative intervention protocols into nonnormative biologies through the championing of values of human variation that have been previously consigned to what Mbembe refers to as the necropolitics of an age (40); and (3) as a movement on its way toward realizing a Deleuzian multiplicity of pluralities within classifications of medical pathology that are growing so expansive that the normative mold of ability and disability are starting to collapse under their own weight.

SEVEN

The Capacities of Incapacity in
Antinormative Novels of Embodiment

> This negative, "differential" notion (of madness as pathology) first appeared
> in the eighteenth century, to explain variations and diseases rather than
> adaptations and convergences.
>
> —MICHEL FOUCAULT, *THE HISTORY OF MADNESS* (385)

> I would tell all the stories I knew
> in which people went wrong
> but the nervous system
> was right all along
>
> —ADRIENNE RICH, "PIERROT LE FOU"

INTRODUCTION: NOVELISTIC
DESCENT WITH MODIFICATION

Coming on the heels of our assessment of a variety of nonnormative cultural
locations for exploring the participation of disabled persons within biopolitics, this chapter explores some alternative literary representational spaces
developing in post-1960s U.S. and U.K. literature. While in the previous
chapter we analyzed how single impairment user groups were being transformed by the perspectives of those living with surgically adapted bodies into
adulthood on blog sites, here we group contemporary novelistic approaches
to disability. These novels which we will refer to throughout as antinormative novels of embodiment, represent crip/queer bodies as productive difference in order to reveal ways to approach peripheral embodiment as what
Kevin Floyd describes as a "certain kind of skilled labor" (*Reification* 155).
Taken collectively these narratives provide a repertoire of tools to expose

examples of what Darwin called in *Origins of the Species* (1859) "descent with modification" (the random, mutating path of evolution that links all organisms to a shared evolutionary history of ancestral structures and potentially adaptive futures) (378). Antinormative novels of embodiment represent forms of narrative adaptation moving consciously away from traditions of representational deployments of disability as a metaphor of individual and/ or social collapse, as we analyze in *Narrative Prosthesis: Disability and the Dependencies of Discourse*. Here we want to build on our prior analyses of productive nonnormative filmic and internet forms by examining alternative neoliberal narrative spaces as allowing movement toward an alternative representational tradition of those living lives in peripheral embodiments.

Within the antinormative novel of embodiment plot turns increasingly rely on the revelation of the normative body's secreted "dysfunctionality," the perennial operations of embodiment that cover over in-built biological inefficiencies, disjunctures, weaknesses, and incapacities. In order to reverse the usual line of diagnosis imposed upon disabled bodies, these novels emphasize normalcy as reliant on a mechanistic adherence to scripts of pathology in other bodies to maintain fictive formulas of normative embodiment. Within embodied scripts of normativity the disabled body is culturally positioned as a derivative identity, secondary and inferior to norms of able-bodiedness.

Yet, while the normative body may emerge as little more than a cultural phantom of expectations, a historically reiterated and overvalued pattern of how bodies must do things and appear, within the antinormative novel disability is redeployed in the service of displacing hegemonic able-bodied norms. Within these plots the able-bodied hegemon—rendered sensible as an amalgam of median capacities and forged in the exclusionary space between dynamic bodies and normative architectures, aesthetics, and functionalities—emerges as a fetishized product of "bare life" while referencing disability as the dissonant expression of a distant kinship (the displacement of proximity from the norm suggested by our use of the phrase "peripheral embodiment"). Alternatively, the antinormative novel of embodiment explores disability as revelatory of variation's potential for innovation; and, in its wake, identifies normative embodiment as an impossible attainment of a body's smooth functioning to which post-Fordist strategies of neoliberal inclusionism stubbornly cling.

Throughout this chapter and as a follow-up to our critiques of inclusionist practices developed under neoliberal education (cripistemologies) in chapter 2, we will refer to the self-congratulatory emphasis of nationalist post-Fordist tolerance as representative of a specific set of tactics indicative of neoliberal representational forms. Neoliberalism advances economic rationalism into formerly noneconomic spheres; in doing so, as Wendy Brown explains, a "'mismanaged life' [such as disability] becomes a new mode of depoliticizing social and economic powers," one that blames individual insufficiencies rather than the inequalities of social conditions ("Neoliberalism" 42). If, as we have argued throughout this book, neoliberalism requires vigilance on behalf of full bodily capacitation, then disability serves as a key indicator of "bodies falling away from true"—a failure of personal upkeep to adequately maintain one's embodiment within an acceptable range of social norms of ableist comportment (Elkins, *Magic Kingdom* 223).

Here, then, and in the parlance of new disability materialisms we might say that within neoliberalism, disability operates in at least two distinct domains: (1) disability actively references the United States' claims to global exceptionalism—the inclusive adoption of policies toward disabled people as a sign of the nation's embrace of diversity in neoliberalism; and (2) antinormative novels of embodiment employ disability's radical potential to unseat traditional understandings of normalcy as subject integrity, cognitive coherency, and typical functionality. The first mode involves disability as a sign of neoliberalism's tolerance of difference (i.e., a rhetoric of inclusionism realized by claims to American exceptionalism); the second mode unveils *the capacities of incapacity* that disability embodies as a key strategy in the antinormative novel of embodiment's neomaterialist revelation of imperfection as a creative, biological force.

By identifying the novels under discussion here as "neomaterialist" or "immanent materialist," we seek to identify their formative role as part of a tradition of alternative thinking regarding the agency of materiality developing within neoliberalism but also hostile to its more reductive integrations (Braidotti 202; Connolly 179). Neomaterialist thought is sometimes characterized as a return of the body or a more materialist corporeality after the pervasive recourse to cultural agency found in the interpretations of social constructivist thought. Neomaterialism characterizes a threat to neoliberal concepts of tolerance for nonnormativity because, as Rosi Braidotti characterizes it, the reaction to "this trend has caused both the neoliberal and the neo-Kantian thinkers to be struck by high levels of anxiety about the sheer thinkability of the human future" (202).

In neomaterialism living matter becomes an agent in its own right rather than passively imprinted, inert space of matter within a hierarchically organized overvaluation of the human as a product of acculturation. Within neomaterialism corporeality (both human and nonhuman) becomes a subject rather than an object, and this alternative emphasis results in the rethinking of "a biocentered perspective (that) affects the very fiber and structure of social subjects" (Braidotti 201). While disability and impairment have been subject to imprisoning cultural concepts of inferiority, neomaterialisms reactivate the materiality of any form of differential embodiment as a potentially active, agential, and adaptive site of species innovation. In Elizabeth Grosz's terms, "[As a neomaterialist] I develop a concept of life, bare life, where freedom is conceived not only or primarily as the elimination of constraint or coercion but more positively as the condition of, or capacity for action, in life" (*Nick of Time* 140). The readings that follow regarding the representational tactics of disability evolved within antinormative novels of embodiment explicate the creative agencies of crip/queer materialities as instances of adaptive knowledge and strategies of the pursuit of being that exceed neoliberal normative scripts of tolerance for those "engaging [the] discrepant materialisms" of peripheral embodiments (Kruks 258).

CREATIVITY IN CHAOS

Richard Powers's 1993 novel, *The Gold Bug Variations*, tries to capture the haphazard process by which four basic codings, the building blocks of life, result in complex human organisms founded on principles of diversity. Within neoliberal efforts to privatize collectively held resources, the Human Genome Project's attempt to copyright a normative map of genetics stands as exemplary. Powers's novel exposes not only the fallacy of such an undertaking, but also why it would miss the very point of genetic diversity as an engine that produces so many organismic variations (i.e., mutations). As one of the novel's characters, the geneticist Dr. Ressler, explains: "We like to think of nature as unerring. In reality, everything it does is an approximate mistake" (606). We might refer to Ressler's theory as neomaterialist in the sense that it recognizes transcription errors as a more fully agential expression of life than its biopolitical ableist corollary, perfectly controlled repetition, which supplies the background for a mechanistic, deterministic, and automaton-like genetic sequencing process as desirable.

To orchestrate a novel about this microscopic domain of bodily relations, Powers's tale begins with an aria about the "wild chaos" of genetic
transcription:

> Gene-raining cascade, proliferating green
> Tints, varieties senseless except for their own
> Runaway joy in the explosion . . .
> All patterns patented: gyro, chute, receiver,
> Fish that track ocean back to first stream
> Or steer pitch black by trapped bacterial beams.
> Can egg-chaos really be all the blueprint needed
> To father out this garden-riot from just seed?
> No end to the program except a breaking out
> In species-mad experiment, sense-shattered shout,
> Instruction-torrent: live, solve, copy This, repeat. (8)

Within this paradigmatic gardening metaphor of genetic sequencing,
standardization-based models of biological replication productively fail by
going awry of their program. Such versions of genetics results in the biological equivalent to replication as akin to Fordist assembly-line processes
of mass production. Those coding fictions designed to promote and foster
repeated product assembly mechanisms that inevitably result in deviations
in final material outputs. Alternatively, we could interpret the replication
process described here, as we believe Powers intends, in a Deleuzian manner where the "play" in an otherwise homogenizing system cultivates revelations of difference. In other words, genetics produces massive variation
within the species rather than the standardized, average, universal body; or,
perhaps more accurately, the massive degree of repetition involved in genetic
sequencing introduces myriad opportunities for difference to emerge. This
reading's emphasis on variation rather than sameness intends to overwrite
Fordist assembly line concepts of heredity as efficiency regulating the generation of species normativity.

The mutation thesis at the heart of *Gold Bug*, that genetic mass production produces accidents resulting in large- and small-scale biological variations, situates the plot in the transitional historical moment of the 1950s, a
period characterized by the competitive international scientific search for
the double helix. Additionally, the 1950s lay at the historical cusp of a transition from liberal humanism to neoliberal biopolitics traced in chapter 1.

While liberalism and neoliberalism involve efforts to engineer predictive patterns of human biology, neoliberalism encourages tightly bounded forms of difference to emerge out of an inherently dynamic, heterogeneous, developmental undertaking. Variation, for Powers, turns the weakness of homogeneous production systems (that is, the objective of reigning in threats of difference in actively maintaining the elusive stability of standardization) into the creative basis for organismic transformation rather than replicability. What Elizabeth Grosz says of Darwin's concept of variation might also be said of Powers's novelistic method as well: "the continuity of life through time . . . is *not* the transmission of invariable or clearly defined characteristics over regular, measurable periods of time (as various essentialisms imply), but the generation of endless variation, endless openness to the accidental, the random, the unexpected" (*Nick of Time* 7).

At one point in *Gold Bug*, the protagonist, Jan, stares at her uncle, Jimmy, now recovering in a hospital bed following a massive brain hemorrhage. Pointedly the stroke occurs while Jimmy subjects himself to a medical examination by doctors representing the health insurance policy sponsored by the company for which he works. The exam is required to solidify his right to a disability claim and also to approve the reinstatement of his life insurance policy after he inadvertently misses a monthly premium payment just prior to his stroke. From the standpoint of the insurance company a missed premium results in a fortuitous error in a regulating system of repetition (the monthly payment schedule), and as such provides a rationale that allows health coverage to be denied (the paid product to be withheld).

When Jan first sees Jimmy in his hospital bed she is surprised by how he looks: "There's nothing wrong with him. In that first moment, he seemed the same person he had ever been" (541). Jan's initial revelation of Uncle Jimmy's "intactness" of a former self exposes a fictive allegiance to a more stasis-oriented idea of human development that even disability can't (immediately) disrupt. But as their postdisability interactions unfold, Jan reacts with discomfort to the fact that Jimmy now speaks in monosyllables and can no longer effectively control some motor skills. The key threat posed by disability is that it promises to upend able-bodiedness's allegiance to the fiction of constancy and coherence: the body as seamless, continuous, and invulnerable to the incursions of difference.

With a researcher's impulse to bury embodiment's unwanted alterations in abstraction, Jan runs to the medical library in order to read about prognoses of recovery from a stroke. Like Auguste Adone (played by Nick

Nolte) in *Lorenzo's Oil* (1992)—a film that would easily fall into this classification of neoliberal narratives of antinormative embodiment—when
the protagonist is overcome by the degree of pathologizing language used
to characterize his son's disability diagnosis in a medical encyclopedia, Jan
becomes quickly overwhelmed by the negativity of the pathological cata-
logues she encounters:

> There was aphasia, loss of speech, alexia, loss of reading, agraphia, loss
> of writing, and agnosia, loss of recognition. Everything a person pos-
> sessed could be taken away. . . . I grabbed at every slight ray of optimism.
> Children's brains could re-wire, recover from blows that would wipe out
> mature adults . . . I was so high strung that I even found, hidden in the
> technical folds, rare benefits from a well-placed lesion. Violent person-
> alities woke up from apoplexy as loving as a newborn. Pasteur's massive
> stroke altered his work for the better. Dostoevsky's visionary power fol-
> lowed from lifelong epileptic seizures. Research proved nothing except
> that no one could predict injury's outcome. (544)

Reading the medical records, a field whose pace "consigned all texts to the
pyre every two years," leaves Jan with a feeling of ambiguous guilt in "hoping
for [a] kinder, comprehensive solution" (544). Her catalog of miraculous biological repairs and historical rescues from impairment read like a search for
alternative positive potentials regarding disability outcomes. The list takes
on the case of a catalog of positive images consistent with early efforts by
disability studies in the humanities to reclaim disability as something other
than pathology and biological deviance.

   In the wake of giving up on a way to return Jimmy to his former self,
Jan remembers an insight passed on to her by Ressler: "the nervous system
is like a language; the circuitry remains active, historically dynamic while
appearing on the surface to be fixed and unchanging" (543). The memory
of this point about subterranean alterations and reroutings of neural networks enables Jan to read beyond what she initially encounters as Uncle
Jimmy's ruined body—"His face had collapsed on one side, as if from a bad
foundation. His mouth sagged down to the left, an eighty-year-old's mouth,
unable to produce anything more than a few raw vowels" (541). Rather than
revulsion at embodiment's complete jettisoning of able-bodied mastery over
its own operations, Jan resists placing Jimmy among the inhuman despite
his medical classification as a "vegetable." In turn, she is able to reimagine

an active life reorganizing itself beneath the topography of an apparently destroyed surface.

The novel's plot ultimately turns upon this very revelation as Jimmy marshals the monosyllables of speech left behind by stroke into "crucial bits of information—passwords, memory locations, patch names—that until then had been the secret domain of the Operations Manager" of the insurance company (576). Ironically, the "data bits" provided by Jimmy allow Ressler to unlock a heavily guarded computer network and sabotage it through random messages sent to employees of the insurance company about the unethical practices of their employer. Point of fact is that because hacking into a computer system requires expertise in binomial commands (I and O binaries), Jimmy's monosyllabic utterances turn out to be exactly fitted to the job.

In a turn becoming increasingly foundational to the alternative workings of the antinormative novel of embodiment, the computer hacking ultimately enables the geneticist to blackmail a corporate profiteer of neoliberal health care coverage into paying for the costs of Jimmy's hospitalization and lifelong recovery. As Jan reports, the conversation between Jimmy and Ressler that enables interference with the company computer system's normative neural network operates in the following manner: "Ressler said only the letters of the alphabet; Jimmy made only grunts. But the transmission was there, intact, awful in its implied risk. Uncle Jimmy was the classic Picardian third: minor his whole life, promoted to major at the last chord" (576). It is this sudden revelation of productive insight about an unexpected capacity within disability that is a key feature of the antinormative novel of embodiment. In the aftermath of rendering Jimmy a "vegetable" disability first appears as a landslide down the normative chain of being. Yet, rather than continuing to serve as a "picardian third" in his life among the able-bodied, Jimmy's stroke results in an opportunity to play a major role in disrupting the cost/risk efficiencies of a national for-profit healthcare network. We call this surprise revelation of alternative capacity the "capacities of incapacity."

The capacities of incapacity underwriting the representational innovations of the antinormative novel primarily turn on the identification of an alternative approach to representations of nonnormative materiality as agentive ("lively" in the parlance of neomaterialisms) rather than passively inscribed as deviant within medical rubrics of pathology and dysfunctionality. The constitution of disability and other alternative materialities as bodies that fail of their normative scripts relies on notions of embodied privilege within neoliberal biopower. These formulas of able-bodied desirability (and its constitutive alternative, crip/queer embodiment's inherent undesirability) depend on a decidedly constructivist notion of life as organized around predictive anxieties of what bodies will prove worthy of "letting live" within the decidedly indeterminate futures of biopolitics. The capacities of incapacity help to demonstrate why normative concepts of embodiment rest on an ability to anticipate what bodies will pay off if more resources are poured into their potentials at the expense of those consigned to less productive, underresourced existences.

Within our notion of the capacities of incapacity the matter and materiality of bodies come to the fore with greater prominence and institutes what Rosi Braidotti calls a "biocentered egalitarianism." A neomaterialist-based, biocentered egalitarianism approaches disability as instances of varied embodiment that openly rework crip/queer bodies through a more active notion of subjectivity as a negotiation of "life-forces" (204). The capacities of incapacity disconnect and reoperationalize the binary relationship between ability and disability into less oppositional modes of interaction. "Alternative ecologies of belonging both in kinship systems and in forms of social and political participation" are inaugurated with respect to alternative ways of being-in-the-world as disabled and a more open grappling with the indeterminate expressions of biological multiplicity that vulnerable embodiment represents (Braidotti 204). Fully in line with Braidotti's claims, our approach refuses more evaluative approaches to mutation that mark some materialities as inherently undesirable, unproductive, and predictively selective. Biocentered egalitarianism discounts the utility of the neoliberal question regarding which bodies will prove most productive in the future (if, in fact, productivity will remain an oppressive measure of usefulness for bodies within neoliberal biopolitics, as we challenge in the afterword).

Thus, in the *Gold Bug* example, the insurance employee, Uncle Jimmy, loses his own coverage and his employer argues that his decision to let his payment lapse at an untimely moment removes the corporation from the responsibility of covering his hospitalization costs. In *History of Madness*, Foucault points out that the one constant in the incoherent history of conceptions of madness is the practice of banishing alterity and then turning around to condemn the banished person on the basis of his/her culpability for choosing exclusion (507). The utilitarian logic of refusing coverage on the basis of making Jimmy responsible for losing his own medical coverage to begin with (this charge is effectively a charge of the individual mismanagement of his health care needs), is later offset by Ressler's hacking of the employee communication web by sending out sporadic messages about ethical quandaries produced by the for-profit provision of health care insurance industry: "Would you mind if your major medical coverage was dropped? Enter Y or N to continue" (617). A later follow-up strand of information pertaining more directly to Jimmy's situation appears on company screens as "A stroke victim is about to be cut loose." Ressler's transition from genetic decoder to computer hacker (another kind of decoding as a form of disability-based resistance), in other words, asks company employees if they would condone Jimmy's treatment as an ethical choice of the company if it were applied to their own situation. Peripheral embodiment becomes a catalyst in this situation for other insurance industry employees to assess their complicity in an industry that depends on excluding people at the moment of their greatest need for health insurance.

The neoliberal normalization of disability initiates a process of cultural rehabilitation on behalf of the few that inevitably operates at the expense of the many. Disability becomes an opportunity in antinormative novels of embodiment to contemplate complicity in unethical profiteering practices naturalized within neoliberalism as a kind of deterministic survival of the fittest. Without Jimmy's stroke and Ressler's intervention to make the disability event into a political cause, company business would continue as usual as a result of the complicity of Jimmy's fellow laborers in denying consumers access to the very immaterial product (i.e., health insurance) they were presumably in the business of mass producing. Further, Jimmy's monosyllabic cracking of the company's computer code proves advantageous to a public restoration of cause and effect—the profit motive in health insurance is exposed as a logic of what David Harvey calls "accumulation by dispossession" (*New Imperialism* 137). Profits amass in the insurance industry as the company promotes as many rationales as possible for reasons why it doesn't have to provide the product consumers have already paid for at the moments they attempt to access it.

BODIES FALLING AWAY FROM TRUE

Whereas Powers's novel *Gold Bug* explores the diversity of systems at the base of neural networks and cybernetic chains, Stanley Elkins's novel *The Magic Kingdom* (1985) takes on the task of staging disability itself as an overarching classification beneath which varieties of alternative embodiments thrive. The unusual assembly of a group of disabled characters—as opposed to the much more common individuation model involving a singular protagonist navigating impairments—parallels the surprise one might experience at running across a plurality of disabled people in public. Outside of day-home field trips for residents to the mall one day a month, special adaptive screenings of movies on specified days at theaters, or the passing of a short bus with disabled charges, we rarely encounter assemblies of people with disabilities in public. Their plurality is hidden as intensely as the individuation of their conditions within the larger diagnostic rubrics of medicine. Without visible multiplicities of disabled people in public spaces disability largely remains comprehended as exceptional, rare, isolated, and disastrous divergences from able-bodiedness. At the center of Elkins's antinormative novel of embodiment is the narrative explication of a multiplicity of disability perspectives, a plurality that nuances experiences of peripheral embodiments within the rarity of a multipronged, pluripotent, collective point of view. The novel sets into motion a neomaterialist impulse that nuances experiences of disability within the subpopulation of a group of nonaligned, jaded, ethnically and class differentiated, diversely embodied disabled youth.

The Magic Kingdom operationalizes peripheral embodiments as an opportunity to explore the alternative subjectivities wrought by navigating the world as disabled people. In the words of Jason Edwards, "What binds a group together as a 'class,' and thus provides it with a capacity for transformative agency, is a set of material practices involved in everyday life and the experience of lived space" (295). The group of disabled youth in Elkins's novel evaluate their lives back in the U.K. as relatively nauseating given their abandonment to grueling forms of medical experimentation and socially imposed experiences of isolation. At the same time, the disabled collectivity believes a trip to Disney World is the last thing they need as a respite from ceaseless regimes of treatment—the two come to seem two sides of the same neoliberal coin. The defensive comments made by parents to their son Liam, who is dying from terminal cancer when he critiques the idea of Disney as the destination for his own memorialization sum up the anemic deflections offered in the face of the collective skepticism felt by all of the crip/queer participants:

> It isn't as if this trip were your memorial or anything. Of course not. What, are you kidding? A clambake in Florida? A binge on the roundabout? A spree at the fun fair? Your memorial? You think your mum and

I would turn something like that into a great bloody red-letter day or go skylarking about like nits in the pump room? I'm shocked I am you should think so, well and truly shocked. (95)

A field trip of freaks that feels like a requiem for lives hurried into their status as corpses hardly qualifies as the fulfillment of this disabled group's make-a-wish postadolescent desires. Elkins, who experienced much of his adult life with multiple sclerosis, opens up the disability experience as a phantasm of able-bodied projections that infantilize the participants well beyond childhood. Normative embodiment can offer no viable narrative of disability futurity outside the parameters of a reduced version of its own homogenizing imaginings.

Yet, over the course of the novel, the group transforms itself through modes of collective agency based on the insights derived from making active comparisons and contrasts between divergent disability experiences. Through Elkins's efforts to imagine alternative worlds in which they won't feel so rejected, the motley crew of crip/queer youth scratches beneath the surface of the Magic Kingdom's simulacra of supports for disabled visitors. As the able-bodied make-a-wish team leader, Eddy Bale, realizes immediately upon arriving in Orlando, Florida, in the midst of a freak snowstorm, the charity trip was ill-conceived at best:

It's ... it's a ... it's a mistake, Eddy Bale thought. And, despondent, realized he'd come all this way and raised all their hopes in a futile cause. Because it was almost gone eleven—never mind the freak storm or rapidly rising temperatures through which the flakes fell, losing their icy edge, their crystalline structures collapsing so that what dropped through the air seemed less like weather than some spilled aspect of the jettisoned, not a freak storm at all so much as a mid-course meteorological correction, and never mind either whatever of accidental, unintentioned beauty the storm, by way of the blind bizarre, happened, like paint in milk, to bring about—and the morning of the first day was damn near shot and the children hadn't even had their breakfasts. (95)

What Bale dejectedly focuses upon is the barrier that a not-quite-freak-snowstorm provides to his amusement park plans. The group is cut off from entering a simulated environment promising to flatten accessibility horizons in an ultimately futile expression of human control over nature. Yet the interruption of a "mid-course meteorological correction" rather than "freak storm" is poetically explored as a deviation with potential, an "accidental, unintentioned beauty of the storm." The warm temperatures melt the hard icy edges of the crystalline precipitation into rounded, homogeneous flakes, but the aesthetic interest resides in their unexpected diversity prior to filtration in the Disney-fied melting pot atmosphere of neoliberal inclusionism.

For Elkins's narrative, such a sudden deviation in the social script (represented by both the disruption of Bale's plans and the freak snowstorm's "accidental, unintended beauty") yields the value of crip/queer embodiments as a departure from expected normative patterns, an unexpected turn in materiality that threatens to destabilize fantasies of control over bodies. If neoliberalism promises to deliver all bodies into the experience of collectively shared pleasures, then a group of disabled kids should revel in the opportunity to be like their able-bodied others.

Yet, in focusing on the normative use of Disney as one that would prop up the disabled group's spirits, Bale misses the more worthwhile aesthetic aspects in the freakish event—the "accidental, unintentioned beauty of the storm, by way of the blind blizzard, happened, like paint in milk." The surprising mixings of "the blind blizzard" that turns Disney into something more akin to the tundra of northern Europe from where they come results in revelations of an alternative aesthetic landscape. The trip refuses to conform to Bale's concept of a reentry mission into the normative context of simulated Florida amusement park adventure. Instead he is left to wander in a much more nuanced, corporeal landscape of "their awful morning catarrhs and constipations, the wheezed wind of their snarled, tangled breathing, their stalled blood and aches and pains like an actual traffic in their bones, all the low-grade fevers of their stiff, bruised sleep" (95). Bale's idea to is provide Disney as an escape from the material urgencies of their bodies, but the demands of "freak" natures—those that outstrip the imposition of a normative human dominion over life—promise to divert attentions to the strange beauties of the ill-fit.

The disabled group's experience in Orlando results in a variety of immersions into unexpected scenes of strange beauty that result from nonnormative bodies using the simulated terrain of Disney World in alternative ways. For instance, Janet Order's aortic transposition—the reversal of the usual routes of oxygenated and deoxygenated blood—gives her skin a decidedly blue cast. In order to better conform (i.e., pass as nondisabled) Janet spends much of her time thinking up specific cultural activities in which her blue body will fit in more seamlessly:

Janet Order looked forward to her dreams. In these dreams she'd found an infinite number of ways in which she was able to take on a sort of protective coloration. Sometimes she was an ancient Briton, one of that old Celtic tribe who painted themselves blue, or she dreamed of Mardi Gras, fabulous celebrations, the party makers behind incredible disguises, her own blue skin almost ordinary among the brilliant hues and shades of the gaudy, garish celebrators . . . Or even, this was tricky, thrilling, as she marched past a reviewing stand, waving a large, heavy Union Jack in front of her in such a way that the flag's staves and superimposed crosses hid her face while her body was protected behind the livid, rippling triangles of the blue field. She felt at these times quite like a fan dancer, quite like a tease. There were thousands of ways to protect herself. She dreamed of blue populations in blue towns and blue cities. She dreamed of herself cold and at peace in water, her lips and face blue in the temperature. Or exposed on a beach, blue and drowned. (68)

Janet's dreams here are not particularly fantastical. She is not transported to fantasy landscapes yet to be realized unlike the pretension of the amusement park she is about to visit. Instead she imaginatively travels through a variety of culturally specific ethnic practices that offer the promise of a more flexible environment of acceptance ("alternative ecologies of belonging," in Braidotti's terms) beyond the promise of passing—a place where a blue girl can participate without the need for extraordinary efforts of social concealment within neoliberal inclusionist practices.

Not only do the disabled protagonists remain actively attentive to local culture alternatives, but they also look longingly to alternatives offered by species other than humans. In largely eschewing rights-based models of normalization as liberation, Elkins and other antinormative novelists of embodiment avoid merely documenting moments of stigmatized embodiment. Instead, disability provides an opportunity to explore rejected embodiments as creative deviations in materiality itself. For Elkins the point is not to map the insufficiency of normative imaginings about disability (although this happens throughout the book), but rather to bestow an artful agency demanded by bodies as they navigate environments engineered to accommodate narrow aesthetic and functional norms.

Disney World, with its entirely human-made simulations of idealized landscapes, turns out to be—in the most Baudrillardian sense—a complete failure of accessibility (Baudrillard, "Disneyworld Company"). After combating the dispiriting effects of inaccessible rides, condescending staff attitudes, the rudeness of nondisabled travelers mashing their way through crowds, and encounters with "mute" characters that turn out to be the neoliberal equivalent to popular consumption's carpetbaggers, the queer male nurse, Colin Bible, takes the entire disabled troupe to the afternoon parade down Main Street USA. In order to better combat the unavailability of Disney World to serve as a hideout—a place of integration—for those with diverse embodiments. In doing so Colin uses the imperfections on display in the assembly of consumptive parade-watchers to alter the group's deepening depression over their capacity to transcend the limits of their incapacities.

Rather than bring them to the hardscape of an accepting, diverse environment (a promise that Disney World makes but completely fails to deliver in its neoliberal transcendence of diversity in normalization), Colin decides to bring the always-already diverse environment to the attentions of his disabled charges in order to demonstrate that their incapacities have openly marked the all-too-human topographies of which they are a part:

> "It breaks your heart," Colin said. "Imperfection everywhere, everywhere. Not like in nature. What, you think stars show their age? Oceans, the sky? No fear! Only in man, only in woman. Trees never look a day older. The mountains are better off for each million years. Everywhere, everywhere. Bodies mismanaged, malfeasanced, gone off. Like styles, like fashions gone off. It's this piecemeal surrender to time, kids. You can't hold on to your baby teeth. Scissors cut paper, paper covers rock, rock smashes scissors. A bit of candy causes tooth decay, and jawlines that were once firm slip off like shoreline lost to the sea. . . . Bellies swell up and muscles go down. Hips and thighs widen like jodhpurs. My God, children, we look like we're dressed for the horseback! (And everywhere, everywhere, everywhere, there's this clumsy imbalance. You see these old, sluggish bodies on thin-looking legs, like folk carrying packages piled too high. Or like birds puffed out, skewed, out of sorts with their foundations.) And hair. Hair thins, recedes, is gone. Bodies fall away from true, I don't know. It's as if we've been nickel-and-dimed by the elements; by erosion, by wind and water, by the pull of gravity and the oxidation of the very air." (223; our italics)

Colin's perspective, informed by his adoption of the gender troubling role of queer male nursemaid to this crip/queer ensemble, gives voice to what might pass as the closest thing to a thesis of the antinormative novel of embodiment: that is, that "bodies fall away from true." The "failure" of normative expectations is "everywhere, everywhere" in that embodiment makes us radically open to the vicissitudes of vulnerability, the mutating manifestations of genetic coding errors, the gradual descent into forms of degeneration that prove nothing more than materiality's inconstancy— the dynamic drift of ever-present, yet not necessarily conscious, transformations of corporeality. Within this alternative narrative scheme normative embodiment is the ruse of engineering an active repression against the dynamic contingencies of embodiment.

The espousal of this perspective places Colin squarely in a tradition of those who lose hope in order to gain the wisdom of a "spongy relation to life, culture, knowledge, and pleasure," something akin to Halberstam's notion of the "queer art of failure" (*Queer Art* 2). Rather than "succeed" by a false approximation of norms—that which Colin refers to as the artificiality of "the true"—the queer art of failure "allows us to escape the punishing norms that discipline behavior and manage human development with the goal of delivering us from unruly childhoods to orderly and predictable adulthoods" (*Queer Art* 3). Within this formulation we might understand Colin's demonstration project at the Disney World parade of anomalous characters as an embodiment of those who fall short of "orderly and predictable adulthoods." Except the cast of anomalous characters on display becomes constituted as the audience of imperfect human characters sharing in a spectacle of difference. Attention moves in this context from the parade of difference represented by freakish cartoon characters to the imperfections of embodiment represented by onlookers positioned as normative.

The revelation leaves the children's differences fully intact. Rather than normalizing their experiences of embodiment in false approximations of how they, through a twist of political correctness or inclusionist rhetoric, fit into normative expectations of embodiment, Colin Bible explains how a lack of fitness is the more epiphanic common denominator of the world. The antinormative novel of embodiment comes of age as revelatory of alternatives to normative ways of living based on a more superficial version of diversity.

THE CAPACITIES OF INCAPACITY

We want to bring these readings toward conclusion by returning to one more of Richard Powers's novelistic universes founded on a plot of acquired disability and end with some parallels to Mark Haddon's "autistic novel," *The Curious Incident of the Dog in the Night-Time*. In *The Echo Maker*, the protagonist, Mark Schluter, is diagnosed with a rare form of traumatic brain injury from a closed head trauma. This situation, taxonomically specified as Capgras syndrome, follows a mysterious accident in which his truck rolls over on an icy Iowa road and pins him in the cab for several hours. Capgras is explained, in the terms of neuropsychology, as a form of identity mis-recognition disorder where the subject experiences itself as alienated from longtime relations now turned foreign. Mark believes his sister, Karin, and his dog, Blackie, have been abducted by aliens and replaced with a mechanical version of themselves. Their robot doubles are, according to Mark, identical in every aspect to the original with the exception of, as Karin puts it, "now he just resents *me* [the present Karin], and thinks *she* [the prior non-robotic Karin] was some kind of saint" (120).

Yet, in trying to make the leap of faith necessary to believe that dynamic organisms remain synonymous with a prior coherent self, Capgras allows the incoherency of selves to dominate and the stasis of consciousness required for recognition to be submerged. Capgras syndrome refuses, in other words, to allow the bearer to overlook the dynamic inconsistencies of perpetually mutating selves. Capgras produces a subjectivity that is "too attentive to small difference" (123). Instead disorganization comes to the foreground, or rather our uncanny ability to subvert diversity in the name of retaining familiarity with another becomes impaired.

This capacity of incapacity results from an epiphany central to disability and other forms of resistant subjectivities on display in antinormative novels of embodiment—namely, that social obligations to the persistence of normativity, a consistency that keeps us static as ourselves into the future, predisposes human actors to squelch the truth of variation as a staple feature of organismic life. In his reading of Derrida's notion of "the gift of time," Pheng Cheah argues that "the structural openness of any material being to the gift of time or the pure event" is based upon an impossible promise of an ultimate arrival at absolute identity (80). In contrast, experiences of severe disability prod those in crip/queer bodies to give up investments in the impossible normalcy of stasis as the foundation of our coherent relations to others.

In an effort to bring Mark back from the "erasure" of Capgras (*Echo Maker* 420), Karin calls in the world-renowned psychologist Gerald Weber to diagnose and "treat" her brother. Rather than remake Mark back into the

prior self he has left behind, Karin's motives are relatively modest: she wants
to convince her brother that a robotic simulation of herself was not installed
during the time of his coma in the hospital ICU. In other words, Karin is
hardly a dyed-in-the-wool normate longing for medical science to retrieve
Mark from the slander of disability. Weber decides to lend his fascination
and expertise with one of the most rare expressions of human abnormalcy
in order to stoke the publication of his next biographical case study. As he
explains to his wife, Sylvie, he's not only never interacted with a case of Capgras before, but, even more astonishingly, he's never been privileged to witness "the naked brain . . . [s]crambling to fit everything together. Unable to
recognize that it's suffering from any disorder" (123).

This point of a failure to recognize the existence of a disorder impeding
normative practices of cognition is completely overturned by novel's end in
what we might call the "crip art of failure." Rather than "treat" Mark, Weber
plans, perhaps in the most innocuous neuropsychological fashion, to provide a bridge for Karin to accept Mark as a changed person who will not
return to preaccident normalcy. As Weber in one of his most noninvasive
interventionist moments explains: "Nobody's ever who they were. We just
have to watch and listen. See where he's going. Meet him there" (58). Consequently, Karin's desire to be revealed as consistent with the sister Mark
has always known becomes the radical object of Weber's "medicine." All of
this may sound relatively "progressive" given the novelistic representational
history out of which disability develops in variations on "kill or cure" plots
(Stemp, "Devices and Desires"), except that Capgras is transformed over
the course of the story into a more accurate mirror of the ways in which the
structures of human cognition actually operate.

While Mark persists in experiencing his "altered" cognition as a new
baseline for a definitively shifting perceptual processing mechanism, Weber
realizes that identity—that which holds ourselves and others in the false
truth of consistency against variation's chaos—is a fraud perpetuated by the
mammalian brain's desperate need to organize the world's disorganization.
During one of his lectures at the university Weber uses a metaphor of the
nation as sovereign state in order to explain to his students the workings of
normative consciousness:

Remember my lecture on anosagnosia, two weeks ago. The job of consciousness is to make sure that all of the distributed modules of the brain
seem integrated. That we always seem familiar to ourselves. . . . We think

we access our own states; everything in neurology tells us we do not. We think of ourselves as a unified, sovereign nation. Neurology suggests that we are a blind head of state, barricaded in the presidential suite, listening only to handpicked advisors as the country reels through ad hoc mobilizations. (363)

Yet Weber's explanation of consciousness fails in important ways to define the significance of Capgras syndrome for his patient. Because he falls back on disciplinary contextualizations of pathology to explain an experience common to all identity bearers, Weber's neoliberal metaphor of consciousness as like the sovereign state of the nation cannot effectively extract itself from concepts of deviancy. The Capgras patient's abnormalcy references his doublingly disabling cognition process as akin to "a blind head of state." As the lecturer thinks to himself in the middle of his discussion: "No hope of showing them [the failure that is the human realization of an integrated consciousness]. He could at best reveal the countless ways the signals got lost" (364). The alternative explanatory system for a more productive emphasis on "unproductive dysfunction" is left for the antinormative novel of embodiment to address.

Whereas *Gold Bug* and *The Magic Kingdom* both resort to an "able-bodied gatekeeper" to offer tutorials to disabled intimates on the thesis of productive mutation (Jan O'Deigh in *Gold Bug* and Colin Bible in *Magic Kingdom*), *The Echo Maker* employs Weber's Capgras "sufferer," Mark, as the source who provides the most useful thesis of his own disability experience, one that emphasizes a way of explaining altered experiences of consciousness by radically requesting Weber's implantation of a bird's amygdala as a substitute to his nonnormative Capgras processing mechanism:

> "My brain, all those split parts, trying to convince each other. Dozens of lost Scouts waving crappy flashlights in the woods at night. Where's me?? ... Can you put one in? You know. Kidnap a Scout, stick another in his place? Same basic crappy flashlight, waving around in the dark? ... I mean transplants. Cross-species mix and match. . . . They put ape parts into people, right? Why not birds? Their little almond thing for our little almond thing." Weber needs only say no, as gently and fully as possible. But something in him wants to say: no need to swap. Already there, inherited. Ancient structures, still in ours. (415–16)

There are several competing matters going on here that one needs to interpret in order to appreciate Mark's colloquial, yet more accurate, rendition of consciousness. First, Mark revises Weber's explanation for Capgras by explaining that the true *failure*, if we can briefly return to Halberstam's critique of normativity in the queer art of failure or Colin's thesis of "bodies falling away from true," is that our brains learn to be inattentive to most of the details that define ourselves in relation to others as a shifting, dynamic process. Coherence is the payoff for all that goes awry in each of us in order to disallow the ongoing work of evolution as perpetual adaptation. Within this revelation Capgras becomes a *truer* experience of consciousness in that it remains attentive to the minutely shifting nature of dynamic organisms—so much so that most of us jettison the details in order to impose the fiction of coherence upon, and for, each other. In Derrida's terms, our recognition of a stable identity in others is predicated on a smoothing function inherent in normative cognition that promises the arrival at an absolute definition of self. This definition will inevitably require myriad revisions of mutating relationships over time but the ruse of constancy at the base of cognition is in the provision of a temporal fix.

Second, Mark grows up on the Platte River in Nebraska, where a yearly migration of cranes takes place (the Great Crane Migration). His intimacy with the massive flying birds that seem to arrive with their lineage of descent from pterodactyls intact makes Mark one who recognizes another series of details that most humans fail to access: our ancestral proximity to birds and other species as a marker of desirability rather than a failure of human dominion over nature. Mark's experience of his disabled body provides an opportunity for the reestablishment of his belonging to the animal world in that Capgras unleashes the tiered layers of human, mammalian, reptilian, and avian (in Mark's evolutionary understanding) ancestry always already present in the brain's palimpsestic species composition. This ironic revelation experienced only as a result of Capgras—or, rather, the capacity of incapacity—provides Powers with an opportunity to employ disability as an agency that operates by virtue of an exposé of normative cognition's defining insufficiency.

Capgras reveals the degree to which normative consciousness is the problem in a world that holds firmly to the binary hierarchy of human superiority and animal inferiority; one that overprizes human agency at the expense of the alternative agencies of nonhuman animals and matter in general. Our ability to sustain a hierarchy between ourselves and other species (including, or perhaps especially, in relation to people with cognitive disabilities, whom Darwin identifies in *Descent of Man* as evidence of "regression of parts" [i.e., a "missing link"]) arrives intact from Descartes's cogito—"I think, therefore, I am"—the cost of the maintenance of our false foundation in rationality as exceptionally human.

In *The History of Madness*, Foucault defines this artificial relationship between the self and disabled others (including madness's terrifying proximity to forms of animality) as the normative subject's conscious effort to measure the distance between his own rationality and an other's unreason: "we must . . . speak of that gesture of severance, the distance taken, the void installed between reason and that which it is not, without ever leaning on the plenitude of what reason pretends to be" (181).

LIKE OKAPI IN THE JUNGLE

A similar revelation of the incapacities of normative cognition can be found in Mark Haddon's *The Curious Incident of the Dog in the Night-Time*, wherein his protagonist, Christopher, who could be described as existing on the autistic spectrum, explains his experience of nonnormative consciousness similarly to that of Capgras as an "overattentiveness to small details." According to Christopher, going into a field of cows results in a level of observation that cannot be accommodated by normative models of "rational" description:

> there were 31 more things in this list of things I noticed but Siobhan said I didn't need to write them all down. And it means that it is very tiring if I am in a new place because I see all these things, and if someone asked me afterward what the cows looked like, I could ask which one. (142)

Like Powers's antinormative characterization strategy, Haddon's formulation of alternative cognition patterns for those on the autistic spectrum reveals a universe of "excessive diversity," if it's possible to use the phrase in a more productive sense, one where loss is revealed as residing in those clinging to reductivist principles of normative consciousness, a form of knowing perhaps best described as ways of not knowing.

At one key point in the novel Christopher diagnoses this problem in those with normative cognition capacities as "glancing": "But most people are lazy. They never look at everything. They do what is called glancing, which is the same word for bumping off something and carrying on in almost the same direction, e.g., when a snooker ball glances off another snooker ball. And the information in their head is really simple" (140). So in one respect this attention to an abundance of details marks one aspect of the capacities of incapacity involved in autistic cognition; in another respect the need to reduce one's susceptibility to overstimulating situations also fuels ways to imagine alternative disability universes. Myriad examples of locating more hospitable ecologies in order to wall off excess detail occur throughout the novel as when Christopher puts his hands over his ears, closes his eyes, and rolls forward until hunched up with his forehead pressed onto the grass when physically accosted by another (4); or when he crawls between the wall of the shed, the fence, and the rainwater tub and covers himself with a fertilizer sack to hide after discovering his father is the murderer of the neighbor's dog, Wellington (127); or when he escapes from a policeman by stowing his body on a luggage shelf during a train ride to London to live with his mother. These activities of shut down, stimming, and self-isolation in tiny places demonstrate the extent to which Christopher actively shrinks the circumference of his interactions with humans in order to protect himself from normate onslaughts.

Further like Mark and his intimate relation to cranes, Christopher pursues a variety of cross-species identifications in his pursuit of alternative ecologies within which he might flourish in his crip/queer capacities of being. Throughout the novel he likens his existence to other animals that enjoy being alone, identifying asociality as a viable option for one who experiences interactions with others as a barrier: "And eventually there is no one left in the world except people who don't look at other people's faces. . . . And they like being on their own and I hardly ever see them because they are like okapi in the jungle in the Congo, which are a kind of antelope and very shy and rare" (198–99). The queer/crip poet Eli Clare (a transgender man with cerebral palsy) declares similarly in the film *Self Preservation: The Art of Riva Lehrer*: "I don't like being around people. I've always led a somewhat willful existence where being alone in Nature is preferable to interacting with other humans" (Snyder 2005). Such expressions of alternative pleasures found in isolation from humans who compose an inaccessible space where interaction with others is the barrier expose ways of being that would find inclusionism a source of oppression rather than liberation.

The antinormative novel of embodiment privileges disability as a failure of realizing expectations of normalcy, a source of innovation that runs consciously counter to sociality's insistence on the all-encompassing power of stigmatizing cultural inscriptions. To be clear, this alternative approach to disability is not a story of overcoming where the limited body exceeds its social expectations in an approximation of normative modes of relating to the world; nor is its representational mechanism one that uses disability as a metaphor for ailments that prove social rather than bodily (as does the story of female hysteria, for instance, in Charlotte Perkins Gilman's "The Yellow Wall-Paper"); and, perhaps most liberational of all, these are not inclusionist stories of the ways in which disabled people are rescued by their similarity to some abstract majority of others. The antinormative novel of embodiment surfaces with a version of nonnormative materiality that proves more innovative for its truthfulness to the imperfections of organicity than its more culturally performative normative cousins. In turn these works also locate an overlooked creativity—the skilled labor—required of living with disabilities as the realization of forms of subjectivity that expand alternatives for living in the world.

Whereas social constructionist-based theories suppress the innovation supplied by corporeality in the name of antiessentialism, antinormative novels of embodiment revel in the degree to which fiction can deploy disability to demonstrate the insufficiency of social investments in normative stasis—a defining feature of a desire for sameness residing at the foundation of neoliberal social domains created by inclusionist practices. The capacity of incapacity to which we are referring as an alternative, corporeal-based methodology turns for its insight on a form of biological materialism reinterpreted as a critique of pathology's normative referencing frame. This immanent materialist approach depends upon reimagining life as life, as that which can never be stable, that which must undergo change both in itself, at the level of individuals, and over generations, at the level of species or populations. In Elizabeth Grosz's poetic explication of alternative materialities that might well be applied to lives such as Christopher's and others occupying center stage in antinormative novels of embodiment:

> Matter is organized differently in its inorganic and organic forms; this organization is dependent on the degree of indeterminacy, the degree of freedom, that life exhibits relative to the inertia of matter, the capacity that all forms of life, in varying degrees, have to introduce something

new. This something new, a new action, a new use of matter, a new arrangement or organization, is brought into existence not through complete immersion in matter but through the creation of a distance that enables matter to be obscured, to be cast in a new light, or rather, to have many of its features cast into shadow. (167)

We would end by offering this explanation of Grosz's paraphrase of Darwin's evolutionary method as a means for understanding the radical literary history of embodiment offered up by antinormative novels of embodiment. A historical outcropping of narrative experiments within neoliberalism's insufficient embrace of disability as diversity. The antinormative novel of embodiment emerges in a post-Fordist fetishistic expansion of the marketing of difference made available by neoliberal biopolitics extant in late liberalism. Such strategies of inclusion effectively undermine the material alternatives that queer and disabled bodies actually provide. The antinormative novel of embodiment's most radical critique develops in an interim space, that which queer narrative theorist Ross Chambers refers to as oppositional narrative's tactical exploitation of "room for maneuver," disability's revelatory capacity to reveal incapacity as a viable alternative to the reification of the value of normativity.

Afterword

Disability as Multitude: Reworking Nonproductive Labor Power

BEYOND SURPLUS LABOR POWER

As we have attempted to demonstrate throughout these pages, one of the contributions of new disability materialisms to the field of identity-based disability studies has been a transformation of concepts of embodied human variation in relation to the advancement of a more agentive materiality. Whereas socially devaluing terms such as *crippled* and *handicapped* marked individual bodies as insufficient, neoliberal concepts of "disability" reorient critique away from bodies and toward inadequately adapted environments. Rather than *différance* in the poststructuralist and psychoanalytic tradition of Derrida, Lacan, and Kristeva, disability identifies material bodies socially shaped and actively adjusted by norms, averages, and narrow aesthetic standards. Consequently, unlike the radical segregation practices of the eugenics era before it, neoliberal disability moves away from late eighteenth-century ideas of individual incapacity (and, ultimately, social Darwinian "unfitness") toward a limited inclusion of populations that experience socially produced exclusions based on bodies that fall away from true, those embodiments exhibiting an incomplete approximation of sensory, cognitive, and/or bodily "typicality."

In other words, as a result of disability studies scholarship and modern-day global disability rights movements working alongside other identity-based efforts at equality, disabled people have shifted from modernity's *exception* (a lineage of defect to be isolated and eradicated) to neoliberal *exceptionality*. In this latter state, the ontology of disability retrieves a formerly fallen object and makes it newly available for *cultural rehabilitation*. While rehabilitation often refers to a productive process of recovery leading to a return to approximations of normative embodiment (and, ultimately, employability), here the term suggests something less optimum. Cultural rehabilitation refers to normalization practices at work within the neoliberal era through which nonnormative (i.e., nonproductive) bodies become culturally docile. This process accomplishes its task of adjustment through a gradual ceding of democratic state power and the duty to govern on behalf of the people to corporate interests both benign and disciplinary. Such practices jettison the value of the commons (literally selling off the collectively held riches of the commonwealth) while enlisting nonnormative bodies in service of inclusionism as a further fetishization of the accomplishments of the neoliberal state's normalcy. Claims to neoliberal exceptionality rely on a largely rhetorical celebration of this accomplishment of inclusion long before any such utopian realizations could be justifiably demonstrated. Or, rather, such arrivals at inclusionist goals prove successful only because their application to marginalized lives is so meager. Throughout this book we have referenced this implementation of neoliberal diversity as the "weakened stain" of inclusionism akin to inoculations from disease that introduce a small amount of virus into a system in order to ward off greater degrees of infection in the future.

Rather than social pariahs, disabled people increasingly represent "research opportunities" in the sense that medical race sociologist Aihwa Ong means when she argues that "treating" ill and disabled Cambodian refugees in the United States increasingly "became the justification for state and local clinics to obtain much-needed funding from the federal government" (96). Rather than a former era's economic "burden," disabled people have become objects of care in which enormous sectors of postcapitalist service economies are invested. In the terms of recent political economy, disability has been transformed into a target of neoliberal intervention strategies—a "hot" ticket item for potential research and policy funding schemes. Disabled people, once thrown out of the labor system on the basis of their lack of normative productivity in a competitive labor market, now find themselves "at hand for [the] purposes of accumulation at a later point in time. Put in the language of contemporary postmodern political theory, we might say that capitalism necessarily and always creates its own 'other'" (Harvey, *Neoliberal-*

ism 141). The historical production of others situates bodies in a position tantamount to un(der)explored geographies: they come to be recognized as formerly neglected sites now available for new opportunities of market extraction that fuels so much of the production end of neoliberal capitalism. Such developments arrive, inevitably, with their own contradictions intact, but they also provide opportunities for rethinking disability as not only alternatively social, but also nonnormatively material, subject.

In this afterword we want to bring our thinking about alternative horizons of disability in a multicultural, transnational, and "postimperialist" world to a close by focusing on the most pragmatic concern of all: disabled people's contributions to the ever evolving creativity of resistant subjectivities. To apply the prefix "post" to these historical movements is not to suggest their "end." Each continues a dynamic legacy of exploitation, travesty, domination that reverberates in the aftermath of a lengthy period of military and cultural subjugation. However, like other "dynamos" (the term Henry Adams used to represent the churning engine of industrial capitalism at the end of the nineteenth century [380]) these systems of exclusion must come to rest of their own inertia or metamorphose into new hegemonic amalgams of activity. These hybrid forms of indenture are made out of the scraps of an older disciplinary machine, and, consequently, the alternative formations of resistance they once spawned are now co-opted. They produce an alternatively minted, prostheticized, even if ultimately compromised, mutating social organism.

As Hardt and Negri argue, rather than feeling doomed about the saturation of imperial power through networks of capitalism we might also see room for potential:

> The immediately social dimension of the exploitation of living labor immerses labor in all the relational elements that develop the potential of insubordination and revolt through the entire set of laboring practices. (*Empire* 29)

International movements of disabled persons have managed to cultivate forms of insubordination within global capitalism by leveraging pressure for increased civil rights and accessible public spaces with reference to other disability movements demanding similar objectives. A rights-based model of social disobedience has proven relatively flexible in translating pressures on international spaces of exclusion into some gains of access to public spaces (although it's important to note that rights-based models are ineffective in non-rights-based settings as they depend upon a grievable system of litigation/governance to enforce).

As individuals who have taught disabled and disability-identified international students since the early 1990s, we have had the privilege of learning about the ever inventive, mutating array of rights-based social model applications imported into various global spaces. In the year 2000 a group of disabled women in South Korea protested a dangerous public lift by setting up tents in an underground subway to contest the state's lack of concern regarding their safety (Eunjung Kim, now disability and women's studies professor at the University of Wisconsin, told us of this story) and it is documented in the film *Turtle Sisters*; during 2008 a Bosnia-Herzegovina disabled student public relations campaign made pedestrians aware of curb cuts for wheelchair and other mobility-impaired users by painting them bright yellow (Vladimir Cuk, now chair of the United Nations group leading the CRPD advancement, told us of this artsy street performance intervention campaign); and in 2004 a Russian disability group blocked entrance to the Moscow underground rail system by staging a protest about the inaccessibility of public transportation on the entry stairs (we learned of this action from our colleagues at "Breaking Barriers: The Moscow Disability Film Festival" during a screening of our films in the mid-2000s). Most recent to the writing of this book thousands of physically and intellectually disabled students gathered in the Indian capital city of New Delhi to protest lack of access to meaningful education and employment. Their specific arguments went beyond inclusion by emphasizing a desire to be taught by qualified teachers trained to meet their needs ("Thousands of India's Disabled Protest"). These protests shared an aim of exposing the inaccessibility of public institutions for disabled participants in the spirit of disability civil disobedience practices organized in the 1980s by the Denver activist group ADAPT (Americans with Disabilities for Accessible Public Transportation). In turn those protests were fueled by the vision of the U.K. group UPIAS (Union of the Physically Impaired Against Segregation), who argued that disability was not in the person but rather in exclusionary interactions encountered within human-made environments. All of these actions occurred as part of political activism taking shape at the level of global disability rights movements using each other's tactics to transform their own local public spaces.

The creativity of these civil disobedience tactics that interfered with able-bodied access in order to emphasize disability-based segregation from the social mainstream turned experiences of exclusion on their head. The protestors transformed their own bodies and prosthetics into barriers, producing temporary inaccessibility for nondisabled users in order to point out the daily impediments faced by people with disabilities. Even in the midst of actively protesting structural barriers disabled activists are narrated as "fragile" and as taking unnecessary chances with their own socially and biologically bequeathed vulnerabilities, rather than as properly resistant subjects. However, as Mike Davis points out in *Planet of Slums*, a proper systemic analysis such as those identified above inverts the terms of recognition by placing the blame for vulnerability in its appropriate place: "'Fragility' is simply a synonym for systematic government neglect of environmental safety" (125). Neoliberal tactics of nongovernance rely on strategies of abandoning the well-being of the commonwealth by directing state energies to the creation of new corporate marketplaces. As a partial response to this abandonment, disability collectives have forged alternative nonnormative discourses in contrast to normative practices of consumption, standardization, and heteronormative belonging that offer important possibilities for collective political action on a global scale.

Theories about new forms of political resistance bear a great deal of significance for disability studies and global disability movements, not only because the forms of political resistance now operative allow some space for disability rights-based interventions on a global scale (witness, for instance, the recent passage of the 2006 United Nations charter on global disability rights [CRPD] by many nations—although, at the time of the writing of this book, there is still no signatory action by the United States), but also because the international disability rights movement provides a key, albeit still relatively localized, example of Hardt and Negri's controversial formulation of militancy within late liberalism:

> The multitude designates an active social subject, which acts on the basis of what singularities share in common. The multitude is an internally different, multiple social subject whose constitution and action is based not on identity or unity (or, much less, indifference) but on what it has in common. (*Multitudes* 100)

Within this definition of coordinated yet nonunified, non-hierarchically organized insurgencies, Hardt and Negri have most consistently cited the Zapatista movement and the "spontaneous" uprisings of protestors during meetings of the G8. Even more recently, we have seen the willy-nilly pro-ductive incoherency of the Occupy Wall Street movement (and its various offshoots in other U.S. cities) as a protest of corporate greed, the "collective yoke of debt," and the evasion of responsibility for accounting to the 99% by the 1% (Hardt and Negri, *Declaration* 35). A demographic sociology of these resistance groups within neoliberalism reveals the participation of members who do not align themselves primarily on the basis of foundational social identity rubrics such as race, class, ethnicity, or gender. Rather, contempo-rary resistance movements bring with them alternative values of living that oppose corporatist models of everyday life. They specifically attack late capi-talist cultural formations in terms of "the *productive* dimension of biopower" wherein lifestyles of over- and underconsumption operate as false universals (Hardt and Negri, *Empire* 27).

It may seem strange to cite disability movements in the context of a defi-nition of multitude that is not based on identity. After all, disability seems to mark a horizon of contemporary identity-based politics based on variable bodily capacities, appearances, and experiences of exclusion developed without common community institutions or practices of everyday life. The disability historian Cathy Kudlick refers to this last-ditch inclusion of disability social movements through the imperative: "Why We Need Another Other" (764). Other than incarcerating institutions themselves (such as nursing homes or congregate care settings), there are no specific cultural institutions for genera-tions of disabled people to gather in on the basis of their status as disabled people (other than, ironically, carceral institutions themselves)—no place to effectively organize, share concerns, or transfer hard-earned information from one generation of disabled persons to another. Yet, for Negri: "the multitude is the power of the singularities that are brought together within cooperative constellations; and the common precedes production" (2005 215). This charac-terization better captures the productive multiplicity that characterizes move-ments of disabled persons' goals at a micro and, ultimately, macro level. As theorized in chapter 4, the politics of atypicality practiced among crip/queer bodies necessitates an identity rubric that actively cultivates productive frac-turings beneath the ever mutating banner of disability.

First, disability does not constitute a shared social condition. Instead, disabled people recognize the intense differences that constitute their bod-ies (what Negri calls "the composition of singularities in a common rela-tionship") as their greatest commonality (*Kairos* 183). The embrace of id-iosyncrasy, functional diversity, and aesthetic impropriety across peripheral

embodiments has both an *empirical* and a *socially derived* utility—empirical
in the sense that disability movements contest inadequate universalist pathological categories of medicine and rehabilitation. According to disability
studies scholars, the imprecision of medical taxonomies of deviance simultaneously pathologizes and groups impairing disparate experiences as shared
when they are more commonly disparate in a phenomenological sense. It is
also socially derived because the "unity" of disabled people fighting for their
rights seeks a radical edge that is essential to revolutionary politics: "The
[multitude], the producers of the common formula from which they are—
nonetheless—excluded, are the motor of the materialist teleology, because
only the multitude of the poor can construct the world under the sign of the
common, pressing relentlessly beyond the limit of the present" (Hardt and
Negri, *Empire* 185). Cross-cultural efforts by disability groups to seize the
commons in the name of universal accessibility for all bodies contests the
neoliberal state's justification of privatization and able-bodied privilege at
the base of modern definitions of citizenship (what, ask politicized disabled
people, bodily capabilities does one need in order to actively participate in
social democracies?). Disability movements, as opponents of "accumulation
by dispossession" to which they are subject, play a critical role in the exposé
of neoliberal practices that disenfranchise people from access to shared public space (Harvey, *Postmodernity* 43).

Beyond these two important applications of disability studies to critiques
of neoliberalism's containment strategies of difference, disability may also
be approached in a manner that, perhaps, no other political theory allows.
Rather than focusing on more traditional Marxist objects of resistance—
such as the "worker" or "the masses" or "class conflict"—Hardt and Negri
expand the boundaries of effective political culture not only beyond identity
(particularly that of nation), but also beyond the critical Marxist category
of *surplus labor power*. Whereas surplus labor power denotes a concept of
an ever available pool of laborers that assists in keeping wages down, job
security for employed people tenuous, scab labor a prevalent threat against
worker agency, and identification between the proletariat, potential proletariat, and the bourgeoisie uncoordinated, the category surplus labor leaves
entire populations outside of the activities of even neo-Marxist resistance
demographics.

Hardt and Negri put the question in this manner:

But can those who are excluded from work still be considered part of
a living labour? Of course, since even the excluded are part of the com-

mon. And the poor person, who is more excluded than anyone, i.e. the singularity at the greatest risk at the edge of being—at the point where Power closes off the teleological striving towards the *to-come*—the poor, therefore, are the most common. For if it is only the common that produces production, those who are excluded but participate in the common are also the expression of living labour. (*Multitudes* 225)

In order to create a less exclusionary definition of subjects beyond notions of labor and surplus labor (both remain tied to definitions of competitive labor markets within the logic of late liberalism), Hardt and Negri use "living labor" to suggest forms of creativity that cannot be reduced to an economic exchange value. This definition of resistant subjects does not simply expand outward to include those who occupy "nonproductive bodies," but rather takes its lead from those whose capacities make them "unfit" for labor as the baseline of human value. In fact, Hardt and Negri propose that the more "risk" individuals experience within capitalism the less likely they are to feel invested in its continuance. As those cultural constituencies left out of the loop of potentially laboring subjects, *nonproductive bodies* are inoculated (in a Nietzschean sense) against participating in the misdirected destabilization of working bodies that so often characterizes the presence of those in the surplus labor ranks.[1]

THE WORK OF "NONPRODUCTIVE BODIES"

Who are the inhabitants of "nonproductive bodies?" What do they have to do with disabled people? Why have they existed below the radar of radical labor theory and political economy for so long? Nonproductive bodies are those inhabitants of the planet who, largely by virtue of biological (in)capacity, aesthetic nonconformity, and/or nonnormative labor patterns, have gone invisible due to the inflexibility of traditional classifications of labor (both economic and political). They represent the nonlaboring populations—not merely excluded from, but also resistant to, standardized labor demands of productivity particular to neoliberalism. Within neoliberalism productivity measures have been increasingly used to assess human value at the individual and population levels.

As many scholars have pointed out, *disability* was first coined in the mid-1800s to designate those incapable of work due to injury. This grouping identified disabled veterans of the Civil War as eligible for various govern-

mental supports—disability pension payments, state provisions of prosthetics, life skills training, and so on. Likewise, the diagnostic category of
feeblemindedness in the same period defined those who, due to the hereditary
transmission of "bad seed," were incapable of participating in a competitive
market-based economy. This group also qualified for levels of public support largely received in centralized, carceral forms of institutional care. As
we argue in *Cultural Locations of Disability*, membership in this latter classification group resulted in the coercion of individuals to *exchange their liberties for social supports* (19). This designation as "nonproductive" developed
in spite of the fact that many institutional residents participated in laboring economies developed within institutional societies: residents farmed
the institution's land, provided housekeeping services to fellow inmates and
administrators, supervised each other on behalf of the institution, and produced products for the state (brooms, clothing, baskets, etc.) at excessively
low (or no) wages. In many cases nothing more was provided in exchange for
their productive labor beyond the "benefit" of living an excluded life within
the walls of the multiply partitioned institution.

Historical forces that went into the transformation of disability into
nonproductive bodies also depended on an unseen network of labor practices where the presumably "insufficient" provided for themselves within
the walls of an undetected informal economy. Institutions operated as if
they were small city-states that actively rendered the labor of the nonlaboring classes invisible while at the same time drawing on their resources.
In many cases a majority of institutions could claim themselves as "self-
supporting." Ironically, such claims effectively disproved the theory upon
which institutions were based: those who could not compete in a competitive labor market should be sheltered from its demands in an institutional world that functioned as a closed circuit of dependency and care.
Instead, institutional residents often made an ideal labor force—those
who could efficiently meet the needs of their own segregated society—
when conditions could be adjusted according to the follow principle: from
each according to his/her ability, to each according to his/her need(s). The
realization of Marx's famous formulation in his 1875 *Critique of the Gotha Program* within institutions consequently posed a threat to reigning
orders of capitalism operating beyond the walls of the institution (27). In
fact, historically capitalists and bourgeoisie alike have sought remedies in
state legislatures across the country to limit the productivity of institutionalized labor forces. In 1903 deaf workers who built phones at the Chicago Telegraph Company went on strike to protest low wages compared to

those made by hearing workers (see illustration titled: "Protest by Signs"). These workers with visual impairments, in turn, went on strike and forced the city to reopen their place of employment on the basis of their status as an exceptional class of laborers.[2] Thus, not only could disabled people uphold the efficiency rigors of manufacturing but they also could organize themselves into striking laborers unjustly displaced from low-wage jobs. These disability labor history details expose the great ironies of institutional life for those who were deemed "nonproductive" on the basis of physical, sensory, and/or cognitive incapacity.

The identification of hordes of people designated as "nonproductive bodies" and located on the outermost fringes of productive economies replaces now antiquated categories such as "the masses." The potential for widespread civil unrest proved compromised because those occupying nonproductive bodies (albeit laboring within adapted workshops supervised by institutional administrations) found themselves engulfed within networks of capital that kept them enthralled to impossibly low levels of compensation and dependent upon the institution for which they worked. Further, as modernity gave way to postmodernity, the antagonistic divisions between workers and capitalists that were anticipated as fueling revolution became increasingly blurred. No longer did one participate in a simple, agonistic division of labor; but for Hardt and Negri (2005), David Harvey (2005), Frederic Jameson (1992), and other political theorists, the biopolitics of late capitalism now saturated every nook and cranny of life and became increasingly confused with a biopolitical *natural order of things*. One could find no outside to capitalist production given that the network of exchange had grown so diffuse and pervasive. Neoliberal capitalism's power came to be increasingly located with its ability to naturalize its own artificial consumptive context across every social interaction. Thus the birth of what Marx anticipated as *social capitalism* (Portes 7–8).

The critical question asked by today's theorists of neoliberal political economy is that which Negri poses to himself in *Kairos, Alma Venus, Multitudo: Nine Lessons to Myself*: "how can this biopolitical (intellectual and co-operative) mass, which we call 'multitude,' exert 'governance over itself'?" (209). In other words, where does resistance manifest itself once a concept of the workers revolution no longer seems tenable, and how will this resistance govern itself without the institution of new hierarchies of inequality?

In order to formulate responses for crip/queer lives to Hardt and Negri's question articulated in their *Multitudes* trilogy, we must unpack the terms in as literal a way as possible. Biopolitical represents the degree to which every aspect of living is ensnared by late capitalism: economic, social, artistic, cultural, and so on. Whereas liberal period capitalism saw division and segregation as its strategy of divide and conquer among laboring parties in a strategically segmented labor production process (i.e., the prior economic production mode of Fordism), postmodern capitalism elevates *cooperation* across spatially, geographically, and culturally diffuse networks that place individuals in contact with each other across disparate geographies. "Multitude" replaces "masses" in that a multitude is defined as productive singularities (material and affective bodies) that cannot be collapsed into a universal formula of normative labor identity. Within this formulation of resistant "bodies" Hardt and Negri essentially recognize *forms of incapacity* as an alternatively galvanizing agent of resistance to neoliberal formulas of containment (variations on practices of neoliberal inclusionism designed to expand the pool of resources on the post-Fordist consumption side of capitalism).

"Nonproductive bodies" represent those who belong to populations designated "unfit" by capitalism. Thus, whereas traditional theories of political economy tend to stop at the borders of laboring subjects, including potential laborers (i.e., surplus labor pools), the concept of nonproductive bodies expansively rearranges the potentially revolutionary subject of leftist theory. If one is "wired" into the system in some manner—and, for Hardt and Negri, there is no such thing as an outside to this formulation—then one actively participates in the global give-and-take of biopolitical life. While such a claim may seem to deflate the potential for significant political action given the seemingly boundless ability of late liberal capitalism to produce subjectivities advantageous to its own livelihood, the alternative proves equally accurate: those whom Fanon designated as experiencing "the immobility to which the colonized subject is condemned" come into greater contact with each other through immaterial communication networks, and the opportunities for "collective" action increase (15). Let us conclude our deliberations here on the productivity of nonproductive bodies with a brief description of how disability collectivities may be recognized as a paradigm of the alternative formula of resistance that is "multitudes."

INSURRECTIONAL POTENTIALS OF NONPRODUCTIVE BODIES

By the end of the nineteenth century efforts to segregate, restrict, and oppress populations identified variously as "feebleminded," "subnormal," "deviant," "epileptic," "blind," "deaf," "deaf-blind" went increasingly transnational. Eugenics, the social engineering project that sought to eradicate defective traits from a nation's hereditary pool, went global. Scientific collectives to study unproductive bodies were formed, restraint policies on social mobility were translated from one cultural context to another with relative ease, categories of pathology proliferated, and parallel nonnormative populations found themselves increasingly the subjects of carceral practices. Policymakers, scientists, psychiatrists, institutional administrators, social workers, and police alike referenced effective restrictions imposed on nonproductive bodies in other nations to put pressure on home legislatures to adopt "firm measures." In other words modern capitalism recognized the utility of international markets in segregation strategies toward disabled people (and others deemed nonnormal) and actively traded in their dissemination (intentional echoes here of Homi Bhabha's Janus-faced articulation of the polyglot nation represented by his term "DissemiNation" [291]).

In *Cultural Locations of Disability* we point out that a devastating irony was at work in the progressive period: as the discourse of disciplinary eugenics became increasingly mobile and international, disabled people—the very subjects of that discourse—found themselves increasingly immobilized (*Cultural Locations* 103). Their labor was not absent, but rather walled off and strictly contained within the parameters of the modern-day institution. Those who were not fit for physical labor in the fields or workshops often found themselves providing caretaking and/or policing their fellow inmates as part of the cost savings of institutional economies. As a result a disability-enabled panoptic system developed as the infrastructure of institutionalization expanded to encompass all discordant corporealities housed within its walls. As Foucault claims, the feebleminded institution of the nineteenth century was truly a realization of Bentham's panopticon (*Discipline and Punish* 200).

A fully Foucauldian transnational biopolitical network burgeoned within this period with disabled people serving as a key vector of globalization's efforts. Within the United States, Canada, and western Europe, nations argued a logic of racial improvement and hereditary purity; in Russia the old czarist lines were disqualified as "inferior" due to the eugenics concept of 'inbreeding'; in Asia entire countries such as Korea found themselves "disabled" by virtue of another (Japan in this case) colonizing power's emasculation of the country. In other words, the discourse of eugenics, applied unevenly and nonuniformly, functioned as a meta-disqualifier of entire populations whose differences (perceived or actual) served as the source of their multi-faceted inferiority. Here we find the historical roots of a global effort to classify bodies as nonproductive and therefore outside of capitalist competitive labor markets all together.

The modern-day disability rights movement, consequently, is not essentially European or American or "Western" by necessity of the fact that wherever the discourse of eugenics could be found (in one form or another), counterinsurgent forces arise. These resistance strategies increasingly surface within populations designated as "nonproductive"; but, for Hardt and Negri, "nonproductive bodies" prove imminently productive because they occupy outposts alternative to biopolitical discourses, lives imagined and realized in contrast to, even counterposed against, more dominant discourses of consumption, productivity, family, and nation. In part these insurrectional communities of nonproductive bodies begin with the insurrectional potentiality of a "politics of atypicality." The sequestration of nonproductive bodies evolves collectivities founded on theories of malleability—the orchestrated efforts of resistant singularities—across the strictly policed borders, classifications, and social relationships indicative of an evolving society of control.

The introduction of this strategic fluidity proves critical to the creation of disability countercultural formations as they rely upon an exposé of the artificiality of late capitalism's "naturalness" as their political alternative. Disabled bodies, as definitively multiple forms of nonnormative embodiment that cannot be universalized even within "condition" groups, rely for their insurrectional force on the nontranscendental nature of their permutating embodiments—to recall our central thesis of comparative scales in chapter 5. This is the impetus for upsetting medical and rehabilitation-based models of pathology that transect the globe, as discussed with respect to social-media-based single-impairment user groups and the evolution of global cybernetic collection points such as Orphanet in chapter 6. Disability rights movements function as counterdiscursive resistance efforts at the global level while sustaining—and even honoring—local differences. This is one of the powerful lessons that Jim Charlton's *Nothing about Us without Us* has brought to disability studies with its comparativist, international interview methodology approach (4).

MEET ME AT THE GLOBAL

Let us bring *The Biopolitics of Disability* to a close with a laundry list of ways in which contemporary crip/queer collectivities produce a viable counternarrative of biopolitics extant in Hardt and Negri's formulation of multitudes.

Disabled persons are made, willingly or not, into the legitimate "nonworkers"—those who are actively excluded from, but who also consciously refuse, productivity as a basis for an adequate measure of human worth. They strain at entrapment in the productive net of neoliberal capitalism that ensnares all in the seemingly benign, inexhaustible practice of consumption as synonymous with life. Many of the disabled people we know prove to be some of the worst consumers on the planet because they have neither the means nor the interest of mistaking meaning with market. For instance, disabled artists and activists in Chicago and London with whom we have worked live sparing, nonconsumptive lives and, yet, this is what we admire about them.

Those who identify as nondisabled also strain to occupy the increasingly common forms of prosthetization that supplement debilitated bodies trying to navigate inaccessible, or, at most, minimally accessible, neoliberal environments. At least to the great degree that this prosthetic discomfort surfaces for those still inhabiting narratives of the natural, organic, and unsupplemented body. As the autistic narrator, Christopher, argues of his neighbors in *The Curious Incident of the Dog in the Night-Time*, "everyone has special needs, like Father, who has to carry a little packet of artificial sweetening tablets around with him to put in his coffee to stop him from getting fat, or Mrs. Peters, who wears a beige-colored hearing aid, or Siobhan, who has glasses so thick that they give you a headache if you borrow them, and none of these people are Special Needs, even if they have special needs" (43–44). As in Christopher's case, disabled people, in turn and by necessity, have surrendered this artificial nostalgia for a version of their bodies as definitively normative, natural, pure, and unsupplemented. In this manner they become one instance of a recalcitrant remainder within the body-rehabilitating and mind-altering augmentative projects of neoliberal biopolitics.

Global capitalist networks increasingly rely on the development of workforces that can manipulate immaterial data across an expanding array of communication networks. Such labor often involves a variety of skills, such as (1) the ability to sit in a stale room with others for hours on end; (2) the capacity to performatively represent oneself as hyperbolically enabled through digital forms of communication; (3) the ability, and even willingness, to function in cybernetic locations completely bereft of the aesthetic body-based criteria that so often result in exclusions of disabled people from service-based and productivity-driven manufacturing employability; (4) substantial amounts of

leisure time that go relatively uninterrupted by the nuisance of caring support networks supplied for most by family, friends, or love interests; and (5)
a willingness to be devoted to one's job because so much of what counts as
an "outside life" has already been rendered unavailable. This catalog of nonnormative capacities of incapacity are meant as only partially tongue in cheek.
As denizens of neoliberal historical contexts, we are increasingly approaching
a paradoxical time that Hardt and Negri and other post-operaist theorists
"prefer to designate as 'altermodern'" (Mouffe 66). In the altermodern, some of
what passed as the undesirability of life in a disabled body ironically translates
into vaguely apprehended examples of survival within the deprivative workplace atmospheres that govern "immaterial forms of production" within neoliberalism (Hardt and Negri, *Declaration* 65).

However, and perhaps more importantly, even outside of the formal
workforce crip/queer people find themselves manipulating data of a political nature across national boundaries. As we cataloged earlier, disabled people's organizations and disabled individuals now routinely exchange survival
strategies and political tactics with other nonproductive bodies in formerly
unreachable locations. The international participation of eugenics discourse
in the earlier part of the last century has been met by an increasingly globalizing discourse of countereugenic efforts. Thus, disability rights movement
leaders now exchange political insurrection strategies with each other in order to pressure their own legislatures into adopting "human-rights-based
platforms" and principles of universal design through comparisons with
other policy- and rights-based action movements. These efforts effectively
turn eugenics-based strategies on their head and can be fueled by immaterial
commerce across global cybernetic networks.

However, aside from rights-based strategies that inevitably reify heteronormative forms of participation, we want to encourage the option of
following out the logic of nonproductive bodies in order to conceive of disability as a potentially effective political foundation for new forms of resistance, particularly in that disability (as the advocates of TAB [the temporarily able-bodied] remind us) potentially cuts across all socio-economic
categories of experience. Yet the founding recognition of crip/queer political
unity based in difference—that which we have called the politics of atypicality or, in Hardt and Negri's terms, the "intensive singularities of resistance"
that cannot be neatly collapsed in a coherent identity. This is one of the
primary lessons of crip/queer embodiments participating in the alternative
resistance practices offered by the politics of atypicality. Such nebulous en-

actments of politics have been critiqued as unworkable—particularly based on an unwillingness to "acknowledg[e] the pro-active role played by capital in this transition" and the continuous social pressure to make marginalities controllable because recognizable (Mouffe 72).

For instance, Chantal Mouffe, one of the most influential theorists of the competing interests of hegemony as central to political identity formation, argues in favor of the necessity of an identity-based approach to difference within a more openly acknowledged agonistics of competing tribes. Without the consolidation of identity camps, argues Mouffe, there is no viable way of conceiving how the post-operaist multitudes will come into being with respect to more spontaneous forms of collective action. Throughout this book we have addressed this critique (and also believe it implicit in Hardt and Negri's formulation of multitudes) by showing how a limited implementation of "inclusionism" on behalf of formerly excluded nonnormative identities opens the door to a more robust engagement with an alternative ethics of crip/queer being. Rather than posit a space outside of neoliberal capitalism, the biopolitics of disability explores how forms of dissent evolve within limiting rubrics of neoliberal diversity. Mouffe would diminish the significance of these counterhegemonic developments by arguing for their status as "'passive revolution,' a situation where demands which challenge the hegemonic order are appropriated by the existing system so as to satisfy them in a way that neutralizes their subversive potential" (*Agonistics* 73). In contrast, we are arguing for an alternative political evolution of disability collectivities: those who consciously operationalize the marginally "proactive" practices of neoliberalism in order to advance a more radical agenda of collectivity across dissimilarities.

Of course, as we explored in chapter 4 regarding the agonistic identity exchanges of film festival participation, we don't mean to overlook the fact that disability collectivities have discovered creative ways of fracturing their own collaborative potential. Particularly on the basis of less productive debates over whose "disabled" and whose "not-disabled," disability hierarchies, tokenism, marginalization of expressive modes (i.e., putting the pragmatics of policy over arts), the neglect of the experiences of disabled people of color, disabled old boys and old girls networks of power brokering, and so on. But there are also a series of productive ways to organize political constituencies that we owe to the creativity of disability rights movements around the world. Namely, since disability movements continue to operate simultaneously at the local and meta-national levels.

To return to Hardt and Negri's thesis of "resistant singularities", crip/ queer bodies prove so integral to late capitalism's post-Fordist contexts because the model upon which capitalist exchange rests has shifted so dramatically. Disability may present one of the most productive intervention objects of all in that it provides an inexhaustible, dynamic, and ever mutating opportunity to renew capital in new geographies of the body. Since disabled bodies persist throughout history, and, especially as a primary product of militarized economies, neoliberal economies produce disability at "home" and "abroad" with alarming frequency. As a result, market economies increasingly reference them among their most prolific target audiences.

MARKETING IMPERFECT IDENTITIES

Thus, postindustrial, neoliberal capitalism as discussed in chapter 1 now finds itself pitched toward *imperfection* as the standard of vulnerable embodiment and the hawking of product supplementations as the solution— diuretics, impotency, indigestion, mobility aids, depression, manias, hearing loss, vision correction, and so on. The body has become a multisectional market; whereas Fordist capitalism cultivated divided worker populations by hierarchicalizing the assembly line based on the functional demands of production, neoliberalism divides us within our own bodies. We are now perpetual members of an audience encouraged to experience our bodies in pieces—as fractured terrains where the "bad" parts of ourselves are ever multiplying. Whereas disabled people were trained to recognize their disabled parts as definitively inferior, the biopolitics of late capitalism trains everyone to separate their good from bad—a form of alienation that feeds the market's penchant for "treating" our parts separately in order to partition further for resource exploitation. The body becomes a terrain of definable localities each colonized by its particular pathologies as dictated by the marketplace. This late capitalist litany of bodily frailties, imperfections, and incapacities gluts advertising networks as the hegemonic product pitch strategy of today. Within this treatment-based environment disability rapidly becomes synonymous with a humanity that we are all seeking to *overcome*. The imperfect is becoming a standard formula of reference for alternative late liberal marketplace profit extraction.

The rise to legitimacy of the therapies as new "comfort industries" results as the twenty-first century opens. We are all subject to the disciplinary regimens of the therapies that have now transcended their medically subordinate position within the health sciences to become our mainstream training gurus for improving on bodily imperfections writ large. Therapies have now gone "cultural" and encourage our mass dedication not to perfection but to the infinite pursuit of embodied "improvement." Once relatively isolated disability rehabilitation regimens are now applicable to all citizens; just as all citizens grow increasingly responsible for policing their own bodies as a foundational aspect of their well-being. Forms of therapy are increasingly becoming the market solution to ever-expanding ideas of debility, and to the degree that one resists therapy one also further resists greasing the neoliberal market skids. Refusal of our crip/queer bodies as perpetual objects of professional labors provides a model of resistance wherein the ways our bodies function does not lead us to fall prey to regimes of standardization. We now find ourselves encouraged not to conform to a general norm but rather condition-based norms that others who presumably share our disability group establish. This is really nothing but a move from a medical model based on an elusive average body to a therapy-based norm of an elusive average *disabled* body.

Today, as we have argued throughout *The Biopolitics of Disability*, neoliberalism thrives on the production of "new spaces" for exploitation, the promotion of the exotic as a strategy of consumption rather than the promise of the homogeneity amid locales of difference. The body itself has become an outpost for this strategy. An "intensive interior" is now cannibalized as new "erogenous zones" of intervention unfold. To combat this tendency crip/queer subcultures rise as a countervaluing mechanism: collectivities that cannot afford to mistake their own artificial productions as more "natural," but rather, following Hardt and Negri, as a self-acknowledged product that seizes the biopolitical terrain as revisable. "Nonproductive bodies" work a revolution within the conception of worker subjectivity. The nonproductive body is not simply a body incapable of working within the narrow standardization efforts of capitalism, but rather, as Hardt and Negri explain, "the way some deviants perform differently and break the norms" in doing so (*Multitudes* 200). These differences may result in a rigid exclusion from dominant economic networks, but they continue to produce and, in turn, be produced: thus, late liberalism may be generally described as a culture of manufactured sentience; one that wires the life of feeling and flesh directly into the circuitry of prosthetic supplementation (i.e., prosthetics from sip 'n puff wheelchair control systems to voice synthesizers to Xbox superhero cyber realities).

DEMOCRACY AND DISABILITY

A true democracy based on variation cannot be collapsed into a totalizing essence/identity/unity. Based on their multiple formulas of difference, crip/queer refusals of the meager inclusionist projects of neoliberalism help to expose transcendence as a false dream of market compensation. If we conceive of disability as a material expression of variation, then embodied difference may be recognized as a paradigm for true democracy. Specifically those made expendable by late capitalism on the basis of a congenital or acquired incapacity serve as an active recognition that normalization functions as little more than a facade – a false front disguising humanity's defining heterogeneity. A "truer" disability-based model of social production is understood as the interdependency of intense singularities working for common goals (the politics of atypicality)—rather than the obverse, which is the functioning logic of capitalism: intense singularities suppressed by incoherent goals of corporate marketplaces and imposed by companies upon those who produce products and profits from which they do not adequately benefit. These are false promises of arrival at new neoliberal normativities.

As we have tried to show in our analyses of alternative corporeal creativities represented by curricular cripistemologies (chapter 2), mainstream and independent disability film productions (chapters 3, 4, and 5), online, single-impairment user groups (chapter 6), and the alternative representational systems of disability at work in antinormative novels of embodiment (chapter 7), politicized, alternative, disability-based social organizations situate their counterdiscursive productions at both the macro and micro levels of experience. At the micro level, differences proliferate and disability dedicates itself to unearthing the productive misfirings of replication schemes from one body to another; at the macro level disability draws together socially debilitating experiences (i.e., lack of employment, ouster from sexual circuits of interaction, exclusionary architectural standards, etc.) and identifies the degree to which global oppression operates on disabled people across cultural contexts. As a result, bands of crip/queer people have produced viable alternatives to consumptive models of capital and the expulsion of bodily imperfection in order to envision a meaningful contrast of lifestyles, values, and investments adapted to life as discontinuity and contingency. A new disability materialist realization of the World Social Forum's rallying slogan: "Another World is Possible" (Chossudovsky).

Notes

Introduction

1. The terms that ultimately translated into the key contention of the social model of disability—disability is in the environment and not in the person—were first articulated in 1974 by a U.K. organization of physically disabled men who called themselves the Union for the Physically Impaired Against Segregation (UPIAS). UPIAS made a complete distinction between impairment (the biological experience of incapacity) and disability (encounters with social exclusion imposed on top of impairments). The contention established the key argument that discriminatory social conditions created disability rather than individual limitations.

2. "Immanent materialism" is the phrase used by William E. Connolly to reference a mode of thinking about materialism that is "not susceptible to either efficient or mechanical modes of analysis . . . It is a mode in which new forces can trigger novel patterns of *self-organization* in a thing, species, system, or being, sometimes allowing something new to emerge from the swirl back and forth between them: a new species, state of the universe, weather system, ecological balance, or political formation" (180). Alongside other participants in the "new materialism" are those such as Jane Bennett, Elizabeth Grosz, Sarah Ahmed, Rosi Braidotti, Diana Coole, and Samantha Frost who recognize that how we think about matter has far-reaching implications for how we think about the human as a lively corporeality. In order address the alternative agency of materiality more adequately, new materialists share three interrelated themes: (1) a posthumanist orientation that conceives of matter as exhibiting agency; (2) consideration of an array of issues within biopolitics and bioethics on the status of life, the human, and the nonhuman; and (3) a "nondogmatic reengagement with political economy, where the nature of, and relationship between, the material details of everyday life and broader geopolitical and socioeconomic structures is being explored afresh" (Coole and Frost 6–7). While none of these theorists explicitly address disability, here we want to think disability as foun-

dational part of this mix to address matter/materiality as agential embodiment. For nondialectical materialists human and nonhuman bodies exceed their cultural positioning as oppressed, excluded forms of deviancy. Such approaches emphasize the manifold pluripotentiality of life to unfold in multiple directions and, in doing so, they permit a corrective to emerge that recognizes the agency of matter as parallel to discussions of social structures of power that have dominated "the cultural turn" in social constructivist discourses for at least two decades.

3. In this work we refer to our analyses as an extension of the field of scholarship referred to as disability studies. We could opt to differentiate our commitment to the intersectional analyses that run throughout as "critical disability studies" in parallel to many of the theorists from whom this work draws for its arguments. For argument positioned on various sides of the "critical disability studies" debate one could refer to Simo Vehmas and Nick Watson's "Moral Wrongs, disadvantages, and disability: a critique of critical disability studies," Helen Meekosha and Russell Shuttlesworth's "What's so 'critical' about critical disability studies?", and Dan Goodley's "Dis/entangling critical disability studies." However, we feel some trepidation with the labeling strategy of frontloading "critical" before "disability studies." We think that such an approach has the unwanted effect of suggesting: 1) disability studies was not already critical; 2) adding an adjective of "severity" to disability studies resonates (i.e. critical) with ideas of medically modulated degrees of impairment; 3) suggests that it's merely an "add-on" in order to distance one's research from those improperly claiming to do disability studies as is prominent in the field of Education. In other words we don't find the distinction significantly instructive to readers as we imagine the unlikely scenario of audience members at a university graduation, for example, hearing someone getting a diploma in disability studies from a school of Education, and thinking to themselves, "hmmmmm ... it's interesting that they're not getting a degree in 'critical disability studies!'" If the methodology of critical disability studies is best characterized as an intersectional one at base and its goal is to complicate binaries born of the social model formula and break the over-emphasis on North American/UK national boundaries, as well as attend to the compounding identities of race, class, gender, and sexuality, is it a break from or an extension of disability studies? If a break then we would suggest the advent of a new name (something like crip/queer theory or intersectional studies). If an extension (i.e. hailing from a philosophical lineage with the social model at its foundations no matter how critical) then we don't see a pressing value in front loading "critical" before disability studies. In other words, we would tend to treat critical disability studies as a further elaboration of the field (the base) that situates its theoretical nuances at the level of alternative disability studies applications (superstructure). Obviously, we're open to argument on these points because we think this question matters greatly in how scholars go on to refer to evolving work in the field. Thus, we refer to work about the intersection of crip/queer bodies in this book as disability

studies despite its fully intersectional analyses which might better place it beneath the rubric critical disability studies. We call this work disability studies because we have, to this point, seen alternative emphases on intersectionality and the differential materialities of crip/queer bodies as a matter of extension rather than break. We also understand that placing "critical" in front of disability studies helps create the field's continuing evolution as a designator of analytical transition, but it's unwieldy, at best, in the poetry of our collective work.

4. In works such as *Discipline and Punish*, Foucault discusses the increasing ineffectiveness of state spectacles of punishment as associated with the state's implication in the very practices it was seeking to punish (i.e., murder, forms of debauchery, theft, crimes against property). Thus, the productive and regulatory controls enacted by biopower can be understood as a shift in tactics on the part of the state where regulation of behavior becomes a matter of internalization—the tendency of citizens to police one's own behavior at the behest of the state. It is also important to point out that Foucault argues that prohibitions and confinement continue but are overlaid with the techniques of state biopolitical regulation of populations. In other words, these are not histories of one form of regulation entirely supplanting another, and thus, the common critique of Foucault as instituting "breaks" as a feature of his historical method is not accurate in this regard.

5. Foucault diagnoses a tactical shift wherein the nature of bodies particular classes could possess were divided off from each other—i.e., individuated and singularized—in order to enthrall corporealities to norms of social status and worldview (*Sexuality* 128). Such an approach to bodies, which first occurred in the upper and bourgeois classes because lower-class bodies were treated as expendable and not worthy of the expertise required for active cultivation, made the sexualized body, for example, an object to care for and exert controls formerly foreign to it. A kind of precious sexuality was recognizably flawed (hysteria, hermaphrodism, and homosexuality being the major examples) yet, at the same time, particular to the class of which it belonged. This flawed sexuality provides a key bridge to understanding how Foucault's *History of Sexuality* serves to connect social control of sexualities with pathologies of embodiment. A pathologized sexuality of symptomatic surfaces could be actively molded from without (i.e., rehabilitated, regulated, and masked to better approximate normalcy), like a sculpture with its stone chipped down to the essence of a figure, ideal, or, more commonly, an average, and then implanted in bodies as a constitutive feature.

6. This foundational practice of the opting out of neoliberal governments from governing through privatization in the selling off of publicly held spaces to for-profit industries is realized through the implementation of eleven tactics that will prove critical to our evolving understanding of neoliberal disability: (1) the free flow of capital across national boundaries (Hardt and Negri, *Empire* 234); (2) the demographic surveillance of a people's habits particularly in relation to risk calculations regarding

health, disease, illness, and mortality (Foucault, *History of Sexuality* 126); (3) the environmental destruction of productive ecosystems through the exploitation of geographical resources and the dumping of hazardous waste (Harvey, *Neoliberalism* 67); (4) the defunding of public provisions of social services, equipment, and supports while claiming to enhance them (Koshy 155–56); (5) a new toleration of formerly devalued populations driven by the press to identify expanding consumptive market niches (Floyd 183); (6) the increasing tendency for government-funded research operations to coax private revenues into their coffers (often from the very people they're intended to serve) (N. Rose 35); (7) the degradation of personal liberties and the militarization of culture on behalf of burgeoning systems of antiterrorist security oversight (Puar, *Terrorist Assemblages* xi); (8) the "corporatization of schooling" that turns educational institutions into profit-making platforms (Giroux, *Dispossessed* 44); (9) governance by deregulation and the reinvigoration of corporate monopolies (Giroux, *Education* 78); (10) the increasing individuation of responsibility for actions in the "realms of welfare, education, health care, and even pensions" (Harvey, *Neoliberalism* 65); and (11) government reliance on experts and elites as trust in individual authority about experience wanes (Miller and Edwards 5).

7. In the centuries prior to the development of the regulatory controls of biopolitics, techniques of power relied primarily on prohibitions, criminalizations, and punishments (such as confinement or the ending of an individual life by state representatives). These corporeal punishment measures established the state's orientation toward those pursuing nonnormative behaviors (i.e., illicit sexualities, mental illness, hermaphrodism, deformities, and disabilities) as aimed at eradicating evidence of the existence of certain kinds of lives from social mainstreams. However, these direct applications of violence visited upon bodies are increasingly supplanted by tactics that target kinds of embodiments (licit and illicit) in less "direct" ways—through the institution of productive modes of control. In other words, practices of barring subjects from pursuing illicit practices, sexualities, and inappropriate ways of being with others through public prohibitions, criminalization through laws, public spectacles of execution, dramatically staged body woundings, amputations (tongues and hands and feet), and family apprehension of wayward members who threaten social reputations become less common. They fail by virtue of implicating the state in violence toward behaviors, practices, and forms of being it seeks to condemn. Of course, the corporeal measures are not displaced in a sudden shift to biopolitical techniques; rather they coexist alongside neoliberal regulatory measures that seep beyond formal institutions into the cultural sphere of production, that which C. Wright Mills called the "cultural apparatus" (238). Throughout *The Biopolitics of Disability* we will show how these technologies of power orchestrate their work in tandem with each other in neoliberalism.

8. In *The Disability Business* Gary Albrecht traces out the expanding monolith of medicine, rehabilitation, government, insurance, business, and social work as they

compete for control over the disability business and, ultimately, the lives of disabled people. In this study we refer to this coterie of for-profit interests as "professions of control" in order to emphasize the ways in which disabled people are marginalized with respect to control over their own consumption of disability goods and services.

Chapter 1. From Liberal to Neoliberal Futures of Disability: Rights-Based Inclusionism, Ablenationalism, and the Able-Disabled

1. In recent theories of corporeality highlighted by social theorists of the body such as Eve Sedgwick (2003), Elizabeth Grosz (2004), and Brian Massumi (2002), environments are sculpted by corporeal creativity as much as they are deterministically channeled into acceptable circuits of heteronormative outputs. Their work collectively provides some tools that disability studies may adopt for ways to recognize the active give-and-take between the virtual (cybernetic/prosthetic) and organismic (biological/affective) as they constitute sites of promise for cultural renewal rather than merely yielding further examples of social determinism (what Sedgwick calls the products of "paranoid criticism" [125] and Massumi refers to as "the cultural solipsism" of constructivism [39]).

Chapter 2. Curricular Cripistemologies; or, Every Child Left Behind

1. A version of this chapter first appeared in a special issue of the *Journal of Literary and Cultural Disability Studies*. We want to thank the editors of that special issue, Robert McRuer and Lisa Johnson, who guided us through a series of revisions. The chapter was inspired by their coining of the term "cripistemologies," which provided a principle beneath which to organize our findings in these collaborative research seminars and teacher trainings in DSE. We also want to thank Beth Ferri for her insights and key suggestions for ways of further rounding out the research that informs many of these arguments. Her scholarly commitments and those of colleagues in DSE serve as continuing motivation for our own work. We share in and benefit from the tradition of thinking that believes disabled students serve as a key starting point rather than minority addendum to the reform of American educational practices. Key revisions of this chapter were made possible by the generous support of the lead author in the 2012–13 Institute for the Humanities chaired by Sidonie Smith and the Department of English at the University of Michigan. A special note of thanks goes to Tobin Siebers, who provided insights, conversation, and personal and collegial support during the composition of this analysis.

2. Ironically, a visit to the ruins of the Temple of Hephaestus in Athens, Greece, requires one to navigate hundreds of slippery marble stairs to gain access. Apparently the irony of such a situation—i.e., that the temple devoted to the only disabled god in the pantheon is inaccessible to those with mobility impairments—escaped

the notice of the Roman architects who fitted the temple with stairs. While a pre-cipitous and somewhat rickety lift can now be taken up to the floor of the Parthe-non thanks to the efforts of disability activists on behalf of visitors to the Paralym-pic Games in 2004, no such accommodation is yet available at the temple of the crook-footed god to disabled visitors seeking access.

3. The absence of discussions in education and special education about adult employment for onetime students with disabilities in the very system that presum-ably provided them an education is palpable. When do we need to begin to con-template the fact that several generations of students with disabilities have now become adults with higher education qualifications? Why should the system that trained such individuals to be productive members of society act surprised—or even aghast—when those individuals, now graduated, come knocking on the door-step (still often inaccessible) of the schools and colleges that educated them for a job? It is also important to point out that charter schools are not legally required to educate students with disabilities based on educational accommodation principles of equal access because of their status as private businesses in the United States.

Likewise, there is a parallel development in rehabilitation and medical profes-sions that oversee the treatment of disabled people but rarely acknowledge the suit-ability of former "patients" as appropriate wielders of expertise in these professions. A third level of professional exclusion occurs in the network known as the Ameri-can University Centers on Developmental Disability (AUCD). Very few institutes in this well-funded system intended to provide supports and training for people with developmental disabilities have hired representatives of the very populations they are intended to serve. Finally, higher education has failed to even scrape the surface of support for professionalizing people with disabilities at universities (pub-lic or private).

4. For important examples of these trade-offs see the essays about professional discrimination experienced by educators and staff with disabilities in institutions of higher education included in Mary Lee Vance's collection, *Disabled and Staff in a Disabling Society: Multiple Identities in Higher Education.*

Chapter 3. Gay Pasts and Disability Futures: Heteronormative Trauma and Parasitism in Midnight Cowboy

1. Here we borrow the term "abandonment" from Elizabeth Povinelli's book *Economies of Abandonment: Social Belonging and Endurance in Late Liberalism,* where she examines contemporary forms of state-sponsored dereliction. The abandonment within neoliberalism of a commitment to the provision of viable social supports for se-verely devalued inhabitants living in poverty such as indigenous populations (Native American and Australian Aboriginal peoples). For Povinelli abandonment references the existence of "a shattering of the life-world in which a person finds herself situ-

ated, but it also might mean maintaining a life-world under constant threat of being saturated by the rhythms and meanings of another. The conditions of excess always sit side by side with conditions of exhaustion and endurance that put into question the neat capture of substance by capital and other biopolitical projects and complicates the simple ethical investment in the thresholds and transitions of becoming within biopolitics" (*Economies of Abandonment* 1691–94).

2. Released in 1969 to an enthusiastic critical reception, *Midnight Cowboy* has been claimed as an archetypal film of the New Hollywood (Filmsite Movie Review). The picture won three Academy Awards including Best Picture, Best Director, and Best Adapted Screenplay. Both Jon Voight and Dustin Hoffman received nominations for Best Actor but, perhaps ironically given their discussion of John Wayne as macho cowboy in Rico's apartment, both lost to Wayne for his performance in *True Grit*. It was the first and only film to win Best Picture with an X-rating (*A Clockwork Orange* was nominated but did not win in its year of consideration). During its initial review by the Motion Picture Association of America the film was given an R rating; however, after consulting with a psychologist, United Artists decided to change the rating to X based on its "homosexual frame of reference" and its "possible influence on youngsters" ("*Midnight Cowboy*," Wikipedia; please see note 18 for further discussion of the controversy over the film's X-rating). *Midnight Cowboy* earned $11 million at the box office during its initial national run and, to date, its total gross is over $44 million dollars (Box Office Information). The film is based on James Leo Herlihy's novel of the same name, which was published in 1965 and the script remains true to the original plot. The British director, John Schlesinger, was in the process of "coming out" gay but claimed he did not want to make a "gay movie" (Goldstein). At the same time, Waldo Salt, the screenwriter who also adapted disability narratives to screen such as *Coming Home* (1978) and *Serpico* (1973), had his own coming out experience: following fifteen years of being blacklisted in 1951 during the McCarthy era, Salt experienced life with the significant impairments of chronic depression and lung cancer ("Waldo Salt Biography"). The shared crafting of "an oddball love story" places both Schlesinger and Salt as visualizers of bodies as symptomatic surfaces upon which rejected social lives can be read (Goldstein). For bringing this model of symptomatic embodiment to life on screen, Schlesinger and Salt won Academy Awards for their collaborative work on the film. Alan Holender served as cinematographer (his first assignment) after being recommended to Schlesinger by the filmmaker Roman Polanski. The opening of the film was shot in Big Spring, Texas, and New York City sequences were largely staged at the corner of Broadway and West Forty-Fourth Street ("*Midnight Cowboy* Locations"). The film was identified in 1994 as one of cultural, historical, or aesthetic significance by the Library of Congress (Wikipedia).

3. Within the locations of "expendability," divisions between outside and inside are purposefully blurred. As the water from a chronically dripping faucet freezes

over during the long winter and the peripherally embodied couple attempt to layer themselves with newspaper wrappings and stolen coats, Rico's precarious health worsens and Joe's immaculate sexuality degrades. After spilling ketchup on his buckskin-simulated chinos, Joe begins to carry his ten-gallon hat like a fig leaf hiding the stain of his illicit sexuality. Likewise Rico's cough progresses, wracking his body as an audible signifier of his approach as a source of contagion, and further exacerbates a hunch that entrenches him within social discourses of malignancy, and thus, unsalvageability. His decrepit body, in turn, starts to haunt Joe's dreams as Rico turns into a zombie-like frequenter of socially liminal spaces such as abandoned hallways, subway nooks, transitioning trains passing by with eerily lit windows, and, ultimately, as a member of the police posse arresting Joe for rape.

4. In Samuel Delany's *The Motion of Light in Water*, late 1950s and 1960s New York City hosted a fluid gay scene that preexisted Stonewall, which he calls "the great outing of gay men"; yet, somewhat to Delany's dismay, Stonewall brings an end to a utopian moment of men-being-with-men largely outside of official forms of social detection. Pertinent to our application of biopolitical endangerments, Delany's description includes *Midnight Cowboy* as a preamble to state indifference of those dying during the HIV/AIDS panic. Importantly, McRuer and Mollow point out that the most explicit crossing of theory between disability and queer studies occurs in the literature of surviving sex in an epidemic (3). These materials inform our own retroactive reading of the film as a presaging of biopolitical mass deaths of HIV/AIDS-infected gay men.

5. The comic book a young girl is reading on the bus, *Wonder Woman* No. 178 cover dated September–October 1968 places the "present time" of the film in the same historical moment of Congress's passage of the Architectural Barriers Act.

6. Just a cautionary comment about neoliberalism's contemporary association of the idea that unregulated corporations could do everything better than big government. This definition of neoliberalism has been promoted retroactively among conservative political forces as the centerpiece of "the Reagan revolution." However, the promotion of unfettered markets as superior to government intervention played no part in any administration's economic platform. Instead, out of the failure of Keynesian economics to control stagflation in the late 1970s, a backup policy of monetarism promoted by conservative University of Chicago economist Milton Friedman argued that the only effective economic intervention the government could make was manipulation of the money supply. This idea is very different from the ideological argument that corporations do better when they go unregulated, and thus, even leftist accounts of neoliberalism need to take this alternative history further into account.

7. Here we use the phrase "magically resolves" in the way the term was deployed by Stuart Hall and the U.K. cultural studies movement. For instance, in *Subculture: The Meaning of Style*, Dick Hebdige explains spectacular styles as a symbolic

disordering of dominant codes of meaning regulated by the parent culture. Bereft of specific political goals of social transformation (such as those particular to countercultural movements such as flower children, hippies, and anti–Vietnam War protestors of the late 1960s and early 1970s), youth subcultures embrace forms of consumption that violate the values and decorum governing normative existences particular to specific historical dominant symbolic orders. In doing so, they momentarily expose the artificiality of conventions of normalcy that seek to make participants invisible, appropriate, and natural within the meanings and modes of hegemonic cultural norms. Yet disruption of the symbolic order results in no pragmatic political agenda of change, and, thus, Hebdige reads such spectacular disruptions as seeking a "magical resolution" of deep-seated social inequalities. Such displays disrupt but do not, in fact, overturn the oppression conditions out of which they are born.

8. In her essay "'A Man with the Same Feelings': Disability, Humanity, and Heterosexual Apparatus," Eunjung Kim explores similar portrayals that rely on the successful sexualization of disabled men and women once their "bodily characteristics of disability social deviancy are removed" (11).

9. By using various conjugations of the verb "to parasite," we intend to draw attention to ways that late capitalism produces economic exploitation as a modus operandi of its smooth functioning. Michel Serres extensively theorizes the term in his book *The Parasite*, in order to gesture at the ways in which strict divisions between host and parasite cannot be maintained. Since parasites live on the cast-off products and in "unlivable" nooks and crannies of a host organism, their lives appear as niche consumers living off the productivity of another. However, as Serres so persuasively demonstrates, capitalism is alive with parasites because its forms of exchange depend upon capitalists at the top of the economic food chain living off of the exploited labor of their workers. Thus, while late capitalism must disguise the fact that an inverse relation between host and parasite exists in order to run seamlessly as a system of exploitation, the fiction of the host is maintained only to accomplish this masquerade of who is living off of whom. *Midnight Cowboy* powerfully demonstrates how Joe's and Rico's effort to operationalize a sexually parasitic economy largely shadows the parasitism of exchange-based sexual systems from top to bottom.

10. The X on the entry door of Rico's condemned apartment building also recalls the film's original X-rating. In response to the controversy of this designation the film precipitated the creation of a new hard R rating because pornographic X-rated films began an unrestricted use of the rating for sex films. This resulted in a stigma associated with X-rated films, and many movie houses would not run them. The alternative R rating was given to the film upon its rerelease in late 1970 across independent theaters.

11. In his argument about the threat of nonreproductive homosexuality to heter-

onormative futures, Edelman explains, "Hence, what*ever* refuses this mandate [i.e., the procreative imperative] by which our political institutions compel the collective reproduction of the Child must appear as a threat not only to the organization of a given social order but also, and far more ominously, to social order as such, insofar as it threatens the logic of futurism on which meaning always depends" (11). Although Rico, as a disabled person whose sexuality has been socially rendered asexual, does not perform as an antirelational disruptive force in the way that Edelman identifies queer nonreproductive lives, his intentional withholding of himself from sexual circuits of affect and exchange can be interpreted as a refusal to participate in a redress of disabled people's dehumanizing asexualization during the eugenics period. They, too, in tandem with queer lives, expose the artificiality of the command to collective reproduction, but the political terms at stake in this refusal have yet to be more thoroughly theorized in disability studies. Our previous book *Cultural Locations of Disability* analyzes the lengthy history of disabled people's extraction from circuits of sexuality on the basis of their threat to "contamination" of the nation's genetic pool. See, for instance, our chapter in that book titled "Subnormal Nation: The Making of a Disability Minority."

12. The models for these alternative living arrangements derive from social experiments of alternative infrastructures forged in late 1960s counter-cultural spaces such as food coops, be-ins, independent living centers, bathhouses, and communes. Such socially experimental arrangements of living together were forged in contrast to heteronormative sexual economies of exchange.

13. Rico's death scene at the end of the film occurs before a bus full of passengers made up of middle-class women whom Enrico imagines exploiting in his fantasy flash-forwards of able-bodied profiteering (that which I'm calling able-bodied "parasitism"). His dying in the middle of this public audience captures the idea of unsalvageable bodies present in our own purview; yet nothing happens as a result of this tragic development, and the bus driver comments, "OK, noting we can do at this point let's just move along." Further the film is shot and set during the Vietnam War, when so many U.S. and Vietnamese people (soldier and civilian) were being killed in droves by assault weapons and the torturous spraying of Agent Orange. Additionally, homosexuality was actively purged in military populations and, ironically, claimed as a rejected identity by antiwar activists seeking to gain the disability designation "unfit," in order to avoid the draft. According to the *Washington Post* 73 percent of U.S. citizens who died in the war were volunteers rather than draftees.

14. Hoffman's iconic line—"Hey, we're walking here!"—provides the most tangible example of devalued identity group claims for social recognition. *Premiere* magazine ranks his performance as Rico Rizzo number 7 in "best performances of all time." Hoffman claims to have kept pebbles in his shoes to make sure his limp would be consistent from shot to shot—an example of a long tradition of disability simulation among method actors (for a more in-depth discussion of this topic see our

analysis of disability-simulation acting methodologies in the performance history of Shakespeare's *Richard III* in *Narrative Prosthesis: Disability and the Dependencies of Discourse*). While Robert Blake was offered the part of Enrico and declined it, Hoffman dressed up in beggar's rags and sought alms from passersby while meeting the film's auditioner on the street corner in order to prove he could fully occupy the part. On a further note of disability avowal/disavowal, the film contained the first recorded use of the word "scuzzy"—which combined the words scummy and fuzzy, but it also has reverberations of the familial term "cousin" buried within it.

15. The intertwining of nonnormative positivist methodologies hinges on their shared commitment to applications of what we identified earlier in the chapter as akin to an application of Theodore Adorno's "negative dialectics" (1970); a rigorous demonstration of the noncorrespondence between what is claimed by the productive outputs of neoliberalism and what actually exists even as techniques of power allow "the claimed world to appear as the best of all actual worlds" (Povinelli 2467). As an intervention into this noncorrespondence between what is claimed and what actually exists, nonnormative materialisms expose the trauma experienced by bodies that fail as a result of nonconformance to heteronormative criteria—particularly in the heavily policed domain of sexuality. This comparative framework is not an effort to organize a hierarchy of capacities for surviving social degrees of intolerance. Instead, we want to counterpose two differential modes of identity integration as newly recognized within neoliberalism with respect to the historically outcast nature of gay and disabled populations.

Chapter 4. The Politics of Atypicality: International Disability Film Festivals and the Productive Fracturing of Identity

1. In Michelle Cliff's essay, "Journey into Speech" (1985), she discusses the aftereffects of racial colonization as "taming my wildness." Even after the military occupation of Jamaica ended, residents experienced a deepening sense of alienation, participating in cultural training that cultivates ideas about Jamaican cultural practices as primitive, inferior, and animalistic. Cliff parallels the experience of postcolonial Jamaican subjects with Victor, the Wild Boy of Aveyron.

2. This theory of disability culture evolving out of mainstream marginalization strategies owes a debt to the work of Deleuze and Guattari in *Kafka: Toward a Minority Literature* (1986). According to the authors, the fashioning of a minority cultural perspective evolves out of three distinct developments in relation to the dictates of a majority culture: (1) a deterritorialization of a community from its proper homeland; (2) an immediacy of individual politics squeezed out from a claustrophobic space set aside especially for those members of the minoritized community; and (3) a collective articulation of a countercultural politics. Each of these instances can be applied to the formation of disability as a minoritarian space for enunciating

the discontents of those who have been systematically, structurally, and aesthetically removed from participation in majority contexts.

3. Harry Laughlin pioneered the "model sterilization law" published by the Chicago Psychopathic Laboratory in 1922. The model's intent was to provide state legislatures and eugenicists across the United States and Canada with some fail-proof language for implementing coercive sterilization practices on people designed as "defectives." According to eugenicists such as Canadian psychiatrist Charles Kirk Clarke, inferior people would continue to pollute the gene pool if left to their own promiscuous ways. This argument encouraged Canada and the United States to pass laws that instituted hierarchies of value among nationalities. In the United States more than 60,000 were sterilized, while in Canada an estimated 30,000 sterilizations were conducted between 1924 and 1969 (http://www.fathersforlife.org/hist/eugenics1.htm). Germany presented Laughlin with an honorary doctorate from the University of Heidelberg. The translation of the model sterilization law into German resulted in the sterilization of more than 400,000 by the conclusion of World War II.

4. A copy of the program for the 2005 London Film Festival can be found at http://www.disabilityfilm.co.uk/.

Chapter 5. Permutations of the Species: Independent Disability Cinema and the Critique of Ablenationalism

1. The films discussed here were screened at Munich's "The Way We Live" International Short Film Festival, www.abm-medien.de.

Chapter 6. Corporeal Subcultures and the Specter of Biopolitics

1. The Modern Language Association ad hoc Committee on Disability Issues faced a similar issue of canon building. In this case, the scholarly organization instructed the coalition of scholars, many who had signed petitions or protested exclusion from the bibliography or academic forums, to put the words "Disability Studies" in the first paragraph of any article that would count as a constituent part of an emerging field. This collecting method allowed for topics as wide-ranging as Beth Haller's studies of the Jerry Lewis telethon to a historical study of crippled saints to share sponsorship and audience for a burgeoning enterprise: topics that could concern a newly enfranchised constituency that was part of a historical moment that had sought and eventually passed the Americans with Disabilities Rights Act. We should add that universities and scholarly organizations were scrambling to assess their obligations for compliance under the series of guidelines while disability rights groups continued to pressure for a new buzzword, "compliance." Post-ADA scholarship was committed, multilocated, and, as implied by Kuppers's work in the

epistemologies of disability theater, The Anarcha Project, anarchic. By netting and affiliating research, instead of a canon, common causes emerged: freaks; Deaf culture; chronic pain; blind history; autobiography; life-writing; textual cultures that yield insight back to lives that defined themselves by, around, and against disability identity. And as "freak" once captured some kind of proud resistant claim, so does "crip" explain the insult and the right to live against the "good cripple" expectations set in place by nonprofits, charities, NGOs, and the terms that manage one's survival as a person disabled by social predicament. Or in radical special education's patois: attitudes create a more significant barrier than incapacity—smuggling back in the excised body as it still twitches around. "Crip," then, quickly shouts the predominately white flavor of disability scholarship, because once a parade of scholarship was under way the participants could be pegged. Many appeared to be white disabled male wheelchair users. Hierarchy creation and dismantling was under way, as happens in anarchic participatory structures. And the effectiveness of resistance makes little sense to people who do experience lives lived with impairment but can be pitted against each other in identity-based divisive and representational competitions by their sponsors: nonprofits, NGOs, charities. On one coast we have resistance to impairment discussions as a means for accomplishing solidarity, and on another we have collectives with many voices and perspectives that seek to instruct each other in the differentials of their bodies and lives.

2. Used as case study for unbearable infant life in *Should the Baby Live?* Peter Singer and Helga Kuhse cite problems in the medical treatment system as rationale for the necessary rationing of life saving techniques such as lack of available surgeons to do repairs, the earth of techniques and available resources for managing "high-upkeep" impairments, as well as even more mundane issues such as the need for more effective ways to manage secretions. In their writings Singer and Kuhse transform the survival struggles of those with severe disability into exemplary extermination candidates. Initially their "extreme" cases included Down Syndrome, esophageal atresia, and Tay Sachs syndrome. As critiques of their sweeping categories of unviable lives disseminated to the public and outcry ensured they continued to prune their examples of unlivable crip/queer bodies to babies born with just brainstems.

3. The Jerry Lewis telethon serves as such a recuperative instrument. Because it collects together all those who would not otherwise find association, it's also a social networking device. Until 1990 it networked with biopolitical consumers via clinics. In 1990 Quest newsletter was born and even featured a short piece on the PhD program in disability studies at the University of Illinois, Chicago. Also during this time it has sought to become an NGO resource in many senses with chat rooms, independent living tips, and timely updates on research. There is blog space that is not used to any significant extent. Compared to other biopolitical websites, the registration is less cumbersome. One doesn't require a doctor's note, but chat groups are

screened. They are also grouped according to diagnostic labels. The labels consist of both twentieth-century researcher/discoverer terms and postgenomic twenty-first-century groups. Shifting taxonomies for the muscular dystrophies could fill a volume of medical history. The point we will emphasize is that splitting and affinities continue to occur, mostly at the genomic level. When diagnoses are made in clinics, dystrophies are ruled out as unlike each other.

On the MDA website identities are sorted beneath some diagnostic labels that were familiar clinical currency, such as limb-girdle, and some are updated to match genomic marking. The name of this game is patient expertise, and while researchers conduct studies it is now under the watchful eye of those with the researched conditions. One could log in to these sites to find the survivor stories most compelling. One finds many success stories. While the MDA site hosts many complaints that it does not supply medically adequate wheelchairs, and wheelchair users do know the ways that a chair becomes a life-or-death item, these can be understood, in the broadest sense, into medical lifestyle choices. MDA supplies some of the better mobility tips. If one's body parts don't move one can hardly find better advisement for strategies to mobilize oneself. While participants do protest as consumers and even suggest that all may be better off consulting with ILCs, there is little program suggested for social change. An "Adults" chat group that does not fit uniformly with the diagnosis ones features an inquiry about personal assistance legislation information from different states. The site now even features an ambassadors-to-Washington section.

Afterword. Disability as Multitude: Reworking Nonproductive Labor Power

1. In *Thus Spake Zarathustra*, Nietzsche's philosopher-protagonist, Zarathustra, gets tired of humanity and takes up a life among the ironically titled "higher men"— those who have been excluded from dominant culture due to their discordant bodies, behaviors, and appearances. We analyze this alternative social formation of disabled people in chapter 3 of *Narrative Prosthesis: Discourses of Disability* (2000).

2. The history of this early disability identity-based labor protest and others conducted by deaf workers in 1903 can be found in the Chicago Disability History Exhibit that ran from April 20 to September 15, 2006, at the National Vietnam Veterans Art Museum in Chicago. We believe these may be the first labor movements by self-identified workers with disabilities.

Filmography

Berocca. Dir. Martin Taylor. Spartan Films. 2005. 13 mins.

Body and Soul: Diane and Kathy. Dir. Alice Elliott. Welcome Change Productions. 2006. 40 mins.

Born Freak. Dir. Paul Sapin. Planet Wild. 2004. 50 mins.

Coming Home. Dir. Hal Ashby. Jerome Hellman Productions. 1978. 127 mins.

The Cost of Living. Dir. Lloyd Newsome. DV8 Films Limited. 2004. 35 mins.

Girl, Interrupted. Dir. James Mangold. 3 Art Entertainment. 1999. 127 mins.

goodnight, liberation. Dir. Oriana Bolden. Hellagetto Films. 2003. 7 mins.

I'm in Away from Here. Dir. C. MacInnes U.K. Shooting People. 2007.

Killer Cure. Dir. Steve Carolan. Shoot Your Mouth Off Films. 2003. 12 mins.

The Men. Dir. F. Zinnemann. Stanley Kramer Productions. 1950. 85 mins.

Midnight Cowboy. Dir. J. Schlesinger. MGM. 1969. 113 mins.

Multi-handicapped. Dir. Fred Wiseman. Zipporah Films. 1986. 126 mins.

Lorenzo's Oil. Dir. George Miller. Universal. 1992. 129 mins.

Outcasts. Dir. Ian Clark. NFTS Production. 2008. 25 min.

Paris Is Burning. Dir. by Jenny Livingston. Miramax Films. 1991. 71 mins.

Rain Man. Dir. Barry Levinson. MGM. 1988. 133 mins.

Sang Froid / Cold Blood. Dir. Pierre Louis-Levacher. Canine Productions. 2002. 6 mins.

Self Preservation: The Art of Riva Lehrer. Dir. by S. Snyder. Brace Yourselves Productions. 2005. 46 mins.

Serpico. Dir. by Sidney Lumet. Artists Entertainment Complex. 1973. 130 mins.

Turtle Sisters. Dir. by Lee Hye Ran. Feminist Video Activism WOM. 2006. 105 mins.

Vital Signs: Crip Culture Talks Back. Dir. S. Snyder and D. Mitchell. Brace Yourselves Productions. 1995. 48 mins.

Waiting for Ronald. Dir. Ellen Gerstein. Lulu Productions. 2003. 21 mins.

Waterdance. Dir. Neal Jimenez and Michael Steinberg. No Frills Film. 1992. 106 mins.

What It's Like to Be My Mother (Jak to jest byc moja matka). Dir. N. McGettigan. Agata Golańska. 2007.

Whole: A Trinity of Being. Dir. Shelley Barry. TwoSpinningWheels Productions. 2004. 15 mins.

A World Without Bodies. Dir. Sharon Snyder. Brace Yourselves Productions. 2002. 26 mins.

X-Men. Dir. Bryan Singer. 20th Century Fox. 2000. 104 mins.

X2: X-Men United. Dir. Bryan Singer. 20th Century Fox. 2003. 133 mins.

Yolk. Dir. S. Lance. Head Pictures.. 2008. 14 mins.

Works Cited

Abbas, Asma. *Liberalism and Human Suffering: Materialist Reflections on Politics, Ethics, and Aesthetics.* New York: Palgrave Macmillan, 2010. Print.

Abbey, Edward. *Desert Solitaire: A Season in the Wilderness.* New York: Touchstone, 1990. Print.

"About UDL." Center for Applied Special Technology. No date. Web. June 1, 2013. http://www.cast.org/udl/index.html.

Adams, Henry. *The Education of Henry Adams: An Autobiography.* Boston: Houghton Mifflin, 1918. Print.

Adorno, Theodore. *Negative Dialectics.* Trans. E. B. Ashton. New York: Seabury, 1973. Print.

Agamben, Giorgio. *Homo Sacer: Sovereign Power and Bare Life.* Trans. Daniel Heller-Roazen. Stanford: Stanford UP, 1998. Print.

Agamben, Giorgio. *State of Exception.* Trans. K. Attell. Chicago: U of Chicago P, 2005. Print.

Albrecht, Gary. *The Disability Business: Rehabilitation in America.* Thousand Oaks: Sage P, 1992. Print.

Albrecht, Gary, Jerome Bickenbach, David Mitchell, Walt Schalick, and Sharon Snyder (eds.). *Encyclopedia of Disability.* 5 vols. Thousand Oaks: Sage P, 2005. Print.

"Aimee Mullins and Her 12 Pairs of Legs." TED2009 (March). March 9, 2009. Web. July 3, 2012. http://www.ted.com/talks/aimee_mullins_prosthetic_aesthetics. html. Video.

Anderson, Benedict. *Imagined Communities: Reflections on the Origin and Spread of Nationalism.* New York: Verso, 2006. Print.

Archer, Margaret. *Being Human: The Problem of Agency.* Cambridge: Cambridge UP, 2000. Print.

Arendt, Hannah. *The Origins of Totalitarianism.* New York: Harvest Books, 1973. Print.

Armstrong, Phillip. "Beyond Human Rights?" *Disability Studies Quarterly* 29.4 (2009). Web. December 10, 2012. dsq-sds.org/article/view/989/1165.

Baldwin, James. *Giovanni's Room*. New York: Dial P, 1956. Print.

Barnes, Colin. "Disability Studies: New or Not So New Directions." *Disability and Society* 14.4 (1999): 577–80. Print.

Baudrillard, Jean. "Disneyworld Company." *Liberation* March 4, 1996. Web. February 19, 2014. http://www.egs.edu/faculty/jean-baudrillard/articles/disney-world-company/.

Beauchamp, Toby. "The Substance of Borders: Transgender Politics, Mobility, and U.S. State Regulation of Testosterone." *GLQ* 19.1 (2013): 57–78. Print.

Berger, James. *The Disarticulate: Language, Disability, and the Narratives of Modernity*. New York: New York UP, 2014. Print.

Berlant, Lauren. "Slow Death (Sovereignty, Obesity, Lateral Agency). *Critical Inquiry* 33.4 (Summer 2007): 754–80. Print.

Bérubé, Michael. "Life as We Know It: A Father, a Son, and Genetic Destiny." *Harper's Magazine* December 1994. Print.

Bérubé, Michael. *Life as We Know It: A Father, a Family, and an Exceptional Child*. New York: Vintage, 1998. Print.

Bhabha, Homi. "DissemiNation: Time, Narrative, and the Margins of the Modern Nation." H. Bhabha (ed.). *Nation and Narration*. New York: Routledge, 1990: 291–321. Print.

"Biosphere 2." Wikipedia. January 18, 2013. Web. January 19, 2013. http://en.wikipedia.org/wiki/Biosphere_2.

Bolt, David. "Tackling Avoidance in the Academy." University of Hope Liverpool Foundation Hour. May 2, 2011. Liverpool Hope University, 2012. Conference presentation.

Box Office Mojo. Box Office Information for *Midnight Cowboy*. No date. Web. March 16, 2013. http://boxofficemojo.com/movies/?id=midnightcowboy.htm.

Braidotti, Rosi. "The Politics of Life Itself and New Ways of Dying." D. Coole and S. Frost (eds.). *New Materialisms: Ontology, Agency, and Politics*. Durham: Duke UP, 2011: 201–18. Print.

Bragg, Lois. "From the Mute God to the Lesser God: Disability in Medieval Celtic and Old Norse Literature." *Disability Studies Quarterly* 12.2 (1997): 165–77. Print.

Braye, Stuart, Kevin Dixon, and Tom Gibbons. "'A Mockery of Equality': An Exploratory Investigation into Disabled Activists' Views of the Paralympic Games." *Disability and Society* 28.7 (2013): 1–13. Print.

Brown, Wendy. "Neo-liberalism and the End of Liberal Democracy." *Edgework: Critical Essays on Knowledge and Politics*. Princeton: Princeton UP, 2003: 37–60. Print.

Brueggemann, Brenda Jo and Debra A. Moddelmog. "Coming-out Pedagogies: Risking Identity in Language and Literature Classrooms." Diane P. Freedman, Martha Stoddard Holmes, and Rosemarie Garland Thomson (eds.). *The Teacher's Body: Embodiment, Authority, and Identity in the Academy*. New York: SUNY P, 2003. 209–34. Print.

Butler, Judith. *Bodies That Matter: On the Discursive "Limits" of Sex*. New York: Routledge, 1993. Print.

Butler, Judith. *Gender Trouble: Feminism and the Subversion of Identity*. New York: Routledge, 2006. Print.

Butler, Judith. *Undoing Gender*. New York: Routledge, 2004.

Butler, Judith and Athena Athanasiou. *Dispossession: The Performative in the Political*. London: Polity P, 2013. Print.

Campbell, Fiona. *The Contours of Ableism: The Production of Disability and Abledness*. New York: Palgrave Macmillan, 2009. Print.

Campbell, Fiona. "Inclusive Education Research and Teaching: Examples of the Impact of Disability Studies." Unpublished paper presented at the "Transformative Difference: Disability, Culture, and the Academy" conference, September 7 and 8, 2011. Leeds University. Leeds, U.K. Conference presentation.

Canguilhem, Georges. *The Normal and the Pathological*. New York: Zone Books, 1991. Print.

Carver, Raymond. *Cathedral*. New York: Alfred A. Knopf, 1983. June 30, 2014. http://nbu.bg/webs/amb/american/6/carver/cathedral.htm. Kindle AZW file.

Chambers, Ross. *Room for Maneuver: Reading the Oppositional in Narrative*. Chicago: U of Chicago P, 1991. Print.

Charlton, James. *Nothing about Us without Us: Disability Oppression and Empowerment*. Berkeley: U of California P, 2000. Print.

Charlton, James. "Peripheral Everywhere." Unpublished paper presented at Temple University, Philadelphia, U.S., in the Geo-Politics of Disability Lecture Series, February 2009. Lecture series presentation.

Cheah, Pheng. "Non-dialectical Materialism." D. Coole and S. Frost (eds.). *New Materialisms: Ontology, Agency, and Politics*. Durham: Duke UP, 2011: 70–91. Print.

Chen, Mel Y. *Animacies: Bio-politics, Racial Mattering, and Queer Affect*. Durham: Duke UP, 2012. Print.

Chivers, Sally and Nicole Markotic (eds.). *The Problem Body: Projecting Disability on Film*. Columbus: Ohio State UP, 2010. Print.

Chossudovsky, Michael. "The Anti-globalization Movement and the World Social Forum: Is 'Another World' Possible?" *GlobalResearch* May 15, 2013. Web. July 3, 2014. http://www.globalresearch.ca/the-anti-globalization-movement-and-the-world-social-forum-another-world-is-possible/5335181.

Clarke, Eric O. "Queer Publicity at the Limits of Inclusion." *GLQ* 5.1 (1999): 84–93. Print.

Cliff, Michelle. "Journey into Speech." Rick Simonson and Scott Walker (eds.). *The Graywolf Annual Five: Multicultural Literacy*. St. Paul: Graywolf P, 1985: 55–81. Print.

Clough, Patricia. *The Affective Turn*. Durham: Duke UP, 2007. Print.

Clough, Patricia. "Future Matters: Technoscience, Global Politics, and Cultural Criticism." *Social Text* 22 3.80 (Fall 2004): 1–23. Print.

Connolly, William E. "Materialities of Experience." D. Coole and S. Frost (eds.). *New Materialisms: Ontology, Agency, and Politics*. Durham: Duke UP, 2010: 178–200. Print.

Coole, Diana and Samantha Frost (eds.). *New Materialisms: Ontology, Agency, and Politics*. Durham: Duke UP, 2011. Print.

Cresswell, Timothy. *On the Move: Mobility in the Modern Western World*. New York: Routledge, 2006. Print.

Darwin, Charles. *The Descent of Man*. New York: Prometheus Books, 1998. Print.

Davidson, Michael. *Concerto for the Left Hand: Disability and the Defamiliar Body*. Ann Arbor: U of Michigan P, 2011. Print.

Davis, Lennard. *Bending Over Backwards: Disability, Dismodernism, and Other Difficult Positions*. New York: NYU P, 2002. Print.

Davis, Lennard. "The End of Identity Politics and the Beginning of Dismodernism: On Disability as an Unstable Category." L. Davis (ed.). *The Disability Studies Reader*. New York: Routledge, 2006: 231–42. Print.

Davis, Lennard. *The End of Normal*. Ann Arbor: U of Michigan P, 2013. Print.

Davis, Mike. *Planet of Slums*. New York: Verso, 2007. Print.

Delany, Samuel. *The Motion of Light in Water*. New York: Plume, 1989. Print.

Delany, Samuel. *Times Square Red, Times Square Blue*. New York: New York U P, 2001. Print.

Deleuze, Gilles and Felix Guattari. *Kafka: Toward a Minor Literature*. Minneapolis: U of Minnesota P, 1986. Print.

Deleuze, Gilles and Felix Guattari. *A Thousand Plateaus: Capitalism and Schizophrenia*. Trans. B. Massumi. New York: Continuum, 1987. Print.

D'Emelio, John and Estelle B. Freedman. *Intimate Matters: A History of Sexuality in America*. Chicago: U of Chicago P, 2012. Print.

Desjardins, Michel. "The Sexualized Body of the Child: Parents and the Politics of 'Voluntary' Sterilization of People Labeled Intellectually Disabled." R. McRuer and A. Mollow (eds.). *Sex and Disability*. Durham: Duke UP, 2012: 69-88.

Dorn, Michael. Eighth Annual Psychology Conference. U of the West Indies. Old Dramatic Theater, Mona Campus, Kingston, Jamaica. March 11–13, 2009. Conference Presentation.

DuBois, W. E. B. *The Souls of Black Folks*. Rockville, IN: Arc Manor, 1998. Print.

Duggan, Lisa. *The Twilight of Equality: Neoliberalism, Cultural Politics, and the Attack on Democracy*. Boston: Beacon P, 2004. Print.

Dwoskin, Stephen. "Whose Film?" A. Pointon and C. Davies (eds.). *Framed: Inter-*

rogating Disability in the Media. London: British Film Institute, 1997: 214–16. Print.

Edelman, Lee. *No Future: Queer Theory and the Death Drive*. Durham: Duke UP, 2004. Print.

"Editorial on Language Policy." *Disability and Society*. No date. Web. September 24, 2010. http://www.tandf.co.uk/journals/authors/cdsoauth.asp.

Edwards, Jason. "The Materialism of Historical Materialism." D. Coole and S. Frost (eds.). *The New Materialism: Ontology, Agency, and Politics*. Durham: Duke UP, 2011: 281–98. Print.

Elkins, Stanley. *The Magic Kingdom*. New York: Dalkey Archive P, 2000. Print.

Elman, Julie Passanante and Robert McRuer. "The Gift of Mobility: Disability, Queerness and Rehabilitation in the Emergent Global Order." Unpublished paper.

Erevelles, Nirmala. *Disability and Difference in Global Contexts: Enabling a Transformative Body Politic*. New York: Palgrave Macmillan, 2011. Print.

Erevelles, Nirmala, and Andrea Minear. "Unspeakable Offenses: Untangling Race and Disability in Discources of Intersectionality." *Journal of Literary and Cultural Disability Studies* 4.2 (2010): 127–45. Print.

Ewart, Chrisopher. "Not Until I Stand Up: Framing a Disability Theory of Value for Contemporary Narrative." Unpublished dissertation at Simon Fraser University. 2014. Print.

Fanon, Frantz. *The Wretched of the Earth*. New York: Grove P, 2005. Print.

Faulkner, William. *The Sound and the Fury*. New York: McGraw-Hill, 1967. Print.

Ferguson, Roderick A. *The Re-order of Things: The University and Its Pedagogies of Minority Difference*. Minneapolis: U of Minnesota P, 2012. Print.

Ferri, Beth A. and David J. O'Connor. *Reading Resistance: Discourses of Exclusion in Desegregation and Inclusion*. New York: Peter Lang, 2006–7. Print.

Finkelstein, Vic. "The Social Model of Disability Repossessed." December 1, 2001. Web. November 30, 2012. http://www.leeds.ac.uk/disability-studies/archiveuk/finkelstein/soc%20mod%20repossessed.pdf.

Floyd, Kevin. *The Reification of Desire: Toward a Queer Marxism*. Minneapolis: U of Minnesota P, 2009. Print.

Foucault, Michel. *Abnormal: Lectures at the Collège de France, 1974–1975*. New York: Picador, 2004. Print.

Foucault, Michel. *Discipline and Punish: The Birth of the Prison*. New York: Vintage Books, 1995. Print.

Foucault, Michel. *The History of Madness*. New York: Routledge, 2006. Print.

Foucault, Michel. *The History of Sexuality*. Vol. 1: *An Introduction*. New York: Vintage Books, 1990. Print.

Friedlander, Henry. *The Origins of Nazi Genocide: From Euthanasia to the Final Solution*. Chapel Hill: U of North Carolina P, 1997. Print.

Gamson, Joshua. "The Organization Shaping of Collective Identity: The Case of

Lesbian and Gay Film Festivals in New York." *Sociological Forum* 11.2 (June 1996): 231–61. Print.

Garland-Thomson, Rosemarie. *Extraordinary Bodies: Figuring Disability in American Literature.* New York: Columbia UP, 1997. Print.

Gilroy, Paul. *Against Race: Imagining Political Culture beyond the Color Line.* Cambridge: Belknap P of Harvard UP, 2002. Print.

Giroux, Henry A. *Disposable Youth: Racialized Memories and the Culture of Cruelty.* New York: Routledge, 2012. Print.

Giroux, Henry A. *Education and the Crisis of Public Values.* New York: Peter Lang, 2011. Print.

Giroux, Henry A. *The Violence of Organized Forgetting: Thinking Beyond America's Disimagination Machine.* San Francisco: City Lights Books, 2014.

Goldschmidt, Richard. *The Material Basis for Evolution.* New Haven: Yale UP, 1982. Print.

Goldstein, Patrick. "*Midnight Cowboy* and the Dark Horse Its Makers Rode in on." *Los Angeles Times.* Web. November 27, 2012. http://articles.latimes.com/2005/feb/27/entertainment/ca-cowboy27.

Goodley, Dan. "Dis/entangling Critical Disability Studies." Disability & Society 28.5: 631-644.

Grosz, Elizabeth. "Feminism, Materialism, and Freedom." D. Coole and S. Frost (eds.). *New Materialisms: Ontology, Agency, and Politics.* Durham: Duke UP, 2010: 139–57. Print.

Grosz, Elizabeth. *The Nick of Time: Politics, Evolution, and the Untimely.* Durham: Duke UP, 2004. Print.

Haddon, Mark. *The Curious Incident of the Dog in the Night-Time.* New York: Vintage, 2004. Print.

Halberstam, Judith. *In a Queer Time and Place: Transgender Bodies, Subcultural Lives.* New York: NYU P, 2005. Print.

Halberstam, Judith. *The Queer Art of Failure.* Durham: Duke UP, 2011. Print.

Halle, Randall. *Queer Social Philosophy: Critical Readings from Kant to Adorno.* Chicago: U of Illinois P, 2004. Print.

Halperin, David. *Saint = Foucault: Towards a Gay Hagiography.* Oxford: Oxford UP, 1997. Print.

Haraway, Donna. *When Species Meet.* Minneapolis: U of Minnesota P, 2008. Print.

Hardt, Michael and Antonio Negri. *Commonwealth.* Cambridge: Belknap P of Harvard UP, 2009. Print.

Hardt, Michael and Antonio Negri. *Declaration.* New York: Argo Navis, 2012. Print.

Hardt, Michael and Antonio Negri. *Empire.* Cambridge: Harvard UP, 2001. Print.

Hardt, Michael and Antonio Negri. *Multitudes: War and Democracy in the Age of Democracy.* New York: Penguin, 2005. Print.

Harvey, David. *A Brief History of Neo-liberalism.* Oxford: Oxford UP, 2007. Print.

Harvey, David. *The Condition of Postmodernity: An Inquiry into the Origins of Cultural Change.* Cambridge, MA: Blackwell, 1990. Print.

Harvey, David. *The Enigma of Capital and the Crises of Capitalism.* Oxford: Oxford UP, 2011. Print.

Harvey, David. *The New Imperialism.* Oxford: Oxford UP, 2003. Print.

Harvey, David. "The 'New' Imperialism: Accumulation by Dispossession." *Socialist Register* 40 (2004): 63–87. Print.

Hebdige, Dick. *Subcultures: The Meaning of Style.* New York: Routledge, 1979. Print.

Herlihy, James Leo. *Midnight Cowboy.* New York: Simon and Schuster, 1965. Print.

Homer. *The Odyssey.* Trans. Robert Fagles. New York: Penguin Classics, 2006. Print.

Huffer, Lynne. *Mad for Foucault: Re-thinking the Foundations of Queer Theory.* New York: Columbia UP, 2010. Print.

Jameson, Fredric. *The Geopolitical Aesthetic: Cinema and Space in the World System.* Bloomington: Indiana UP, 1992. Print.

Jarman, Michelle. "Resisting Good Imperialism: Reading Disability as Radical Vulnerability." *Atenea* 25.1 (June 2005): 107–16. Print.

Kafer, Alison. "Desire and Disgust: My Ambivalent Adventures in Devoteeism." Robert McRuer and Anna Mollow (eds.). *Sex and Disability.* Durham: Duke Up, 2012: 331-54. Print.

Kafer, Alison. *Feminist Queer Crip.* Indianapolis: Indiana UP, 2013. Print.

Kerouac, Jack. *On the Road: The Original Scroll.* New York: Viking, 2007. Kindle AZW file.

Kerry, John. "24 Hours to Decide." *Boston Globe* December 3, 2012. Web. December 3, 2012. http://www.huffingtonpost.com/john-kerry/24-hours-to-decide_b_2231403.html.

Kerry, John. "Our Disabled Deserve Access Abroad." *USA Today* July 21, 2013. Web. March 9, 2014. http://www.usatoday.com/story/opinion/2013/07/21/secretary-of-state-kerry-disabities-treaty-column/2573513/.

Kim, Eunjung. "'A Man, with the Same Feelings': Disability, Humanity, and Heterosexual Apparatus in *Breaking the Waves, Born on the Fourth of July,* and *Oasis.*" Sally Chivers and Nicole Markotic (eds.). *The Problem Body: Projecting Disability on Screen.* Ohio State UP, 2010: 131–56. Print.

Kohl, Herbert R. *"I Won't Learn From You": And Other Thoughts on Creative Maladjustment.* New York: New P, 1995. Print.

Koshy, Susan. "Morphing Race into Sexuality: Asian Americans and Critical Transformations of Whiteness." *Boundary 2* 28.1 (February 2001): 153–94. Print.

Kruks, Sonia. "Simone de Beauvoir: Engaging Discrepant Materialisms." D. Coole and S. Frost (eds.). *New Materialisms: Ontology, Agency, and Politics.* Durham: Duke UP, 2011: 240–280.

Kudlick, Catherine. "Disability History: Why We Need Another Other." *American Historical Review* 108.3 (2003): 762–93. Print.

Kuhse, Helga and Peter Singer. *Should the Baby Live? The Problem of Handicapped Infants*. Oxford: Oxford UP, 1986. Print.

Kunow, Ruediger P. Comments made on the "Age and/as Disability" panel. Modern Languages Association Convention. 11 Jan 2014, Chicago, IL.

Laclau, Ernesto and Chantal Mouffe. *Hegemony and Socialist Strategy*. New York: Verso, 2001. Print.

Langan, Celeste. "Mobility Disability." *Public Culture* 13.3 (Fall 2009): 459–84. Print.

Lee, Spike and Lisa Jones. *Do the Right Thing*. New York: Fireside, 1989. Print.

Lewis, Bradley. "A Mad Fight: Psychiatry and Disability Activism." L. Davis (ed.). Disability Studies Reader 4th Edition. New York: Routledge, 2013: 115-131.

Linton, Simi. *Claiming Disability: Knowledge and Identity*. New York: New York UP, 1998. Print.

Longmore, Paul. "Conspicuous Contribution and American Cultural Dilemmas: Telethon Rituals of Cleansing." D. Mitchell and S. Snyder (eds.). *The Body and Physical Difference: Discourses of Disability*. Ann Arbor: U of Michigan P, 1997: 134–60. Print.

Longmore, Paul. "Screening Stereotypes: Images of Disabled People in Television and Motion Pictures." *Social Policy* 16 (Summer 1985): 31–37. Print.

Lukin, Josh. "Disability and Blackness." Lennard J. Davis (ed.). *The Disability Studies Reader*. 4th edition. New York: Routledge, 2013: 308–15. Print.

Mairs, Nancy. *Waist-High in the World*. Boston: Beacon P, 1997. Print.

Marx, Karl. *The Critique of the Gotha Program*. New York: Wildside P, 2008. Print.

Massumi, Brian. *Parables for the Virtual: Movement, Affect, Sensation*. Durham: Duke UP, 2002. Print.

Mbembe, Achilles. "Necropolitics." Trans. L. Meintjes. *Public Culture* 15.1 (2003): 11–40. Print.

McRuer, Robert. "Compulsory Able-Bodiedness and Queer/Disabled Existence." L. Davis (ed.). *The Disability Studies Reader*. 4th edition. New York: Routledge, 2013: 369–78. Print.

McRuer, Robert. *Crip Theory: Cultural Signs of Queerness and Disability*. New York: NYU P, 2006. Print.

McRuer, Robert. "Disability Nationalism in Crip Times." *Journal of Literary and Cultural Disability Studies* 4.2 (Summer 2010): 163–78. Print.

McRuer, Robert and Julie Passanante Elman. "The Gift of Mobility: Disability, Queerness, and Rehabilitation in the Emergent Global Order." Unpublished talk given at NYU April 22, 2011.

McRuer, Robert and Anna Mollow (eds.). *Sex and Disability*. Durham: Duke UP, 2012. Print.

Meekosha, Helen and Russell Shuttlesworth. "What's so 'Critical' About Critical Disability Studies." *Australian Journal of Human Rights* 51.1: 47-75.

Meronek, Toshio. "The Invisible Punishment of Prisoners with Disabilities. *The*

Nation July 23, 2013. Web. Oct 20, 2014. http://www.thenation.com/article/175404/invisible-punishment-prisoners-disabilities#.

Michalko, Rod. *The Difference That Disability Makes.* Philadelphia: Temple UP, 2002. Print.

"Midnight Cowboy." Wikipedia. March 1, 2013. Web. March 16, 2013. http://en.wikipedia.org/wiki/Midnight_Cowboy.

"*Midnight Cowboy* Locations." October 5, 2006. Web. March 16, 2013. http://exquisitelyboredinnacogdoches.blogspot.com/2006/10/midnight-cowboy-1969-locations.html.

"*Midnight Cowboy* (1969)." Filmsite Movie Review. No date. Web. Mar 16, 2013. http://www.filmsite.org/midn.html.

"*Midnight Cowboy:* John Schlesinger." City University of New York courses: Sex in Film. No date. Web. June 28, 2014. http://userhome.brooklyn.cuny.edu/anthro/jbeatty/COURSES/sex_in_film/midnight.html.

Miller, Clark A. and Paul N. Edwards. *Changing the Atmosphere: Expert Knowledge and Environmental Governance.* Cambridge: MIT P, 2001. Print.

Mills, C. Wright. *The Sociological Imagination.* 40th anniversary edition. Oxford: Oxford UP, 2000. Print.

Mitchell, David. "Institutionalization as Alternative Lifestyle": A Review of Susan Nussbaum's *Good Kings Bad Kings.*" September 8, 2013. Web. January 25, 2014. http://www.truth-out.org/opinion/item/18630-institutionalization-as-alternative-lifestyle-susan-nussbaums-good-kings-bad-kings.

Mitchell, David and Sharon Snyder (eds.). *Encyclopedia of Disability.* Vol. 5: *A History in Primary Source Documents.* Thousand Oaks: Sage P, 2006. Print.

Mitchell, David and Sharon Snyder (eds). *Narrative Prosthesis: Disability and the Dependencies of Discourse.* Ann Arbor: U of Michigan P, 2006. Print.

Morris, Jenny. *Pride against Prejudice: Transforming Attitudes to Disability.* Women's P, 1999. Print.

Mouffe, Chantal. *Agonistics: Thinking the World Politically.* New York: Verso Books, 2013. Print.

Muñoz, José. *Cruising Utopia: The Then and There of Queer Futurity.* New York: NYU P, 2009. Print.

"My Twelve Pairs of Legs." TED.com, 2012. Web. January 1, 2014. http://www.ted.com/talks/aimee_mullins_prosthetic_aesthetics.html.

Negri, Antonio. *Kairos, Alma Venus, Multitude.* New York: Verso, 2001. Print.

Nietzsche, Friedrich. *Human, All Too Human.* Trans. H. Zimmern. New York: Nellan Media LLC, 2010. Print.

Nietzsche, Friedrich. *Thus Spake Zarathustra.* New York: Penguin Group, 1978. Print.

Nussbaum, Martha C. *Frontiers of Justice: Disability, Nationality, Species Membership.* Cambridge: Belknap P of Harvard University P, 2006. Print.

Nussbaum, Susan. *Good Kings Bad Kings*. Chapel Hill: Algonquin Books, 2013. Print.

Oliver, Michael. *The Politics of Disablement: A Sociological Approach*. New York: Palgrave Macmillan, 1990. Print.

Onda, David. "Greatest Unscripted Movie Moments" (in English). No date. Web. March 16, 2013. http://xfinity.comcast.net/slideshow/entertainment-unscript-edmoviemoments/7/.

Ong, Aihwa. *Buddha Is Hiding: Refugees, Citizenship, and the New America*. Berkeley: U of California P, 2003. Print.

"Pediatric Cleft Lip and Palate." Medscape Reference. March 23, 2009. Web. December 10, 2012. http://emedicine.medscape.com/article/995535-overview#showall.

Portes, Alejandro, A. "Social Capital: Its Origins and Applications in Sociology." *Annual Review of Sociology* 24: 1–24, 1998. Print.

Povinelli, Elizabeth. *Economies of Abandonment: Social Belonging and Endurance in Late Liberalism*. Durham: Duke UP, 2011. Kindle edition.

Powers, Richard. *The Echo Maker*. New York: Picador, 2007. Print.

Powers, Richard. *Gold Bug Variations*. New York: Harper Perennial, 1992. Print.

Powers, Richard. *Three Farmers on Their Way to a Dance*. New York: Harper Perennial, 1992. Print.

Price, Margaret. "Defining Mental Disability." L. Davis (ed.). *Disability Studies Reader 4th edition*. New York: Routledge, 2013: 298-307. Print.

Price, Margaret. *Mad at School: Rhetorics of Mental Disability and Academic Life*. Ann Arbor: U of Michigan P, 2011.

Price, Janet and Margrit Shildrick. *Feminist Theory and the Body: A Reader*. New York: Routledge, 1999. Print.

"Protest by Signs." Disability History Museum. Curated by Sharon Snyder and David Mitchell. May 2007. Web. February 26, 2014. http://accessliving.org/index.php?tray=content&tid=top826&cid=546.

Puar, Jasbir. "Coda: The Cost of Getting Better: Suicide, Sensation, Switchpoints." *GLQ* 18.1 (2011): 149–58. Print.

Puar, Jasbir. "Prognosis Time: Towards a Geopolitics of Affect, Debility, and Capacity." *Women and Performance* 19.2 (July 2009): 161–73. Print.

Puar, Jasbir. *Terrorist Assemblages: Homonationalism in Queer Times*. Durham: Duke UP, 2007. Print.

Ranciere, Jacques. *The Politics of Aesthetics*. London: Bloomsbury Academic, 2013. Print.

Rich, Adrienne. "Pierrot Le Fou." *Poems: Selected and New, 1950–1974*. New York: W.W. Norton, 1975. Print.

Rich, B. Ruby. *Chick Flicks: Theories and Memories of the Feminist Film Movement*. Durham: Duke UP, 1998. Print.

Rich, B. Ruby. "Collision, Catastrophe, Celebration: The Relationship between Gay and Lesbian Film Festivals and Their Publics." *GLQ* 5.1 (1991): 79–84. Print.

Richter, Zach (pseudonym: Newtown Autistic). "Ableliberalism: On the Purely Aesthetic Nature of Neoliberal Commitments to Accessibility and Universal Design." *Stims, Stammers, and Winks: A Catalogue of Awkward Gestures.* June 2014. Web. June 26, 2014. http://stimstammersandwinks.blogspot.com/2014/06/ableliberalism-on-purely-aesthetic.html.

Rose, Jacqueline. *Sexuality in the Field of Vision.* New York: Verso, 2006. Print.

Rose, Martha L. *The Staff of Oedipus: Transforming Disability in Ancient Greece.* Ann Arbor: U of Michigan P, 2003. Print.

Rose, Nikolas. *The Politics of Life Itself: Biomedicine, Power, and Subjectivity in the Twenty-First Century.* Princeton: Princeton UP, 2006. Print.

Rose, Tricia. "'All Aboard the Night Train': Flow, Layering, and Rupture in Post-industrial New York." *Black Noise: Rap Music and Black Culture in Contemporary America.* Hanover: Wesleyan UP, 1994: 21-61. Print.

Sandahl, Carrie. "Queering the Crip or Cripping the Queer? Intersections of Queer and Crip Identities in Solo Autobiographical Performances." *GLQ* 9.1–2 (2003): 25–56. Print.

Schipper, Jeremy. *Disability and Isaiah's Suffering Servant.* Oxford: Oxford UP, 2011. Print.

Schrager, Norm. "*Midnight Cowboy* Review." No date. Web. March 16, 2013. http://movies.amctv.com/movie/1969/Midnight+Cowboy.

Sedgwick, Eve Kosofsky. *Touching Feeling: Affect, Pedagogy, Performativity.* Durham: Duke UP, 2003. Print.

Serres, Michel. *The Parasite.* Minneapolis: U of Minnesota P, 2007. Print.

Shakespeare, Tom. "Cultural Representations of Disabled People: Dustbins for Disavowal?" *Disability and Society* 9.3 (1994): 283–99. Print.

Shakespeare, Tom. *Disability Rights and Wrongs.* Oxford: Routledge, 2006. Print.

Shakespeare, Tom and Nicholas Watson. "The Social Model of Disability: An Outdated Ideology?" *Research in Social Science and Disability* 2 (2002): 9–28. Print.

Shildrick, Margrit. *Dangerous Discourses of Disability, Subjectivity and Sexuality.* New York: Palgrave Macmillan, 2012. Print.

Shildrick, Margrit. *Embodying the Monster: Encounters with the Vulnerable Self.* Thousand Oaks: Sage P, 2002.

Shildrick, Margrit. *Leaky Bodies and Boundaries: Feminism, Postmodernism, and (Bio)Ethics.* New York: Routledge, 1997. Print.

Siebers, Tobin. "A Sexual Culture for Disabled People." R. McRuer and A. Mollow (eds.). *Sex and Disability.* Durham: Duke UP, 2012: 37–53. Print.

Siebers, Tobin. *Disability Aesthetics.* Ann Arbor: U of Michigan P, 2010. Print.

Siebers, Tobin. "Disability and the Theory of Complex Embodiment—For Identity

Politics in a New Register." L. Davis (ed.). *The Disability Studies Reader*. 4th edition. New York: Routledge, 2013. Kindle edition.

Siebers, Tobin. *Disability Theory*. Ann Arbor: U of Michigan P, 2008. Print.

Smile Train. "Every Year Children in Developing Countries Are Born with Disfiguring Cleft Palates." 2012. Web. December 10, 2012. https://secure.smiletrain.org/site/Donation2?2060.donation=form1&df_id=2060&s_src=SEARCH_GoogleGrants&s_subsrc=Search_Brand&mkwid=s7maK15iA&pcrid=16582052521&gclid=CMLK3NCPkLQCFelDMgodBGEApw.

Smith, Phil. *Whatever Happened to Inclusion? The Place of Students with Intellectual Disabilities in Education*. New York: Peter Lang, 2010. Print.

Snyder, Sharon and David Mitchell. "Afterword—Regulated Bodies: Disability Studies and the Controlling Professions." David M. Turner and Kevin Stagg (eds.). *Social Histories of Disability and Deformity*. New York: Routledge, 2006: 175–89. Print.

Snyder, Sharon and David Mitchell. *Cultural Locations of Disability*. Ann Arbor: U of Michigan P, 2006. Print.

Snyder, Sharon and David Mitchell. "Introduction: Ablenationalism and the Geopolitics of Disability." *Journal of Literary and Cultural Disability Studies* 4.2 (2010): 113–25. Print.

Snyder, Sharon and David Mitchell. "Re-engaging the Body: Disability Studies and the Resistance to Embodiment." *Public Culture* 13 (2001): 367–89. Print.

Snyder, Sharon, David Mitchell, and Gary Albrecht (eds.). "Sumerian Prophecies." *The Encyclopedia of Disability*. Vol. 5: *Primary Source Materials*. Thousand Oaks: Sage P, 2006. Print.

Stemp, Jane. "Devices and Desires: Science Fiction, Fantasy and Disability in Literature for Young People." *Disability Studies Quarterly* 24.1 (2004). Web. February 18, 2014. http://dsq-sds.org/article/view/850/1025.

Stiker, Henri-Jacques. *A History of Disability*. Ann Arbor: U of Michigan P, 1997. Print.

Stone, Deborah. *The Disabled State*. Philadelphia: Temple UP, 1984. Print.

"The Jaw-Dropping Prison Pipeline No One Talks About." Colorlines: Lifecycles of Inequality. 2014. Web. Oct 20, 2014. http://www.upworthy.com/the-jaw-dropping-prison-pipeline-no-one-talks-about?g=3&c=ufb1.

Thomas, Carol. *Female Forms: Disability, Human Rights, and Society*. London: Open UP, 1999. Print.

Thomson, Rosemarie Garland. *Extraordinary Bodies: Figuring Disability in American Culture and Literature*. New York: Columbia UP, 1997. Print.

"Thousands of India's Disabled Protest to Demand Equal Rights." February 4, 2014. Web. July 3, 2014. http://disability-ecafe.net/nadi-Zorin.

Turner, Brian S. "Disability and the Sociology of the Body." G. Albrecht (ed.). *Handbook of Disability Studies*. Thousand Oaks: Sage P, 2001: 252–66. Print.

Turner, David and Kevin Stagg (eds.). *Social Histories of Disability and Deformity: Bodies, Images and Experiences*. New York: Routledge, 2006. Print.

Union of the Physically Impaired Against Segregation (UPIAS). Policy Statement. March 12, 1974. Web. November 30, 2012. www.leeds.ac.uk/disability-studies/archiveuk/UPIAS/UPIAS.pdf.

Vehmas, Simo and Nick Watson. "Moral Wrongs, Disadvantages, and Disability: A Critique of Critical Disability Studies." *Disability & Society* 29.4: 638-650.

Virilio, Paul. "The Third Interval: A Critical Transition." V. A. Conley (ed.). *Rethinking Technologies*. Minneapolis: U of Minnesota P, 1993: 3–12. Print.

"Waldo Salt Biography (1914–1987)." *Film Reference*. No date. Web. November 27, 2012. http://www.filmreference.com/film/56/Waldo-Salt.html.

Ware, Linda. *Ideology and the Politics of (In)Exclusion*. New York: Peter Lang, 2004. Print.

Warner, Michael. *The Trouble with Normal: Sex, Politics, and the Ethics of Queer Life*. Cambridge: Harvard UP, 1999. Print.

Wendell, Susan. *The Rejected Body: Feminist Philosophical Reflections on Disability*. New York: Routledge, 1996. Print.

White, Patricia. "Queer Publicity: A Dossier on Lesbian and Gay Film Festivals." *GLQ* 5.1 (1991): 73–93. Print.

Weheliye, Alexander G. *Habeus Viscus: Racializing Assemblages, Biopolitics, and Black Feminist Theories of the Human*. Durham: Duke UP, 2014. Print.

Winerip, Michael. "A Second Act for Biosphere 2." *New York Times* June 10, 2013. Web. July 2, 2014. http://www.nytimes.com/2013/06/10/booming/biosphere-2-good-science-or-bad-sense.html?_r=0.

Index